New England's Covered Bridges

New England's Covered Bridges

A *Complete Guide*

Benjamin D. Evans and
June R. Evans

University Press of New England
Hanover and London

Published by University Press of New England,
One Court Street, Lebanon, NH 03766
www.upne.com
©2004 by University Press of New England
Printed in Singapore
5 4 3 2 1

CIP data appear at the end of the book.

This book was published with the generous support of Richard Walbridge Spaulding.

Photograph facing the title page: Hemlock Bridge, Oxford County, Maine.

This book is dedicated to

all of the covered bridge societies, governmental agencies,

and enthusiastic "bridgers" for their continued efforts

toward the preservation and restoration of covered bridges.

Contents

Preface

We have always had a passing interest in covered bridges. June's interest dates back to her childhood when she spent all her summers on a farm owned by a family member in Columbia County, Pennsylvania. Her best friend lived a short walk down the country lane past the farmhouse, and a short distance beyond her home was a lovely, historic covered bridge—the Stauffer Covered Bridge. That bridge was frequented not only by the children as their playhouse, with the stream it spanned as their wading pool, but by many of the local residents as a lovely place to hold a weekend or holiday picnic. The bridge was destroyed by Hurricane Agnes in 1972, but the memories of it have remained.

Our joint interest in covered bridges dates back to the early years of our marriage when we visited Franconia Notch in Grafton County, New Hampshire. On that visit, Ben photographed the Flume Bridge, which crosses the Pemigewasset River. He then used this photo to create an amateur painting of that picturesque bridge. The painting has hung prominently in our home since that time.

Three of the most important days on our calendar occur in the month of December. Starting with December 20 and extending to December 31, we celebrate our wedding anniversary, Christmas, and Ben's birthday. In 1990, June presented Ben with a new camera, a Nikon 8008, as a gift for these three special days. Early in 1991, after a light snowfall, we set out to experiment with Ben's new gift. Since there is a cluster of historic covered bridges quite close to our home, we decided to make them the focus of our experimental run. The results were excellent and prompted us to begin a collection of covered bridge photos. However, June's interest in history led us to the Lehigh County Historical Society's library, where she tried to obtain historical data that we could include with the photos in our album. That was the beginning of an intense covered bridge project that extended over the next nine months.

It was not long before we had photographed all the covered bridges surrounding our home county, Lehigh, and we had also traveled into all the counties southeast of the Susquehanna River, photographing nearly half of the covered bridges in the state, and had started to fill a second album with photos and historical and anecdotal information about each bridge. With the encouragement of family and friends, this photographic collection led to the publishing of the first edition of *Pennsylvania's Covered Bridges: A Complete Guide*. The manuscript of the book reached our publisher's office in October 1991, and the finished publication was on the shelves of bookstores in our home state and surrounding states by October 1993. By November of 1998, sales had been so successful that a second printing was necessary. In January 2000, the new director of the University of Pittsburgh Press, our publisher, contacted us about preparing a second edition of the book. Consequently, after considerable review of the status of covered bridges in the past decade, we decided that a second edition would certainly be beneficial to the "bridging" community. Many changes, most of them positive, had taken place in the past ten years. Therefore, between March and June of 2000, we made a far more organized documentation tour of 221 Pennsylvania covered bridges. At that time, 216 of them were considered to be authentic, historic structures.

After having researched and documented Pennsylvania's covered bridges twice in ten years, it was only natural that we should begin to expand our "bridging" interest into other areas. The New England states have always attracted us. From the rugged coastline of Maine to the Appalachian Mountain range that extends through much of New England, the scenic landscapes and the lovely, quaint towns nestled in the quiet valleys had drawn us on many summer vacation trips. In more recent years, after retiring and gaining more year-round freedom, we returned there frequently to enjoy other seasons of the year. New England, consequently, was the area in which we decided to concentrate our next efforts.

After looking for publications that would help us on these future "bridging" excursions, we discovered that while there were a few guidebooks on individual states, most of them excellent, there was no one guide that would provide the kind of information we like to have before we set off on a new excursion. Consequently, with the encouragement of our local "bridging" associates, we decided that we would make *New England's Covered Bridges: A Complete Guide* our next publication. The total number of covered bridges still remaining in the six-state area would make this publication nearly the size of our two former books. We counted over two hundred covered spans that would have to be visited, documented, and photographed.

Having made this decision, the next thing to determine was the criteria on which we would base the inclusion and documentation of a given covered bridge. In addition to the historic, authentic covered bridges that remain on public roads, there are also many covered bridges that have been built on private property. Consequently, we decided that we would include every remaining historic and/or authentic covered span, as well as other "covered bridge" structures that have received recognition in various state publications or on state tourist maps available to the "bridging" enthusiast. However, the latter would be included only if they had the appearance of an authentic covered bridge; that is, the supporting truss structure, even if built on a "stringer" base, would have to fall into one of the recognized truss designs. These bridges have often been classified as "romantic shelters" or "modern structures" by our "bridging" associates.

We have made every effort to validate all the information contained in this book; however, we do not claim that the information is without error. As we have noticed in our "bridging" experiences, some information is subject to change or is still not accessible to us in any available resource. We would, therefore, appreciate any substantiated corrections or additions for use in future editions of this book. We hope that this volume will not only bring reading and viewing pleasure but will provide the inspiration and necessary information to readers who will actually visit many of these treasures of the New England heritage.

Acknowledgments

To the following people we are sincerely grateful:

Our family, friends, and associates who encouraged us to consider the possibility of publishing this guide.

Richard Donovan, third vice president of The Theodore Burr Covered Bridge Society of Pennsylvania, Inc., and cataloger of covered bridges for the National Society for the Preservation of Covered Bridges, who provided guidance to locate some previously undocumented covered bridges and who enthusiastically contributed information from his vast storehouse of covered bridge knowledge every time we called on him.

James Garvin, architectural historian for the New Hampshire Division of Historical Resources, who efficiently and promptly provided answers to the many questions we sent his way regarding the bridges of his state, especially information regarding his role in the authentic rehabilitation of New Hampshire's covered bridges.

Dan Brock, an enthusiastic, knowledgeable bridger from Vernon, Connecticut, who was able to supply us with many facts about the covered bridges of the New England states. If answers were not readily available, he knew where to make the contacts to acquire the necessary facts.

Joseph Nelson, president of the Vermont Covered Bridge Society, author of *Spanning Time—Vermont's Covered Bridges*, and author of *VERMONTBRIDGES .COM*, website of the Vermont Covered Bridge Society, for his permission to quote and/or paraphrase any of the material contained therein.

The New Hampshire Department of Transportation, which prepared the excellent publication *New Hampshire Covered Bridges, "A Link with Our Past,"* for permission to quote and/or paraphrase material contained therein.

William Dunton, Big Adventure Center, Bethel, Maine, designer and builder of the three newest Paddleford truss bridges in Maine, for the opportunity to discuss his building experiences and the courtesies extended to us when we visited his entertainment center to document and photograph the Big Adventure Bridge.

Suzanna Bunta, public relations manager, and Lynn Befa-Negreni, manager of the Visitors Center, Old Sturbridge Village, for the courtesies extended to us when we visited the village to document and photograph the Dummerston/Vermont Bridge.

Amey Bassett, marketing director, New Hampshire Division of Parks and Recreation, for introducing us to the knowledgeable staff at the Flume Gorge Visitors Center.

Beverly Hunt, managing ranger on duty at the Flume Gorge Visitors Center, Franconia Notch, New Hampshire, for her expertise on the Flume Bridge and Sentinel Pine Bridge, information made available to us from the center's files, and the courtesies extended when we visited the gorge to document and photograph the two bridges therein.

Jerry West, manager of Lost River Gorge, Kinsman Notch, New Hampshire, for sharing his experiences in supervising the construction of the Allen Hollis Footbridge in Lost River Gorge, and the courtesies extended to us when we visited the gorge to document and photograph the bridge.

Barbara and Neil McGowen, volunteers at the Maine Forest and Logging Museum, Orono, Maine, for the courtesies extended to us when we visited the museum to document and photograph Leonard's Mills Bridge and for introducing us to Vernon Shaw, overseer of the museum property.

Vernon Shaw, overseer of the Maine Forest and Logging Museum, Orono, Maine, and director of the crew of volunteers who built Leonard's Mills Bridge as part of the museum's re-created nineteenth-century logging village.

Charles M. Borders, Foster, Rhode Island, for the details surrounding the building and rebuilding of the Swamp Meadow Bridge, Foster, Rhode Island.

Richard Walbridge Spaulding, Cabot Plains Farm, Cabot, Vermont, builder of the A. M. Foster Bridge, for the background information on the construction of that bridge.

Ellen and Robert Robbins, South Barre, Vermont, former owners of the Robbins Nest Bridge, and to Robert, builder of the bridge, for the information regarding its construction.

The authorities at the state historic preservation agencies who efficiently provided answers to our inquiries about their agencies' role in the rehabilitation of their state's covered bridges—Paul Loether, coordinator, Certified Local Government and Historic Restoration Fund Programs, Connecticut Historical Commission, Historic Preservation Division; Kirk F. Mohney, assistant director, Maine Historic Preservation Commission; James L. Garvin, architectural historian, New Hampshire Division of Historical Resources; Sarah Zurier, Rhode Island Historical Preservation & Heritage Commission; and Eric Gilbertson, deputy state historic preservation officer, Division for Historic Preservation, Vermont.

Stephen H. Roper, historic bridge specialist, Massachusetts Highway Department, for his contributions regarding covered bridges listed on the National Register of Historic Places.

The owners of private covered bridges, all of whom responded positively and enthusiastically when contacted for permission to document and photograph their bridge for inclusion in this guide—Terry and Deborah Allen, Ferrisburg Artisans Group, Ferrisburg, Vermont (Spade Farm Bridge); Sam Ankerson, Shelburne Museum, Shelburne, Vermont (Shelburne Museum Bridge); Richard Balser and Missy Middleton, South Pomfret, Vermont (Teago/South Pomfret Bridge); Susanna Bunta, public relations manager, Old Sturbridge Village, Sturbridge, Massachusetts (Dummerston Bridge); Kevin Casey, chief operating officer of MJABC, LLC, Moodus, Connecticut (Johnsonville Village

Bridge); Kathleen Davidson, Branch Brook Campground, Campton, New Hampshire (Turkey Jim Bridge); William Dunton, Big Adventure Center, Bethel, Maine (Big Adventure Bridge); Jeanne A. Elliott, Lyneburke Motel, Lyndonville, Vermont (Sanborn Bridge); William and Marian Gray, Ashfield, Massachusetts (Grays Sugarhouse Bridge); Stephen and Susan Gross, Wilmington, Vermont (High Mowing Farm Bridge); Cathy Harper, West Stratton Development Corporation, Stratton, Vermont (Snow Bridge); Ellen S. Hurwitz, New England College president, Henniker, New Hampshire (New England College Bridge); Susan Jukosky, Brundage-Cater Family Trust, Grafton, New Hampshire (Brundage Bridge); Robert Keating, Jack O' Lantern Resort, Woodstock, New Hampshire (Jack O' Lantern Bridge); Thomas J. Kreffer, Sandgate, Vermont (Kreffer's Crossing Bridge); Mr. and Mrs. Frank G. Lewis, Woodstock, Vermont (Frank Lewis Bridge); Michael Mallett, Wentworth Golf Club, Jackson, New Hampshire (Wentworth Golf Club Bridge); Anthony Martel, Barnard, Vermont (Seven Cedars Farm Bridge); Peter Mohn, vice president of sales, Grafton Cheese Co., Grafton, Vermont (Cheddar Bridge); Eileen Murray and Kurt Janson, Calais, Vermont (Kent's Corner Bridge); Paul and Dennis Nugent, Northfield, Vermont (Chamberlin Bridge); Dan Roulier, Worthington Pond Farm, Somers, Connecticut (Worthington Pond Farm Bridge); Priscilla Sawyer, Magnolia, Massachusetts (Sawyer Pond Bridge); Dwight and Debra Scott, Ashfield, Massachusetts (Creamery Bridge); John Sell, Barre, Vermont (Robbins Nest Bridge); Richard Walbridge Spaulding, Cabot Plains Farm, Cabot Plains, Vermont (A. M. Foster Bridge); Lee and Robert Stoddard, Dolphin Mini Golf Enterprise, Boothbay, Maine (Kenneth E. Stoddard Shell Museum Bridge); Charles Thorndike, Marshfield, Vermont (Martin Bridge); Mr. and Mrs. Andrew Titcomb, Perkinsville, Vermont (Titcomb Bridge); Dan and Nancy Wanek, Glen, New Hampshire (Bartlett Bridge); and Jerry West, Lost River Gorge manager, Woodstock, New Hampshire (Allen Hollis Footbridge).

The numerous town clerks whose offices we visited and contacted by telephone or email for information regarding covered bridges in their vicinity. Every one responded in a most efficient and courteous manner.

The numerous other persons we encountered in our travels who gave us directions, anecdotal information, encouragement, or just pleasant conversation.

Most significantly, we extend our sincere gratitude to the staff of University Press of New England for their enthusiastic support during the preparation of this guide to New England's covered bridges and to William R. Hively, the copyeditor contracted by the Press, for his superb, meticulous editing of our original manuscript.

New England's Covered Bridges

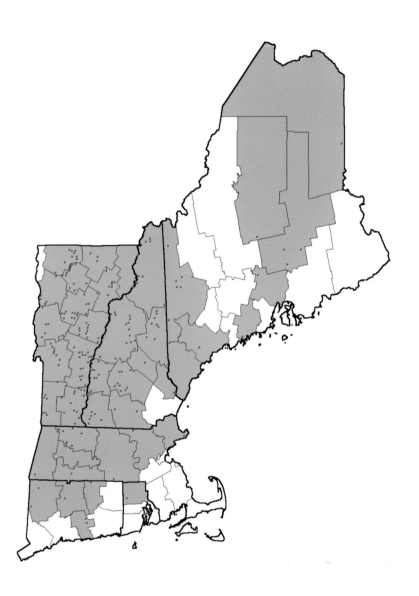

Introduction

I. Covered Bridges in New England

After a brief period of time traveling around the New England countryside, one can readily understand the need for some sort of crossing to bridge the numerous brooks, creeks, and streams as well as the much larger waterways. Rivers such as the Connecticut, Housatonic, Ottauquechee, Sago, Swift, White, and many others created serious obstructions to the travels of our founding fathers.

Many of the crossings were simple, uncovered log spans set on pilings or other solid material along the edge of the waterway, sometimes supported in midstream with a pier or series of piers. Spring freshets and sudden rainstorms frequently destroyed these early crossings, placing a financial burden on the local residents for appropriate replacements. Many bridges of this type were erected and rebuilt numerous times prior to the beginning of the nineteenth century.

It was not until 1805 that the first covered span appeared in the United States. It was the Permanent Bridge that crossed the Schuylkill River in Philadelphia, built by Timothy Palmer from Connecticut, as an uncovered structure. A Philadelphian, Judge Richard Peters, a member of the bridge company, was convinced that covering the intricate trusses would greatly extend their life expectancy. Consequently, the bridge company commissioned Adam Traquair and Owen Biddle to design and build the covering. It was opened for travel on January 1, 1805. This structure gave Pennsylvania the distinction of having the first covered bridge in the United States. After the structure was covered, Palmer gracefully agreed that with this "newfangled refinement" the bridge "might last thirty or forty years." After being rebuilt and widened in 1850–51, it stood until it was destroyed by fire on November 20, 1875. One year after the Permanent Bridge was completed, Palmer built his next bridge, a tightly enclosed and roofed structure that extended from Easton, Pennsylvania, to Phillipsburg, New Jersey.

Following the erection of these two covered spans, similar spans sprung up all over the Northeast. Designers and builders by the name of Theodore Burr of Torringford, Connecticut; Ithiel Town of Thompson, Connecticut; Colonel Stephen H. Long of West Hopkinton, New Hampshire; William Howe of Spencer, Massachusetts; Peter Paddleford of Littleton, New Hampshire; and Thomas Willis Pratt of Boston, Massachusetts, became well known among the communities requiring these magnificent new structures. Their designs became the ones relied upon by bridge builders all over the Northeast.

During the nineteenth and the early part of the twentieth centuries, the erection of nearly one thousand covered bridges was recorded in New England's archives. However, the ravages of time, storm, flood, neglect, and the destructive nature of society's vandals have reduced the number of remaining historic, authentic truss, covered bridges to fewer than two hundred. Fortunately, during the 1950s a movement began among covered bridge enthusiasts to save, preserve, and rehabilitate these lovely treasures created by artisans long past but not forgotten.

II. Locating Covered Bridges

Many times the hunt is half the fun of "bridging." The search for a particular bridge will often take you into some of the most interesting, remote, and scenic areas of a state. While there are still some bridges that exist along heavily traveled main roads, most of them are located on secondary town roads, frequently unpaved. It is quite surprising to find that many of the rural roads, maintained by town highway departments, still have dirt or gravel surfaces.

The primary resources that we used to locate bridges were the various state atlases and gazeteers published by DeLorme Mapping Company; the *World Guide to Covered Bridges* (*WGCB*), 1989 edition by Bill Helsel, prepared by the National Society for the Preservation of Covered Bridges (NSPCB); *Spanning Time—Vermont's Covered Bridges,* by Joseph C. Nelson; *Covered Bridges of Vermont,* by Ed Barna; and *New Hampshire Covered Bridges: Map & Guide* and *Vermont Covered Bridges: Illustrated Map & Guide,* both published by Hartnett House Map Publishers. The DeLorme publications and the two Hartnett House maps locate nearly all of the covered bridges with an easy-to-find icon. The *WGCB* is presently available only as a computer diskette, which is being updated on a regular basis. The directions to bridge locations contained in this guide are given in tenths of a mile along specific route numbers or from given locations. These were helpful, except that we were often traveling from a different direction and had to interpret the instructions in reverse or the directions were given from a town some distance from the bridge, making them difficult to follow.

Another source of information for location of the "romantic/modern" shelters as well as some of the questionable historic, authentic bridges was our good friend and fellow "bridger" Richard Donovan. Richard is a storehouse of covered bridge information and the person individually responsible for assigning specific numbers to all the bridges listed in both publications of the NSPCB: the *World Guide to Covered Bridges* and *Romantic Shelters,* by Arthur F. Hammer. Armed with these valuable resources, we were able to plan systematic routes to visit, document, and photograph over two hundred bridges included in this guide.

For the serious "bridger," this new guide to the covered bridges of New England should make locating the bridges relatively easy. Using it, together with a copy of the respective state's highway map, should provide a delightful "bridging safari." Keep in mind, however, that while road names and signs were in existence during our research of 2002 and 2003, there is no guarantee that they will still be there when you venture forth on your next safari. If one has it readily available, a copy of the state's DeLorme *Atlas & Gazetteer,* mentioned above, will also be helpful.

For those who have one of the more contemporary directional aids—a GPS receiver—the GPS coordinates of every bridge have also been provided. These have been recorded as close as possible to the bridge portal. The GPS coordinates can also be found along the top, sides, and bottom of each page of the more recent editions of the respective DeLorme *Atlas & Gazetteer.*

A few typical road signs, in any event, are indicative of a covered bridge in the area:

Bridge/Weight Limit 3 Tons/1300 ft. Ahead
Covered Bridge Road
Low Clearance/Bridge Ahead/11′ 6″ Clearance
Road Closed/Bridge Out
Covered Bridge Ahead

III. The Structure of New England's Covered Bridges

Truss Types Used in New England

A bridge is a structure built across a gap in the terrain, most often created by a flowing run, creek, brook, stream, or river. The simplest bridge structure is called a "stringer" bridge, and the most primitive of these consists of a single log laid across the gap from one bank to the other. In order to carry a load of any consequence, two logs can be laid some distance from each other with planks joining the two to span the opening. Even this simple span deteriorates rather quickly when exposed to the elements, hence the need to cover it to preserve its supporting framework.

Information about covered bridges dates back over eight hundred years to the bridges in China "with very handsome roofs" recorded by Marco Polo in journals of his travels. A covered footbridge, the Chapel Bridge, in Lucerne, Switzerland, dates to 1333. Although lost to arson in 1993, which also destroyed two-thirds of the magnificent artwork that hung in the bridge, the landmark bridge was restored and reopened in 1994. There are still several hundred covered bridges standing in Europe that date back to the sixteenth century; and, while there are also specific plans for wooden bridges that date to 1570, few of the bridge builders in Europe paid attention to them. Those basic truss designs were described in *A Treatise on Architecture,* volume 3 of a four-volume work by Andrea Palladio, an Italian mathamatician, sculptor, and architect. In this volume he illustrates the basic queenpost truss, a multiple kingpost truss, and two other trusses that combine the arch with vertical timbers and diagonal braces. His treatise was translated into English in 1742, but it seems that he was far ahead of his time.

Twenty distinctively different truss designs have been used throughout the United States, many of them bearing a resemblance to those of Palladio, but only twelve specific truss designs or combinations thereof have been used in New England. There are also ten stringer-type covered bridges documented in this guide.

The stringer bridge is not a truss design, by definition. The true truss system consists of timbers or timbers and metal rods assembled in a triangle, the triangle being the only two-dimensional figure that cannot be distorted under stress. Each bridge consists of two truss systems, one on either side of the structure. The line drawings that follow illustrate the basic pattern of each truss. There have been many variations to these designs depending upon locale, builder, and materials available. The heavy, solid lines in the drawings represent solid timbers. Fine, dashed lines represent the exterior shape of the bridge's side, and in the diagrams of the Howe and tied arch trusses, the heavier dotted lines represent other structural timbers that are not part of the truss. The dashed lines in those two drawings represent metal rods.

1. THE KINGPOST TRUSS

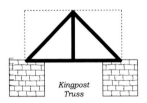

Kingpost
Truss

This is the oldest and simplest truss design used in bridge construction. Initially it was used under the roadway rather than above. It consists of a chord (horizontal timber), a kingpost (vertical timber), and two diagonals. It is used primarily for short spans of approximately twenty to fifty feet (see the Pine Brook/Wilder Bridge in Washington County, Vermont). There are only seven kingpost truss bridges, or variations thereof, remaining in the New England States—one in Massachusetts and six in Vermont.

2. THE MULTIPLE KINGPOST TRUSS

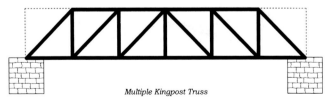

Multiple Kingpost Truss

The multiple kingpost design was developed to span longer distances, frequently up to one hundred feet. The design consists of one kingpost in the center with several right-angle panels on each side of the center, and all diagonals pointing toward the center (see the Dingleton Hill Bridge, Sullivan County, New Hampshire). There are still seventeen trusses of this design remaining in the New England States—one in Connecticut, five in New Hampshire, and eleven in Vermont.

3. THE QUEENPOST TRUSS

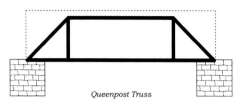

Queenpost Truss

The queenpost truss system followed the kingpost in design chronologically. It, like the multiple kingpost truss, was a modification of the kingpost truss and used to span longer distances, frequently up to seventy-five feet. In this truss, a rectangular panel was placed between the two triangles that originally faced the center vertical kingpost timber. The upper horizontal member of that rectangle, however, was below the horizontal upper chord of the exterior side framework (see the A. M. Foster Bridge, Washington County, Vermont). Frequently, additional diagonal timbers were placed between the corners of the central rectangle. There are still twenty-eight true queenpost trusses remaining in the New England States—one in Maine, one in Massachusetts, three in New Hampshire, and twenty-three in Vermont. There are two examples of the queenpost and kingpost trusses being used together, one in New Hampshire (the Carlton Bridge in Cheshire County) and one in Vermont (the Red Bridge in Lamoille County). There are three examples of the queenpost truss being used to strengthen or modify another truss, one in New Hampshire (the Dalton Bridge in Merrimack County) and two in Connecticut (Bulls Bridge and West Cornwall Bridge, both in Litchfield County). And there is one unique combination of the queenpost truss being used with a multiple kingpost truss and an arch—the Taftsville Bridge in Windsor County, Vermont.

4. THE BURR TRUSS

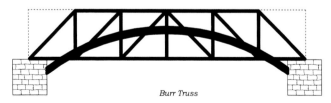

Burr Truss

One of the earliest and most prominent bridge builders in our country was Theodore Burr from Torrington, Connecticut. His career began in New York, where he built a bridge spanning the Hudson River in 1804. Burr's truss design soon became one of the more frequently used systems. The Burr arch truss, as the design became known, used two long arches that rested in the abutments on either end and typically sandwiched a multiple kingpost structure (see the Quinlan Bridge in Chittendon County, Vermont). While there are a large number of Burr truss bridges built throughout the United States, only eleven of them are found in the New England area—one in Massachusetts, one in New Hampshire, and nine in Vermont.

5. THE TOWN TRUSS

Town Truss

The Town truss was named for its originator, Ithiel Town, who also came from Connecticut. He designed and built his first bridge in 1820. His design is sometimes called the "lattice truss," and a quick glimpse at the pattern formed by its members readily explains the nickname (see the Comstock Bridge in Franklin County, Vermont). In some areas the Town truss became very popular because it used smaller-dimension lumber than other trusses, required a limited amount of framing and hardware, could easily be built using unskilled laborers, and could span distances up to two hundred feet. A heavy concentration of them were built in the New England area, a total of seventy-six—three in Connecticut, one in Maine, five in Massachusetts, twenty-two in New Hampshire, one in Rhode Island, and forty-four in Vermont. Several of these are combined with other trusses—three in Vermont are combined with the kingpost truss, one in Connecticut and two in New Hampshire are combined with the Burr-type arch, two in Connecticut are combined with the queenpost truss, and two railroad bridges in New Hampshire use a very substantial double Town truss.

6. THE LONG TRUSS

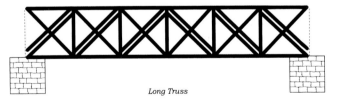

Long Truss

The Long truss was the design of a U.S. Army engineer, Colonel Stephen H. Long of Hopkinton, New Hampshire. In 1830, at the beginning of the railroad era, Long developed and patented this truss. It uses a panel design, similar to the multiple kingpost truss, wherein the single diagonal brace pointing toward the top center is replaced with two diagonals, side by side, that sandwich one counterbrace diagonal in each panel (see the Smith Millennium Bridge in Grafton County, New Hampshire). Even though Long was a New Englander, his truss never became very popular there. There are only eight Long truss covered bridges still standing in the New England states—two in Maine, one in Massachusetts, and five in New Hampshire.

7. THE WARREN TRUSS

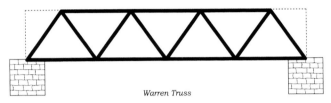

Warren Truss

The Warren Truss is a relatively simple, lightweight truss designed and patented in 1838 by two Englishmen, James Warren and T. W. Morzani. It is better known as a steel railroad bridge truss than as a covered bridge truss. It is still being used in both England and the United States as a railroad bridge truss. However, according to Raymond E. Wilson, in a 1971 article in *Technology Review,* a publication of the Massachusetts Institute of Technology, the truss was "used to some extent in the Middle West and later on the West Coast, due to easy assembly and maintenance." The truss consists of a series of diagonals placed in the shape of a W with no vertical posts, rods, or panels (see the Cocheco River Pedestrian Bridge, Strafford County, New Hampshire).

8. THE HAUPT TRUSS

Haupt Truss

In 1839, Herman Haupt of Gettysburg, Pennsylvania, patented his "improved lattice truss" as a response to the "lattice truss" designs of Ithiel Town of 1820 and 1835. General Haupt was better known for his role as a military figure than as a bridge designer; however, he was a recognized engineer and designer who graduated from West Point in 1835. He used the analytical methods he had developed to design a more efficient lattice truss with diagonal members positioned only at locations that required support. According to Raymond E. Wilson, in one of his popular writings on covered bridges that appeared in *Technology Review* in 1971, Haupt's patents "show a panel-type truss using single-latticed diagonal braces, each spanning three short panels and also braced with a full-length kingpost, serving in place of an arch." Although a number of his bridges were built in various parts of the country, only two remain. The one that most closely resembles the original Haupt patent is the Bunker Hill Bridge in Catawba County, North Carolina. The one that remains in New England is quite a modification of the original design and is located in Thetford Center, Vermont (see the Sayers Bridge, Orange County, Vermont).

9. THE HOWE TRUSS

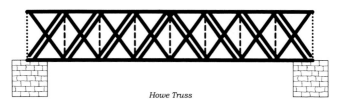

Howe Truss

William Howe of Massachusetts patented the Howe truss design in 1840. It is really an elaboration on the multiple kingpost design whereby two heavy metal rods are substituted for the vertical timbers. Variations on this pattern add a second diagonal timber to the original single diagonal of the multiple kingpost and/or another diagonal timber running in the opposite direction between the vertical rods (see the Packard Hill Bridge, Grafton County, New Hampshire, and the Columbia Bridge, Coos/Essex Counties, in the New Hampshire/Vermont section). Some accounts indicate that the Howe design provided a bridge that was stronger than any all-wood structure; as a result, it became the forerunner of iron bridges. There are 124 Howe truss spans in the United States today. Eleven of these are found in New England—one in Connecticut, two in Maine, two in Massachusetts, two in New Hampshire, two in New Hampshire/Vermont, and two in Vermont.

10. THE PRATT TRUSS

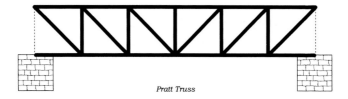

Pratt Truss

Thomas Willis Pratt, born 1812, the son of a prosperous Boston architect, was responsible for the development and patent of the Pratt truss. He was considered a child prodigy when at the age of twelve he drew complicated working plans for a new home that his father planned to build. After his engineering education he was employed during the 1830s by the Norwich & Worcester Railroad in Connecticut, first as an aide, then as a division engineer, and eventually as the superintendent of the company. In 1844, while living in Norwich, he secured a patent for a panel-type truss with structural members primarily opposite those used by Howe in his truss. Where Howe used solid timbers, Pratt used steel rods; and where Howe used steel rods, Pratt used solid timbers. In its original design, the Pratt truss was difficult to adjust, so some of the diagonal braces were removed, leaving only the ones that sloped upward toward the end of the bridge. This principle, when applied to steel railroad bridges, was used extensively throughout the country into the twentieth century. The truss as used in covered bridge construction was primarily a timber structure, as shown in the drawing (see County Bridge, Hillsborough County, New Hampshire). There are five documented uses of the Pratt truss in the New England states—one in Connecticut, one in Massachusetts, two in New Hampshire, and one in Vermont. One of these, the Lincoln Bridge, Windsor County, Vermont, is quite different and probably more closely related to the original Pratt patent. It is described at greater length on the Lincoln Bridge page. In the other four bridges, the truss looks like the one in the drawing—an inverted multiple kingpost truss.

11. THE PADDLEFORD TRUSS

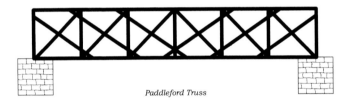

Paddleford Truss

The Paddleford truss was developed by Peter Paddleford of Littleton, New Hampshire. Prior to designing his truss he had successfully built several Long truss bridges. Paddleford's truss is primarily a modification of the Long truss wherein longer stiffening diagonals are set into channels on the vertical and diagonal members they cross or simply pinned to them with trunnels. In appearance, it might also be described as a multiple kingpost truss with additional stiffening diagonals that cross and are anchored to every two vertical timbers starting at the the lower inside to the upper outside of the bridge (see the Lovejoy Bridge, Oxford County, Maine). There are still twenty-five Paddleford truss bridges in the New England area—eight in Maine, fourteen in New Hampshire, and three in Vermont. Eleven of these are examples of a Paddleford truss that has been reinforced with an arch, similar to that used in the Burr truss or the tied arch truss.

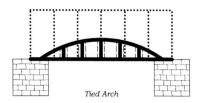

Tied Arch

The arch has been used in bridge construction for many years. Two different arch truss designs were diagrammed in Andrea Palladio's 1570 *Treatise on Architecture.* However, no record has been found to identify the designer of the tied arch as it has been used in the covered bridges of New England. Only three bridges, all in Vermont, have been built using the tied arch truss (see the Best Bridge, Windsor County, Vermont). All of them are relatively short bridges with an average span of forty-one feet. The truss consists of a laminated arch of five to seven layers of two-by-ten-inch planks bent over two-by-ten-inch vertical posts. The vertical posts are spaced intermittently between the arch and the lower chord. These posts, in turn, are tied to both the top of the arch and the bottom of the lower chord with three-quarter-inch metal suspension rods using blocks, washers, and nuts for adjustment. Sometimes additional diagonal rods are used. The truss supports the live load carried by the bridge deck. The sides and roof of a tied arch bridge are usually a simple post and beam, barnlike structure. An arch has occasionally been added to other existing truss structures to increase the live load limit. Some of these may also be of the tied arch variety.

IV. Working to Preserve New England's Covered Bridges

In her book *Covered Bridges Today,* Brenda Krekeler writes, "At one time the United States had as many as 12,000 covered bridges." By the 1950s that number had dwindled to less than 1,500. In 1950, the National Society for the Preservation of Covered Bridges was formed by a group of covered bridge enthusiasts who realized that "these spans bear truthful witness to much that is American Culture and Heritage" and that something had to be done to save them. Shortly thereafter, other statewide and local organizations sprang up around the country with the express purpose of helping to "preserve this country's surviving Covered Wooden Spans." The Vermont Covered Bridge Society is one of these statewide organizations.

State governments, too, have become aware of the need to preserve these historic treasures. In the state of Maine, in 1959, the legislature took a major step toward covered bridge preservation by enacting a law to preserve these structures. The law provided that state money could be used in the preservation and renovation of covered bridges. In 1961, the Department of Transportation started the process of renovating the remaining ten authentic covered spans.

Funding the restoration of covered bridges is always one of the most serious drawbacks to immediate action. The National Historic Covered Bridge

Preservation Program (NHCBPP) has been created to assist both state and local bridge restoration projects. This program was established by Section 1224 of the Transportation Equity Act for the Twenty-first Century (TEA21). It provides funding to help the states in their efforts to preserve, rehabilitate, or restore the nation's historic covered bridges. To be included in this program a bridge must be listed or eligible for listing on the National Register for Historic Places. Between 2000 and July 2002, the sum of $5,623,034 from a total $20,800,750 was allocated to Connecticut, Maine, Massachusetts, New Hampshire, and Vermont for restoration of covered bridges in their respective states.

On the local scene, interested citizens in towns all across the six-state area have organized, in many cases, to save and preserve or restore just one or two bridges. In the small rural town of Langdon, New Hampshire, the Langdon Covered Bridge Association undertook the task of saving and restoring the only two covered bridges still standing within its town line. This organization managed to raise the necessary funds to completely restore the Prentiss Bridge, originally built in 1874. Restoration began in 2000, with the rededication of the bridge taking place in 2002. The McDermott Bridge is the next bridge targeted by the association's restoration efforts. Perhaps by the time you visit the bridge that task will have been realized. This is only one example of many such efforts that are taking place throughout the country.

Interest in covered bridge preservation and restoration now, in the early years of the twenty-first century, reflects a depth of concern that is becoming even stronger. The three-day National Historic Covered Bridge Best Practices Conference, "the first of its kind to collect and benchmark" the large amount of information that exists on covered bridges, was convened on June 5, 2003. Perhaps it was quite natural that the conference would be held at the University of Vermont, in the New England state that can claim the largest number of remaining covered bridges. This event was open to anyone who wished to attend— state and local highway engineers, state and county covered bridge maintenance personnel, volunteers charged with raising funds for the preservation of covered bridges, local and national covered bridge preservation organizations, historic preservationists, general contractors, structural engineers, covered bridge historians, the traveling public, and community members. The intent of the conference was to promote dialogue on the diverse ideas, experience, techniques, and practices for historic covered bridge preservation.

It is only natural, too, that all the state historic and museum commissions have become involved in this wave of activity to preserve and restore these remarkable treasures of our nation's heritage. The role that they are playing is the subject of the next section.

V. The Rehabilitation of New England's Covered Bridges

Every state has a historic preservation office or commission. While their names may vary from state to state, their function is primarily the same. These offices become involved in approving all restoration procedures whenever funding for the rehabilitation is provided by either state or federal sources. They also become involved, if requested, in any restorations that are funded totally by local fund-raising efforts. In their efforts to oversee and approve these restorations, these commissions follow *The Secretary of the Interior's Standards for Rehabilitation with Illustrated Guidelines for Rehabilitating Historic Buildings,* published in 1990. The following list of "Standards for Rehabilitation," which appears in the beginning of the publication, summarizes the secretary of the interior's standards:

1. A property will be used as it was historically or be given a new use that requires minimal change to its distinctive materials, features, spaces, and spatial relationships.
2. The historic character of a property will be retained and preserved. The removal of distinctive materials or alteration of features, spaces, and spatial relationships that characterize a property will be avoided.
3. Each property will be recognized as a physical record of its time, place, and use. Changes that create a false sense of historical development, such as adding conjectural features or elements from other historic properties, will not be undertaken.
4. Changes to a property that have acquired historic significance in their own right will be retained and preserved.
5. Distinctive materials, features, finishes, and construction techniques or examples of craftsmanship that characterize a property will be preserved.
6. Deteriorated historic features will be repaired rather than replaced. Where the severity of deterioration requires replacement of a distinctive feature, the new feature will match the old in design, color, texture, and, where possible, materials. Replacement of missing features will be substantiated by documentary and physical evidence.
7. Chemical or physical treatments, if appropriate, will be undertaken using the gentlest means possible. Treatments that cause damage to historic materials will not be used.
8. Archeological resources will be protected and preserved in place. If such resources must be disturbed, mitigation measures will be undertaken.
9. New additions, exterior alterations, or related new construction will not destroy historic materials, features, and spatial relationships that characterize the property. The new work shall be differentiated from the old and will be compatible with the historic materials, features, size, scale and proportion, and massing to protect the integrity of the property and its environment.
10. New additions and adjacent or related new construction will be undertaken in such a manner that, if removed in the future, the essential form and integrity of the historic property and its environment would be unimpaired.

The 160 pages of this document clearly outline "recommended" and "not recommended" procedures to be followed in the entire restoration process.

Some states have even gone beyond this and established a more extensive set of guidelines for the rehabilitation process. It seems that all efforts are being taken to preserve and restore the historic integrity of New England's covered bridges so that those remaining can be seen and enjoyed for many generations to come.

VI. The Guide to New England's Covered Bridges

This guidebook contains at least one photograph of and statistical information on every authentic covered bridge still standing in New England as well as some "romantic/modern" bridges. The descriptive and statistical data include the following:

Name   The name of the bridge, listing the most common name first when a bridge is known or has been known by more than one name. The most common name has been taken from a variety of documented sources as listed in the bibliography, the state publications, or a more recent posting of a name on or near a bridge.

Location   The location of the bridge, usually based on the nearest locality and town in which the bridge is situated. Throughout the New England states the geographic area of the state is divided first into counties, then into towns within each county, and finally into various localities within each town. The exact classification of these localities varies from state to state. They may be identified as a city, a village, a hamlet, a gore, a settlement, or a district, among other possible local names. For the purpose of uniformity, the word "locality" will refer to any of these populated areas within a given town. For example, "In Ashuelot, a locality within the Winchester town line" means that the bridge is located in Ashuelot, one of several populated areas within the town boundaries of Winchester.

Directions   Directions to the bridge given in tenths of a mile from the nearest locality, or road junction within a locality as portrayed in any of the *Atlas & Gazeteer*s for the various states published by the DeLorme Map Co., Yarmouth, Maine, or found on most of the official road maps published by the specific state.

GPS   The Global Positioning System coordinates taken at the portal of the bridge closest to the point of access as indicated in Directions.

Year   Year of construction as found in a variety of documented sources listed in the bibliography, the state publications, or a more recent posting of a date on or near a bridge.

Truss   The truss design used in the construction of the bridge.

Waterway   The run, brook, creek, stream, or river that the bridge spans.

In Use   "Yes" indicates usage for all traffic. Other usage is specified. Verified on an actual visit to the bridge in 2002 or 2003.

Number of Spans   Data as personally observed and as verified in all our documented sources. A "+" following the number indicates that a pier has been added as additional support.

Owner   Determined from all sources available. See bibliography.

Builder   Determined from all sources available. See bibliography.

Length   Measured on an actual visit to the bridge in 2002 or 2003. The actual length measured from portal to portal. In the case of a sloping portal, the measurement was taken approximately four feet above the road surface.

Width   Measured on an actual visit to the bridge in 2002 or 2003. Inside measurement determined from one side of the portal to the opposite side of the same portal.

Condition   Recorded as personally observed with untrained eyes and verified with various articles appearing in printed and website publications.

Number   The number originally assigned to the bridge as listed in the *World Guide to Covered Bridges* (*WGCB*) and modified by our state covered bridge society, The Theodore Burr Covered Bridge Society of Pennsylvania, Inc., in March 1996 to replace the first two digits with the state abbreviation. Therefore, the first two letters represent the state; the next two digits represent the county, assigned alphabetically; and the last two or three digits represent a specific bridge within a county, assigned in the order data were received by the *WGCB* compilers. The original intent of the compilers was to assign the last two digits according to the chronology of the bridge construction date. However, because information on many of the bridges was received after the first edition was compiled, this sequence was broken. A letter replacing the final digits of the number indicates that the bridge is a "romantic/modern" shelter—capital letter for vehicle usage, lowercase for pedestrian traffic. A "(2)" following the six-character bridge number indicates that the bridge has been replaced with primarily new material on the site of the original bridge.

Register   The date on which the bridge was listed in the National Register of Historic Places. "Does not qualify" indicates that the bridge does not meet the guidelines established by the National Register; that is, it is a new bridge, it is not old enough (at least fifty years old), or it has been rebuilt with too much new material. If a registered bridge has been rebuilt with too much new material and is still listed on the register, the date listed is for the original bridge.

Miscellaneous Anecdotal Information   Interesting bits of information about the bridge gleaned from a variety of sources, such as those listed in the bibliography, or personally observed on our visits to the bridges in 2002 and 2003.

The bridges in this guide are arranged in alphabetical order, first according to state name, second according to county name, and third according to the most common bridge name. If a bridge is located between two states, the states are alphabetized according to the one that occurs first in alphabetical order. Likewise, if a bridge occurs between two counties, the counties are alphabetized according to the one that occurs first in alphabetical order. The map opposite page 1 and the map on the title page of each state display the approximate geographic location of each bridge.

VII. Covered Bridge Terminology

abutment   The structure that supports the end of the bridge or accepts the thrust of the Burr arch and supports and retains the bridge approach, usually built of stone, bedrock, timbers, or concrete.

angle block   A block of wood or metal, triangular in shape, placed at the junction of a post, brace, counterbrace, or arch, serving as a seat. These are commonly found in the Howe truss.

approach   The road surface leading into the bridge.

bed timber   A timber placed at the four corners of a bridge between the abutment and the bottom chord. The basic function of the timber is to more evenly distribute the bearing weight. It is a timber that can easily be replaced when deteriorating due to rot.

bent   A type of support placed under the bridge perpendicular to the longitudinal members of the deck sometimes resembling a sawhorse, occasionally used as a temporary scaffolding in the building process, either original or restoration. It may also be used to support an open bridge approach, a weak or damaged bridge, or even as a substitute for an abutment. (See Bump Bridge, Grafton County, New Hampshire.)

bolster beam   A timber that extends beyond the abutment between the abutment and the lower chord of the truss. Commonly found in a Town truss.

brace   A diagonal structural member that slants toward the top center of the truss.

buttress   A vertical outside timber or iron rod attached at the bottom to an extended floor beam and at the top to an upper member of the truss to give lateral support. It is sometimes called a sway brace.

camber   An upward curve of the bridge deck.

chord   One of the two horizontal members, upper or lower, of the truss system extending from end to end of the bridge.

compression member   A truss member subjected to stress by pressing together (see tension member).

corbel   A timber that projects from the end post of a portal to support an overhanging gable end. It is sometimes used as decoration.

counterbrace   A diagonal structural member that slants toward the top of the truss, away from the center.

dead load   The weight of the bridge itself, independent of traffic (see live load).

deck   The surface of the bridge that carries the traffic.

double barrel bridge   Common name given to a covered bridge with two lanes separated by a center divider. The divider may be a truss, another structural member of the bridge, or simply a partition.

floor beam   A transverse member between the lower chords that supports the decking and live load.

gabion   A galvanized wire box filled with stones used to form retaining walls along a stream or bridge approach.

joist   Timbers laid longitudinally on the floor beams. It is these members that support the floor planks.

key   A wedge-shaped piece inserted into a joint to tighten it.

knee brace   (1) A timber shaped at a right angle cut from a tree branch or root with that shape naturally, used to reinforce a joint between an upright truss member and upper lateral joist (see the North Hartland Bridge (West Twin), Windsor County, Vermont). (2) A short timber placed at a forty-five-degree angle to reinforce a joint between an upright truss member and an upper lateral joist.

live load   The dynamic or moving weight, such as a vehicle, carried by the bridge (see dead load).

parapet   A wall rising above the road level, usually as an upward extension of the wingwall.

pier   Structure(s) located between the abutments to support a multispan bridge. A midstream support added to an existing span.

portal   The opening at either end of a bridge. The face of that opening.

post   A vertical member of a truss that is perpendicular or near perpendicular to the bottom chord.

rod   A slender metal bar used as a vertical or diagonal member of a truss between the upper and lower chords. Truss members could be tightened by adjusting nuts against metal washers and shim blocks or by adjusting turnbuckle.

runners   Lengthwise planks, usually laid over crosswise planks, in the tire track area of the bridge deck, probably added sometime after the invention of the automobile to reduce the noise from loose planks.

span   The horizontal space between two supports of the bridge.

stress   The resistance of an object to external force such as that realized in both a compression member and a tension member.

tension member   A truss member subjected to stress by pulling apart (see also compression member).

trunnel   A wooden peg, usually oak, used to fasten timbers in bridge building, sometimes replaced with galvanized bolts. Also called a treenail.

turnbuckle   A link with a screw thread at one or both ends for tightening a rod.

wingwalls   Stone or concrete extensions of the abutment that contain the fill as the road approaches the bridge.

CONNECTICUT

LITCHFIELD

TOLLAND

WINDHAM

HARTFORD

MIDDLESEX

NEW LONDON

NEW HAVEN

FAIRFIELD

Connecticut

"The Constitution State"

At one time, the state of Connecticut, even though small in size, included over sixty covered highway and railroad bridges. Because of its topography, most of these stood in the western part of the state crossing rivers like the Housatonic, Naugatuck, and Farmington. There are records of only a dozen known to have existed east of the Connecticut River. Most of the covered railroad bridges served predecessors of the New Haven Railroad. They were all very high structures, built with very heavy timbers and covered with thousands of board feet of siding. They were built in towns like Bridgeport, Greenwich, Jewett City, Milford, Norwich, and Waterbury.

Connecticut's greatest contributions to the covered bridge scene were the men who designed and built them. Theodore Burr, designer of the extensively used Burr truss (primarily outside of New England), came from Torringford, a prosperous hill town in the western part of the state. Ithiel Town, designer of the widely used Town lattice truss, was originally from Thompson but made his home in New Haven. Then there were the builders—Colonel Ezra Brainerd of East Hartford, Samuel Mack of Lyme, Jonathan Walcott of Windham, and Zenas Whiting of Norwich. Most of them, however, achieved their recognition in the covered bridge world outside of their home state.

The first covered highway bridge in Connecticut was built as early as 1818. It was the massive 974-foot-long Hartford Toll Bridge designed by Ithiel Town and built by Town and Isaac Damon of Northampton, Massachusetts. The original investment to build the bridge was $40,000. Tolls were collected for seventy years to provide a return on the initial investment. Finally, in 1889, the five towns that benefited most from the use of the bridge purchased it and made usage of it free.

An interesting tale is told about the sign that once hung on the portal of the Hartford Bridge. In his book *Covered Bridges of the Northeast,* Richard Sanders Allen relates:

> This sign differed slightly from the usual "walk your horses" admonition. The story goes that a farmer's wife from over beyond East Hartford was in a hurry to get to market on a Saturday morning, and drove a bit too fast to suit the conscientious constable stationed on the old bridge. Hauled into court, the lady was about to plead guilty and pay her fine when a smart lawyer interceded, leaping to the astonished lady's side.
>
> "May it please Your Honor," he shouted, "I move this case be thrown out of court!"

"How so?" asked the judge.

"Your Honor, the sign on the Hartford Bridge reads 'Ten dollars fine for any man to ride or drive faster than a walk on this bridge.' Your Honor, the horse was a mare and my client is a woman!"

In the uproar that followed the case was dismissed.

Unfortunately, the Hartford Bridge was destroyed by fire on the night of May 17, 1895. Flames that started in the East Hartford end of the bridge spread through the entire 974 feet of the tinder-dry bridge within ten minutes while a crowd of twenty thousand townspeople lining the banks of the Connecticut River looked on.

Today, in the twenty-first century, only three historic covered bridges still exist in Connecticut. They are all highway bridges, but only two of them carry vehicular traffic, and these two both span the Housatonic River—Bulls Bridge and West Cornwall Bridge, both in Litchfield County. The third is a bypassed but restored bridge located in a roadside park—the Comstock Bridge in Middlesex County. All the covered railroad bridges have disappeared, being replaced, where railroad bridges were still required, by contemporary twentieth-century structures. In addition to the three historic bridges still standing in the state, there are two twentieth-century covered bridges—the Huckleberry Hill Bridge, a covered footbridge in Hartford County built in 1968, and the Johnsonville Village Bridge in Middlesex County, built in the later part of the century by Thomas Kronenberger, a contemporary covered bridge builder. There is also one very contemporary bridge, just completed in 2002 by another contemporary builder, Ron Oulette, now residing in Connecticut—the lovely Worthington Pond Farm Bridge in Tolland County. Since Connecticut is a relatively small state, it is possible for the conscientious "bridger" to visit all six covered bridges in one day.

Huckleberry Hill Bridge

Location: In Countryside Park, within the Avon town line.

Directions: In Unionville, at the junction of CT 4 and CT 177, go northwest on CT 4 for 0.6 mile to Huckleberry Hill Road, turn right (north) onto Huckleberry Hill Road, and go 1.7 miles to Countryside Park on the left (west) side of the road. The bridge can be seen straight ahead to the right as the park is entered.

GPS: 41° 47.159N 072° 54.512W (coordinates recorded in parking lot close to the bridge)

Year: 1968   **Truss:** Pratt variant   **Waterway:** Pond outlet
In Use: Foot traffic only   **Number of Spans:** 1   **Owner:** Town of Avon
Builder: Unknown   **Length:** 35 ft. 7 in.   **Width:** 8 ft.   **Condition:** Good
Number: CT-02-02   **Register:** Does not qualify

This lovely little footbridge, located in a roadside park, is really not an authentic covered bridge designed to carry vehicular traffic. We have included it in our guide to New England's covered bridges primarily because it has been documented and given an "official" number in at least one other covered bridge source of information, the *World Guide to Covered Bridges,* 1989 edition, published by the National Society for the Preservation of Covered Bridges.

The bridge is quite substantially constructed using a traditional covered

bridge truss design, a variation of the Pratt truss. It will adequately support the live load of the foot traffic it was built to accommodate and even that of a small to medium-size farm tractor. Resting on concrete abutments, it has a deck of lengthwise planks and a roof of asphalt shingles. The lower halves of the sides are covered with wide vertical boards, the upper halves with a lattice treatment, and the gable ends are also covered with wide vertical boards. The entire structure is painted brown. It certainly adds an early American charm to this quiet, roadside park setting.

LITCHFIELD COUNTY

Bulls Bridge

Location: Approximately 2.7 miles north of Gaylordsville within the Kent town line.

Directions: In Gaylordsville, at the junction of CT 55 and US 7, go north on US 7 for 2.7 miles to Bulls Bridge Road, on the left (west); turn left to the parking areas on both east and west ends of the bridge.

GPS: 41° 40.544N 073° 30.537W

Year: 1842   **Truss:** Town with queenpost   **Waterway:** Housatonic River
In Use: Yes   **Number of Spans:** 1   **Owner:** Town of Kent
Builder: Unknown   **Length:** 109 ft.   **Width:** 14 ft. 1 in.
Condition: Very Good   **Number:** CT-03-01   **Register:** Apr. 26, 1972

Bulls Bridge derives its name from Isaac and Jacob Bull, who built an ironworks nearby in 1760. They are also credited with the first of at least five wooden bridges that spanned the Housatonic River Gorge at this location. The present bridge, however, was the first covered bridge on record at this site.

This bridge has a truss structure that we have seen only two other times in our "bridging" experiences. It is exactly the same as the one used for the West Cornwall Bridge, also in Litchfield County, and one in Pennsylvania, the Schoffield Ford Bridge in Tyler State Park, Bucks County. It is a Town truss sandwiched between two long queenpost trusses. Information on "Connecticut's Historic Covered Bridges" found on the Connecticut Department of Transportation Website indicated that the queenpost trusses may have been added during one of the bridge's renovations. Another rather unusual feature of this bridge is the four heavy, ten-inch-square vertical columns that are anchored to the bottom and the top chords of the truss system on each side of the bridge. The photograph of the interior quite clearly shows these features.

Bulls Bridge spans the Housatonic River at a parklike setting in which trails lead down to the river, where one can view the strong overflow from the power dam located above the bridge. The bridge rests on concrete abutments and has curb-high concrete wingwalls. It has a deck of ten-inch diagonal planks, a roof of cedar shakes, and both the sides and portals are covered with unpainted, horizontal boards. The only side openings are four small windows spaced at equal distances along each side.

This very substantial bridge has a documented construction date of 1842 and has been well maintained. Records indicate that the bridge was raised above the river to its present location when the hydroelectric power station was built upstream between 1901 and 1904. In 1949, the State Highway De-

Truss structure and vertical support columns of Bulls Bridge.

partment improved the bridge by replacing much of the lower chords and all the trunnels in the lattice truss. Further improvements were made in 1969 when large plate girders were installed beneath the deck of the bridge to increase its live load limit. This necessitated the lengthening of the siding boards to conceal the girders from view. When we visited the bridge in August 2002 and again in February 2003, the bridge was in very good condition. It appeared to have been recently refurbished, but we have no data to verify that fact. Even though the present bridge has seen many revisions, it still maintains the character of the original span, reminding us of a time when wood was the primary building material available.

West Cornwall/Hart Bridge

Location: In West Cornwall, a locality within the Cornwall town line.

Directions: In West Cornwall, at the junction of CT 128 and US 7, go east on CT 128 for 0.1 mile to the bridge.

GPS: 41° 52.292N 073° 21.846W

Year: 1864   **Truss:** Town with queenpost   **Waterway:** Housatonic River
In Use: Yes   **Number of Spans:** 2   **Owner:** Town of Cornwall
Builder: Unknown   **Length:** 173 ft. 2 in.   **Width:** 14 ft. 2 in.
Condition: Very Good   **Number:** CT-03-02   **Register:** Dec. 30, 1975

According to some sources, the year of construction of this long, Town lattice truss structure was 1841. This was supposedly the year in which a bridge was erected to replace one washed away by the flood of 1837. However, according

to information contained in the Connecticut Historic Bridge Inventory, a project undertaken by the Connecticut Department of Transportation in cooperation with the Federal Highway Administration and the Connecticut Historical Commission, Michael R. Gannett has shown the correct date to be 1864. This same report indicates that the Connecticut Department of Transportation rehabilitated the bridge in 1973 by inserting a steel deck to bear the weight of contemporary traffic. This project won the Federal Highway Administration's award for outstanding historic preservation.

The renovated deck structure, beneath the original wooden deck, consists of two very heavy metal I beams, which in turn support a molded metal superstructure that runs the entire length and width of the bridge. These metal supports in turn rest on the stone and mortar abutments and a central concrete pier, which is thought to remain from the original 1837 bridge. There are also additional, lighter weight, crosswise and diagonal I beams between the two main heavy beams. The basic truss design of the bridge is exactly the same as that of the Bull Bridge, also in Litchfield County. One of the sources attained by the state inventory indicates that the secondary queenpost trusses may have been added during an 1887 refurbishing of the bridge. The bridge has a roadbed of crosswise planks, a roof of cedar shakes, and is covered with boards and battens on the sides and vertical boards on the portals. There are seven windows on each side with metal mullions embedded in the supporting framework. The entire structure is painted barn red. This bridge has been in use for a long time, and it appears that in its present condition it will be functional for many more years.

MIDDLESEX COUNTY

Comstock Bridge

Location: Approximately 7 miles west of the locality of Colchester, within the East Hampton town line.

Directions: In Westchester, a locality within the Colchester town line, at the junction of CT 16 (Colchester Ave.) and CT 149, go west on CT 16 for 2.1 miles to Comstock Bridge Road, on the right (north); turn right and go 0.1 mile to the parking area adjacent to the bridge.

GPS: 41° 33.206N 072° 26.928W (coordinates recorded in parking lot close to the bridge)

Year: 1936   **Truss:** Howe   **Waterway:** Salmon River
In Use: Foot traffic only   **Number of Spans:** 1+   **Owner:** State
Builder: Unknown   **Length:** 94 ft. 6 in.   **Width:** 14 ft.
Condition: Very Good   **Number:** CT-04-01   **Register:** Jan. 1, 1976

Our sources of information indicate that this bridge was originally built in 1873 and reconstructed by the Civilian Conservation Corps in 1936. As it stands now, it is completely bypassed by a new concrete bridge on CT Route 16 spanning the Salmon River. It is located in a roadside park setting protected with security cameras and has both portals gated to prevent vehicular traffic of any kind. However, it is readily traversed on foot. The typical Howe truss structure rests on cut stone and mortar abutments that extend to short road-level wingwalls on the west end and a cut stone and mortar pier at the east end. A pony truss structure extends for a distance of thirty-five feet seven and one-half inches from the pier at the east end of the bridge proper to another abutment of dry stone at the far eastern bank of the river. The east end abutment is extended to form short, below-road-level wingwalls. The restored bridge has an almost new appearance except for the weathered siding. Its deck is covered with random-width lengthwise planks, the roof with cedar shakes, and the sides and portals with unpainted vertical boards. There is no additional steel reinforcing. According to a sign posted on the east end of the bridge, the bridge has been donated to the state by the towns of Colchester and East Hampton.

Johnsonville Village Bridge

Location: In Historic Johnsonville Village, approximately 2 miles southwest of Moodus, a locality within the East Haddam town line.

Directions: Just south of Moodus, at the junction of CT 149 South and CT 151 North, go north on CT 151 for 0.5 mile to Johnsonville Road; turn left (southwest) onto Johnsonville Road and go 0.3 mile to an overgrown lane on the left (east) side of road marked by two concrete posts (sometimes closed with a chain). The lane is just north of the millpond of Historic Johnsonville Village. Follow it for several hundred yards to the bridge, which is located at the Moodus River inlet to the millpond. Ownership of Johnsonville Village has changed, but the new owners have given permission to enter the property to visit the bridge.

GPS: 41° 29.743N 072° 27.986W (coordinates recorded along Johnsonville Road at the concrete posts marking the lane to the bridge)

Year: Unknown   **Truss:** Multiple kingpost with arch
Waterway: Moodus River   **In Use:** Foot traffic only   **Number of Spans:** 1
Owner: Private   **Builder:** Thomas Kronenberger   **Length:** 60 ft. 2$\frac{3}{4}$ in.
Width: 13 ft. 8$\frac{1}{2}$ in.   **Condition:** Good   **Number:** CT-04-07
Register: Does not qualify

This covered bridge is tucked away in an almost obscure location in the rural area of East Haddam. A number of years ago a local resident started to collect a variety of historic objects and buildings and arranged them on his property in an area he called Historic Johnsonville Village. One of the structures he had replicated was a covered bridge typical of many found in the New England states. It was expertly constructed by a local bridge builder, Thomas Kronenberger, on the property across the Moodus River where it flows into a millpond, which is also part of the village. The trusses of the main bridge are multiple kingpost trusses overlaid on each roadway side of the truss with a single, nine-ply arch. The arch does not go through to the abutment, as a Burr truss arch would, but rests on the bottom chord. The bridge has a pedestrian walkway, also supported with a multiple kingpost truss. The deck is covered

with lengthwise random-width planks, the roof with cedar shakes, and the sides and portals with unfinished vertical boards. The entire structure rests on stone and mortar abutments that are extended to short, road-level wingwalls. This lovely structure certainly adds a great deal of early American charm to its historic village setting.

Worthington Pond Farm Bridge

Location: 3 miles northeast of Somers, a locality within the Somers town line.

Directions: In Somers, at the junction of CT 83 and CT 190, go east on CT 190 for 0.2 mile to Battle St.; go left (northeast) on Battle St. for 1 mile to Turnpike Road, cross over Turnpike Road (Battle St. becomes Mountain Road), and continue for 1.7 miles on Mountain Road to the entrance to Worthington Pond Farm on the left. Turn left into the farm; the bridge is just ahead to the left 0.1 mile, located over the pond outlet.

GPS: 42° 01.018N 072° 24.822W

Year: 2002   **Truss:** Town with arch   **Waterway:** Pond outlet
In Use: Yes, private   **Number of Spans:** 1   **Owner:** Dan Roulier
Builder: Ron Ouelette   **Length:** 61 ft. 8$\frac{3}{4}$ in.   **Width:** 13 ft. 7$\frac{1}{2}$ in.
Condition: New, excellent   **Number:** CT-07-02
Register: Does not qualify

A glimpse at the truss and overhead support structure of the magnificent Worthington Pond Farm Bridge.

The Worthington Pond Farm Bridge is a structure of the twenty-first century. While it cannot be considered a historic covered bridge, it has been built using the tried-and-true methods of the covered bridge builders of the nineteenth century. The owner, Dan Roulier, and his builder, Ron Ouelette, examined a number of covered bridges across the country before settling on this particular design and truss structure. All the timbers used for the construction of the bridge were harvested from the land on which the bridge is built. The trees were cut and the lumber sized and stacked to dry during 2001. In January 2002, construction on the bridge began. The basic truss structure, a Town truss, was assembled entirely with trunnels, exactly as it would have been built in the mid-1800s. Additional strength is added to the truss with a beautifully laminated arch. The entire structure was erected at a cost of $85,000.

Another interesting feature of the bridge is a row of six dormers that extend from the roof on the south side. Mr. Roulier claims that these were added to provide additional illumination to the bridge interior. Although seemingly hidden away on the Worthington Pond Farm property, the bridge will be used extensively for a variety of special events such as hayrides, weddings, social events, and political meetings. The revenue generated from these activities will be donated to charities together with the proceeds of the maple sugaring enterprise that is also conducted on the farm. Next time you're in Connecticut, be sure to look for this beautiful structure.

MAINE

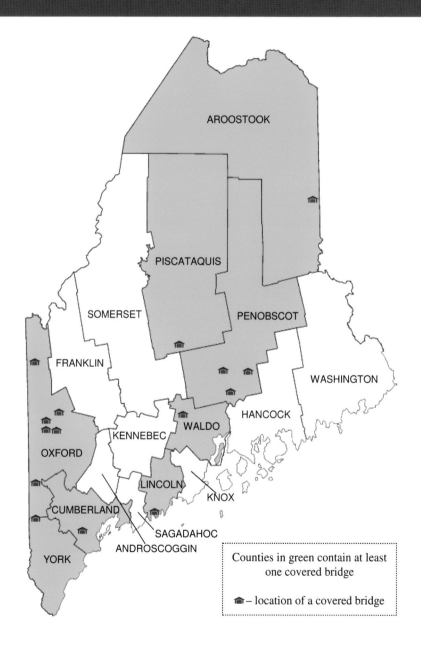

AROOSTOOK

PISCATAQUIS

SOMERSET

PENOBSCOT

FRANKLIN

WASHINGTON

HANCOCK

OXFORD

KENNEBEC

WALDO

CUMBERLAND

LINCOLN

KNOX

YORK

SAGADAHOC

ANDROSCOGGIN

Counties in green contain at least
one covered bridge

🏠 – location of a covered bridge

Maine

"The Pine Tree State"

Although Maine is the largest of the New England states, it has had relatively few covered bridges in comparison with its two closest neighbors to the west, New Hampshire and Vermont. While these states can boast of having had more than 300 and more than 500 covered spans respectively, Maine can claim having had only about 120. Most of these were located in the southwestern part of the state, where the topography is a large, rocky tangle of mountains, lakes, and rivers. Today, most of the surviving historic covered bridges are still located primarily in the same area. Six of them are located in the three most southern and western counties—York, Cumberland, and Oxford. Two are located in the south central area—one in Penobscot County and one in Piscataquis County. And there is one remaining historic bridge located in the far northeast, the farthest north of any covered bridge in the United States—the Watson Settlement Bridge in Aroostook County.

In addition to the historic spans, six more recent covered structures are documented in this guide—four of them built in the later part of the twentieth century and two of them as recently as 2000 and 2001. The Kenneth E. Stoddard Shell Museum Bridge was built in 1993 in the southern coastal area—Boothbay, Lincoln County. Leonard's Mill Bridge was built in 1987, and the Cole Land Transportation Museum Bridge was built in 1994 in the south central area—Penobscot County. The three most recent structures were built by the same builder. William Dunton, owner of Big Adventure Center, Bethel, Maine, built two lovely Paddleford truss footbridges in Bethel—one in the Big Adventure Center in 1999 and the most recent, along the Bethel footpath, completed in 2001. Both of these bridges are located in Oxford County, quite close to the frequently visited, painted, and photographed Artist's or Sunday River Bridge. Mr. Dunton also built a third Paddleford truss footbridge at Field of Dreams in the Town of Unity, Waldo County, in 2000.

Records indicate that the earliest covered crossing was built in the city of Augusta in 1819 by Timothy Palmer, the same Palmer who built the first bridge to be covered in the United States in the city of Philadelphia, Pennsylvania. Following it, over 120 bridges could be found crossing the waterways of the Pine Tree State. It is really quite surprising that, with the large amount of timber available, there were so few bridges built. However, the thrifty town fathers felt that only a major artery crossing a waterway was worthy of a stout covered span.

Covered bridges have always been vulnerable to the ravages of nature—flood and ice—to human destruction by fire, and, of course, to replacement by a more modern structure. Consequently, the number of covered bridges in

Maine gradually decreased until there were only nine historic spans remaining. In 1959, the Maine legislature took a major step toward preserving the remaining historic structures. It passed a law allowing state money to be used to preserve and rehabilitate these bridges. In 1961, a program of covered bridge restoration was begun, and it continues to the present day. In January 2003, on one of the coldest days of that winter, we found a Maine Department of Transportation bridge crew replacing the wooden shakes on the Sunday River Bridge. Hopefully, the remaining covered bridges of Maine will be found standing, and in fine condition, for generations to come.

Watson/Watson Settlement Bridge

Location: Approximately 3.4 miles southeast of the locality of Littleton, within the Littleton town line.

Directions: South of Littleton, at the end of the I-95 exit 62 ramp, go north on US 1 for 4.1 miles to Carson Road on the right (east), turn right onto Carson Road, and go 2.5 miles to the bypassed bridge on the left (north). If approaching Maine from New Brunswick, at the end of the I-95 exit 62 ramp, go north on US 1 for 4 miles to Carson Road on the right (east), turn right onto Carson Road, and go 2.5 miles to the bypassed bridge on the left (north).

GPS: 46° 12.600N 067° 48.043W

Year: 1911 **Truss:** Howe **Waterway:** Meduxnekeag River
In Use: Foot and snowmobile **Number of Spans:** 2
Owner: Town of Littleton **Builder:** David and William Adams
Length: 168 ft. 8 in. **Width:** 17 ft. 7½ in. **Condition:** Fair
Number: ME-02-01 **Register:** Feb. 16, 1970

This is the most recent of the historic covered bridges in Maine and also the most northern and remote of the state's remaining historic spans. While most of the covered bridges were built in the mid to late nineteenth century, this bridge was not built until the early part of the twentieth century. Most accounts, including the civil engineering plaque at the bridge site, indicate that

the bridge was built in 1911 by David and William Adams; however, the *World Guide to Covered Bridges,* published in 1989, and *Covered Bridge Ramblings in New England,* published in 1959 by C. Ernest Walker, list it as 1903, and a sign on the bridge portal says 1902. The name of the bridge is derived from the Watson homestead that was located near the bridge site. When the road from Woodstock, New Brunswick, to Littleton, Maine, was rebuilt in 1984, the nearly century-old bridge was bypassed and closed to vehicular traffic. In 1959, by an act of the Maine legislature, the Maine Department of Transportation (MDOT) was given the responsibility of saving and renovating all of the state's historic bridges. According to information posted on the Federal Highway Administration's website regarding the National Historic Covered Bridge Preservation Program, the state of Maine applied for and received a grant of $840,000 in 2002 for the restoration of the Watson Bridge. The preliminary design report and plans are completed by MDOT. The project will include replacement and straightening of truss members as needed, replacement of structural roof and deck supports, replacement of the present roof with cedar shakes, replacement of damaged decking and siding, and installation of timber approach guardrails. When completed, clear fire-resistant material will be applied to the entire structure. Bids for the project are scheduled to be advertised in March 2004; construction should begin in May and be completed by December 2004.

CUMBERLAND COUNTY

Babb Bridge

Location: 3.2 miles north-northwest of South Windham, within the Windham town line.

Directions: In South Windham, at the junction of ME 237 and US 202/ME 4, go north on US 202/ME 4 for 1.1 miles to the junction with River Road. Turn left (northwest) onto River Road and go 1.6 miles to Covered Bridge Road on the left (south); turn left onto Covered Bridge Road and go 0.5 mile to the bridge.

GPS: 43° 45.963N 070° 26.865W

Year: 1864, rebuilt 1976   **Truss:** Queenpost   **Waterway:** Presumpscot River
In Use: Yes   **Number of Spans:** 1   **Owner:** State   **Builder:** Unknown
Length: 76 ft.   **Width:** 13 ft. 9 in.   **Condition:** Very good
Number: ME-03-01 (2)   **Register:** Does not qualify

There is some question in the mind of the authors of this guide concerning the correct date of construction of the first covered bridge that stood at this site.

According to the *Maine Covered Bridge Finder*, by E. B. and D. K. Robertson, and a newspaper article that appeared in the *Portland Press Herald* on May 7, 1973, written by press writer Bryan Raymond, the original bridge was built in 1843. According to the covered bridges website displayed by the Maine Department of Transportation, the *World Guide to Covered Bridges*, and *Covered Bridges of Maine, a Guide*, by Andrew R. Howard, it was built in 1864. Whatever the date, that bridge, which was built originally for $318, served the towns of Gorham and Windham well until it was destroyed by fire on May 6, 1973, apparently an act of vandalism. When plans were being prepared to replace the covered span with a concrete bridge, a large segment of the local population objected. The selectmen of both towns requested that the state Department of Transportation authorize the replacement of the bridge with an exact replica of the original Babb Bridge. The state agreed and appropriated $75,000 for the new structure. Plans called for a new bridge that not only looked like the original but was built with the same historically authentic techniques. The lumber was milled in Gorham by Nelson Wagner, and the bridge was erected by a state Department of Transportation crew. Through the joint efforts of people from all walks of life—covered bridge societies, historical societies, private citizens, and companies and organizations that donated lumber, labor, and monies—the new bridge was dedicated on July 4, 1976.

Kenneth E. Stoddard Shell Museum Bridge

Location: On the Dolphin Mini Golf enterprise, along ME 27, within the Boothbay town line.

Directions: Along US 1, east of Wiscasset, at the junction of US 1 and ME 27 South, go south on ME 27 for 7 miles to the junction with Hardwick Road on the left (east). The miniature golf course and covered bridge are on the southeast corner of this junction.

GPS: 43° 54.429N 069° 36.947W (coordinates recorded in the mini golf parking lot)

Year: 1993 **Truss:** Town
Waterway: Artificial stream on Dolphin Mini Golf enterprise
In Use: Yes, to house seashell collection **Number of Spans:** 1
Owner: Private **Builder:** Lee Stoddard **Length:** 55 ft. 3½ in. **Width:** 14 ft.
Condition: Excellent **Number:** ME-08-02 **Register:** Does not qualify

Kenneth E. Stoddard had been a collector of seashells from all corners of the world. When he became ill in the early 1990s, his two sons, Bob and Lee, promised to build a museum to house his large collection of shells. However, they did not want just the usual rectangular building that houses many such projects; they wanted something different. They had always been attracted to

covered bridges; and, being aware that their neighboring state to the west had quite a few spans of varying kinds, they spent time visiting and photographing some of New Hampshire's structures. The one that fascinated them the most was the bridge at Ashuelot. So, around 1991, they carefully measured the major timbers of that span and returned to Boothbay, where they erected a late-twentieth-century, reduced replica of that bridge on their entertainment center, the Dolphin Mini Golf enterprise. The bridge, an authentic Town lattice truss span, is positioned over their artificial stream between the miniature golf course and the ice cream pavilion. It resembles the Ashuelot Bridge in all respects except for size. Lee related to us that he had some difficulty convincing the local authorities that his lattice truss structure could support the weight of not only itself but the museum within. However, after an eighteen-month delay, he was permitted to erect this memorial to his father, who, unfortunately, did not live to see its completion. Other than a contribution box at the entrance of the museum, there is no admission to view the lovely shell collection that the museum displays. Although this museum-bridge is not in the immediate vicinity of any of Maine's other covered bridges, if one is traveling the coastal route of this fascinating state, it is certainly one to locate. Keep in mind that this area operates during the usual spring, summer, and fall tourist season. The shell museum, an open, walk-through structure, is closed and locked during off-season and nonbusiness hours.

OXFORD COUNTY

Bennett-Bean/Bennett Bridge

Location: 1.9 miles south of Wilsons Mills, within the Lincoln Plantation.

Directions: In Wilsons Mills, at the junction of ME 16 and Parmachenee Road on the north, go south on ME 16 for 1.7 miles to Littlehale Road (entrance to Aziscoos Valley Campground), turn right onto Littlehale Road, and go 0.2 mile to the closed bridge.

GPS: 44° 55.154N 071° 02.264W (coordinates recorded in parking area near the bridge)

Year: 1898   **Truss:** Paddleford   **Waterway:** Magalloway River
In Use: Foot and snowmobile   **Number of Spans:** 1   **Owner:** State
Builder: Mason Brothers   **Length:** 92 ft. 8 in.   **Width:** 15 ft. 2 in.
Condition: Fair   **Number:** ME-09-03   **Register:** Feb. 16, 1970

An interesting historical account of this bridge exists in *Covered Bridges of Maine, a Guide,* written by Andrew R. Howard in 1978. Here are a few highlights arranged chronologically: the first meeting of the bridge committee was

held on June 6, 1898; Horace Bennett and Fred Taylor completed the erection of the first abutments, constructed of logs, on July 11, 1898, at a cost of $280.00; framing and raising of the bridge was done by Mason Brothers, bridge builders of Bethel, Maine, at a cost of $500.00; lumber for the bridge was purchased from Hiram P. West & Sons of Upton, Maine, and had to be rafted twenty-five miles to the bridge site at an additional cost of $2.00 per thousand feet; R. A. Storey, a member of the bridge committee, was paid $1.50 per day to supervise the six-day rafting trip; James A. Turner's mill in Wentworth Location provided the planks for the bridge floor, 1,120 feet of planks, at a cost of $14.56; the approaches to the bridge were completed in October; and, on November 17, 1898, the town voted to accept the bridge and relieve the committee of any further responsibility. The bridge was covered one year later, and the log abutments were replaced with split stone at a later date.

As recently as 2001, the Maine legislature has again pledged that it will be "responsible for the management of and all costs for maintenance and rehabilitation" of its historic bridges. The Bennett Bridge is one for which the state has applied to the National Historic Covered Bridge Preservation Program (NHCBPP) for funds toward an $850,000 restoration program. In its request the state wrote: "Previous work has been done on the bridge to repair or replace deteriorated members. The bridge remains composed of solid sawn and laminated timber beams, and vertical plank siding. The roof is of corrugated metal. Currently the easterly truss is leaning downstream. The truss has been temporarily braced at the portals by cables and steel rods secured to the ground. Proposed work includes restoring the trusses back to plumb, replacing deteriorated elements; and replacing the metal roof with an original wooden roof." The NHCBPP has awarded $581,404 toward that project.

Bethel Walking Path Bridge

Location: On the walking path leaving the northwest corner of Davis Park in the locality of Bethel, within the Bethel town line.

Directions: Davis Park is located at the northeast corner of ME 26 (entering Bethel from the east) and Parkway. Or entering Bethel from the west on US 2, at the junction of US 2/ME 5/ME 26 and Parkway, turn right (east) onto Parkway and go 0.4 mile to Davis Park on the left (east).

GPS: 44° 24.839N 070° 47.215W (coordinates recorded in parking lot near the bridge)

Year: 2001   **Truss:** Paddleford   **Waterway:** Swamp area in park
In Use: Foot, bicycles, and snowmobile   **Number of Spans:** 1
Owner: Town of Bethel   **Builder:** William Dunton   **Length:** 50 ft. 1 in.
Width: 10 ft. 3$\frac{1}{2}$ in.   **Condition:** Excellent   **Number:** ME-09-07
Register: Does not qualify

In 2001, when the Town of Bethel was looking for a way to bridge a swampy area along its recently created footpath, William Dunton, local bridge builder and owner of Big Adventure Center, volunteered to build a covered bridge. The bridge he erected was very similar to the Sunday River replica he built on the miniature golf course of his Big Adventure enterprise. This bridge, too, is an authentic Paddleford truss span built in true nineteenth-century fashion with hand-turned hardwood trunnels for the essential joinery. During the winter months, the bridge and footpath become a well-traveled snowmobile trail.

Big Adventure Bridge

Location: On the north edge of the locality of Bethel, within the Bethel town line.

Directions: In Bethel, at the junction of US 2/ME 5/ME 26 and Parkway, go north on US 2/ME 5/ME 26 for 0.4 mile to North Road on the left (west); turn left onto North Road to the Big Adventure parking area.

GPS: 44° 25.061N 070° 47.899W (coordinates recorded in Big Adventure parking area near the bridge)

Year: 1999   **Truss:** Paddleford
Waterway: Stream on Big Adventure miniature golf course
In Use: Foot traffic only   **Number of Spans:** 1   **Owner:** William Dunton
Builder: William Dunton   **Length:** 49 ft. 11 in.   **Width:** 8 ft. 5 in.
Condition: Excellent   **Number:** ME-09-06   **Register:** Does not qualify

In 1999, when preparing a focal point for the eighteen-hole miniature golf course at Big Adventure Center, builder and owner of the center William Dunton went to one of his favorite historic structures—the Sunday River Covered Bridge, well known also as the Artist's Covered Bridge—located just a short distance north of his entertainment center in Bethel, Maine. There he took measurements of all the essential elements of the bridge and returned to his minigolf course, where he personally erected an exact replica of the bridge reduced by 50 percent. The resulting structure provides the "fairway" entrance to the twelfth hole of the Big Adventure mini golf layout. It, like the Artist's Bridge, is a Paddleford truss, true in every detail, even to the scaled-down trunnels, which are used to provide the essential joinery, and the scaled-down cedar

shakes on the roof. Other interesting features of the course are the artificial stream that meanders through the layout, an old-fashioned gristmill with a working waterwheel powered by water fed to a sluice by a miniature waterfall, and the Dunton mine located under the waterfall. This attractive bridge and miniature golf layout is located on the northern edge of historic Bethel, Maine, an interesting town to visit when you're visiting Big Adventure to see the covered bridge. If you happen to meet Bill Dunton while you're visiting, that, too, will be an extra. He is quite an interesting craftsman.

Hemlock Bridge

Location: 3 miles north of the locality of East Fryeburg, within the Fryeburg town line.

Directions: In East Fryeburg, at the junction of US 302 and Hemlock Bridge Road on the north and Denmark Road on the south, go north on Hemlock Bridge Road for 2.9 miles to the bridge. Or, in Fryeburg, at the junction of US 302 East and ME 5 (Lovell Road), go north on ME 5 for 6.2 miles to Frog Alley on the right (east), turn right onto Frog Alley, and go 2.1 miles to the bridge. Neither of these access roads is maintained from Nov. 1 to May 1.

GPS: 44° 04.770N 070° 54.173W

Year: 1857   **Truss:** Paddleford with arch
Waterway: Channel of Saco River   **In Use:** Yes   **Number of Spans:** 1
Owner: State   **Builder:** J. Berry   **Length:** 134 ft. 6 in.   **Width:** 18 ft. 5 in.
Condition: Good   **Number:** ME-09-02   **Register:** Feb. 16, 1970

This covered bridge is located in a very lovely, secluded, tranquil portion of Oxford County where it spans a channel of the Saco River. When we visited it in May 2003, only one bicyclist passed by while we spent nearly an hour documenting, measuring, and photographing the structure. Because it is located on a floodplain, it was built on sturdy cut granite abutments that rise a considerable distance above the river channel and extend to road-level wingwalls. The bridge was built with a Paddleford truss by J. Berry (there is no record of Berry's first name). At some time during its existence an arch of the Burr type was added to lend additional support to the truss. The arch consists of fifteen laminated two-by-eight-inch planks and is seated in a concrete cap poured on top of the original granite abutments. Mention of this arch is made in documentation of the bridge in writings prior to 1984. There is also a record of additional work having been done on the bridge in 1988 when it was "reinforced to carry local traffic." This may be when the four steel I beams were added beneath the deck, which consists of crosswise planks with a wide lengthwise runner in the center. The bridge is an unpainted structure, completely covered with random-width, vertical board siding on the sides, and horizontal clapboard siding on the portal gable ends. The only openings in the side are six small windows on each side of the span. The roof is covered with wooden shakes. This is a wonderful place to linger; but, if you visit during the blackfly or mosquito season, carry an insect repellent with you. It will make your visit far more enjoyable.

Lovejoy Bridge

Location: In South Andover, on Covered Bridge Road, within the Andover town line.

Directions: Just west of Rumford Point, at the junction of US 2 and ME 5, go north on ME 5 for 7.6 miles to Covered Bridge Road on the right (east), turn right onto Covered Bridge Road, and go 0.1 mile to the bridge. Or, in Andover, at the junction of ME 120 and ME 5, go south on ME 5 for 3.1 miles to Covered Bridge Road on the left (east), turn left, and go 0.1 mile to the bridge.

GPS: 44° 35.604N 070° 44.023W

Year: 1867   **Truss:** Paddleford   **Waterway:** Ellis River   **In Use:** Yes
Number of Spans: 1   **Owner:** State   **Builder:** Unknown   **Length:** 76 ft. 4 in.
Width: 16 ft. 1 in.   **Condition:** Good   **Number:** ME-09-01
Register: Feb. 16, 1970

Once, again, there is a bit of difference regarding the date of origin of this bridge; however, the difference is only one year. Some sources place it at 1867, others at 1868. When it comes to historic significance, that difference of one

year will matter little. This is an excellent example of a Paddleford truss covered bridge (see the interior photo). Town records indicate that the bridge was constructed at a cost of $743.47 and built with square-sawn spruce. This is a relatively small price by today's standards, but not when compared to contemporary wages: a carpenter received about $0.65 for a ten-hour workday, a man with a team of horses might receive $1.50, and man with a yoke of oxen could charge $2.00.

The bridge served the area quite well until a heavy sand truck crossed the span in 1983 and crashed through the floor into the river. This, obviously,

Paddleford truss of the Lovejoy Bridge.

closed the bridge until repairs could be made. It was reopened in 1984 with a reinforced deck and with height barriers, sometimes referred to as "headache bars," placed at the entrances to the bridge. On our visit to the bridge in January 2003, it was quite an impressive sight with its naturally weathered board and batten siding and its horizontal clapboard portals painted white with red trim, which contrasted with the new fallen snow landscape. The bridge rests on stone abutments that have been laid dry and extend to road-level wingwalls. The snow-covered roof appeared to be covered with wooden shakes. This is one of the nine remaining historic covered spans that are being maintained by the state Department of Transportation, Bridge Maintenance Department.

Sunday River/Artist's Bridge

Location: 6.2 miles north-northwest of the locality of Bethel, within the Newry town line.

Directions: In Bethel, at the junction of US 2/ME 5 and ME 26 and Parkway, go north on US 2/ME 5/ME 26 for 2.5 miles to Sunday River Road on the left (west), turn left (northwest) on Sunday River Road, and go 3.7 miles to the bypassed bridge. (After 2.2 miles follow signs to the covered bridge. A road to ski slopes bears left; the road to covered bridge continues straight and then bears right.) Or, from Newry, at the junction of US2/ME 5 with ME 26, go south on US 2/ME 5/ME 26 for 3.0 miles to Sunday River Road on the right (west), turn right (northwest), and follow directions above for the Bethel approach on Sunday River Road.

GPS: 44° 29.527N 070° 50.607W

Year: 1872   **Truss:** Paddleford   **Waterway:** Sunday River
In Use: Foot traffic only   **Number of Spans:** 1   **Owner:** Town of Newry
Builder: Nahum Mason   **Length:** 99 ft. 4$\frac{1}{2}$ in.   **Width:** 18 ft. 2 in.
Condition: Good   **Number:** ME-09-04   **Register:** Feb. 16, 1970

The first name of this lovely bridge is derived from the waterway that it crosses. An interesting story about the origin of the second name appears in *Covered Bridges of Maine, a Guide,* by Andrew R. Howard:

> Miss Alcenda Kendall, a resident interested in local history, discovered how the name "Artist" bridge originated. When built, the bridge had no special name. John J. Enneking, before he became a famous artist, was vacationing at the Locke House, later called the Locke Mountain House, at North Bethel. The artist sketched along the Sunday River, many times near the bridge. The Lock House residents began calling it the Artist bridge, and the name was taken up by the local residents.

Other accounts simply say it is because it is the most painted and photographed bridge in the state. All sources, except the *World Guide to Covered Bridges,* place the date of origin as 1872. The *WGCB* lists it as 1870. In 1958, when a new concrete bridge was built just a short distance downstream, the Artist's Bridge was bypassed, but not forgotten. It now stands in an attractive, parklike setting beside the main road, where it is still the fascination of many visitors. There are also stories of its having been used occasionally by clergymen as a site for baptisms in a shallow part of the stream beneath the bridge.

On our second visit to the bridge, on a very cold morning in January 2003, we found a crew of craftsmen from the Bridge Maintenance Department of the Maine Department of Transportation, busily occupied replacing the wooden shake roof. This structure is still greatly respected by the state, which is keeping a watchful eye on its well-being.

Porter-Parsonsfield/ Parsonsfield-Porter Bridge

Location: Just south of Porter between the Porter town line and the Parsonsfield town line.

Directions: In Porter, at the junction of ME 25 and ME 160, go south on ME 160 for 0.2 mile to the bypassed bridge on the east (left) side of the highway.

GPS: 43° 47.481N 070° 56.271W (coordinates recorded in parking lot close to the bridge)

Year: 1876   **Truss:** Paddleford with arch   **Waterway:** Ossipee River
In Use: Foot traffic only   **Number of Spans:** 2
Owner: Towns of Parsonsfield and Porter   **Builder:** J. Berry
Length: 186 ft. 6 in.   **Width:** 18 ft. 9½ in.   **Condition:** Excellent
Number: ME-09-05/ME-16-01   **Register:** Feb. 16, 1970

According to the date displayed on the nameplate on the bridge's portal, this bridge was built in 1876 and completely and beautifully restored in 1999. Other printed dates indicate that the bridge might have been built in 1858 or 1859. Construction costs of the bridge and its continued maintenance and restoration have been shared equally since its origin by the towns of Porter and Parsonsfield, although there was some controversy at the time the bridge was

Paddleford trusses with arches of the Porter-Parsonsfield Bridge.

being planned. According to Richard Sanders Allen in *Covered Bridges of the Northeast,* the selectmen of Porter argued that Parsonsfield would get more use from the bridge and consequently should pay more for its construction and maintenance. To settle the question, the selectmen met midway on the old uncovered span that once crossed the Ossipee River. One of the more vocal gentlemen pulled out his jackknife and tossed it into the midpoint of the old rickety floor and said: "The Town of Parsonsfield shall build so far, and no further!"

It appears that the two towns still share equally in the preservation of this old structure. In 1960, the old bridge was bypassed by a modern steel and concrete structure, and it appeared that the old span would be left to fade away. However, the two towns had the 123-year-old structure completely rehabilitated in 1999. It now stands proudly on cut stone abutments extended to road-level wingwalls with a central pier also of cut stone. The portals are covered with horizontal clapboard siding painted white with green trim, and the sides are covered with unpainted vertical board siding. The roof is covered with shakes and the deck with lengthwise planks. The substantial Paddleford trusses reinforced with arches consisting of twenty-one heavy, laminated timbers are quite noticeable in the photo of the bridge's interior.

Cole Land Transportation Museum Bridge

Location: On the property of the Cole Land Transportation Museum, Bangor, just southwest of the city limits.

Directions: From I-95, exit 45B, continue to the first traffic light, turn left, pass the Holiday Inn on the left and continue to Perry Street; turn left onto Perry Street and go 0.5 mile to the museum. It is not necessary to pay an admission fee to the museum to visit and/or photograph the bridge.

GPS: 44° 47.103N 068° 48.303W (coordinates recorded in the museum parking lot)

Year: 1994   **Truss:** Howe (modified)   **Waterway:** Dry gully
In Use: Foot traffic only   **Number of Spans:** 1
Owner: Cole Transportation Museum
Builder: Ted Purvis and Andy LeClair   **Length:** 72 ft. 3 in.   **Width:** 9 ft. 9$\frac{1}{4}$ in.
Condition: Excellent   **Number:** ME-10-23   **Register:** Does not qualify

The facts about this bridge are all presented to visitors of the museum on a document titled "Our Covered Bridge," which is displayed inside the span. In 1994, this bridge was added to the exterior display grounds of the Cole Land Transportation Museum to display the role of the covered bridge in the history of transportation in our country. Its design, based on the patented Howe truss

of 1840, was created for the project by Habib Dagher of the University of Maine together with students of the Civil Engineering Department. It was built by carpenters Ted Purvis and Andy LeClair with assistance from students from the university. The materials used were eastern hemlock timbers for the trusses, white pine board and battens for the siding, and cedar shingles all harvested and milled in Maine. Its construction was partially funded by a grant from Cooperative Forestry, USDA Forest Service. Material and services were donated by Thomas DiCenzo Co., Herman, and the Robbins Lumber Co., Searsmont, Maine. There is an admission fee charged to enter the museum; however, since the bridge is located on the exterior grounds, it can be seen year-round from the parking lot. We visited the bridge in May 2003 during the regular operating hours of the museum. It is possible, however, that there may be times the bridge is closed to visitors. The document mentioned above also states: "The bridge is open during normal Museum hours from May 1st to November 11th."

Leonard's Mills Bridge

Location: On the grounds of the Maine Forest and Logging Museum, Inc., 5.6 miles northeast of the locality of Eddington, within the Bradley town line.

Directions: In Eddington, at the junction of ME 9 and ME 178, go north on ME 178 for 4.4 miles to Government Road on the right (east), turn right onto Government Road, and go 1.2 miles to the parking area for Leonard's Mills, at the Maine Forest and Logging Museum. (After 1 mile on Government Road, the road to the museum bears right.) There is no admission fee to the museum, but donations are gratefully accepted in a donation box inside the covered bridge.

GPS: 44° 52.449N 068° 38.215W (coordinates recorded in the museum parking lot)

Year: 1987   **Truss:** Stringer (Bailey) with Town   **Waterway:** Blackman Stream
In Use: Foot traffic only, and maintenance vehicles   **Number of Spans:** 1
Owner: University of Maine   **Builder:** Vernon Shaw and Paul Atwood
Length: 52 ft. 5$\frac{1}{2}$ in.   **Width:** 13 ft. 6$\frac{1}{4}$ in.   **Condition:** Good
Number: ME-10-A   **Register:** Does not qualify

At first glance, this is an old, historic covered bridge. It has been made to appear so by the local volunteers who assist in the erection and maintenance of a reconstructed nineteenth-century logging community on the grounds of the Maine Forest and Logging Museum, Inc. The details behind the construction of the bridge are quite interesting. In 1964, the Leonard's Mills project acquired a U.S. government military surplus Bailey bridge to provide a substantial bridge across Blackman Stream. This crossing is the primary entrance into the "historic" village. However, as the village grew, the steel panel, stringer-type bridge simply did not fit the nineteenth-century setting of the village. Vernon

Shaw, who has been caretaker, overseer, and head maintenance person of the museum for a number of years, provided the following details. In 1987, Paul Atwood designed a Town lattice truss covering for the steel span. With the assistance of local volunteer retirees, who worked every Wednesday, Vernon and Paul built the Leonard's Mills Covered Bridge. They cleverly concealed the steel stringer members of the Bailey bridge, which actually rests on a steel pad on each of its four corners rather than the typical stone or concrete abutment, and they covered the deck in typical nineteenth-century fashion with crosswise planks and lengthwise plank runners in the traffic area. The sides, both of which have three windows, are covered with unpainted, weathered, vertical board and batten siding, and the portals with similar material in random widths. The roof is covered with regular roof shingles. Anyone visiting the covered bridge should also plan a little extra time to appreciate the other historic logging village structures that have been assembled at this museum, largely with the assistance of the volunteers, most of whom are retirees.

Robyville Bridge

Location: 3.8 miles northwest of the locality of Kenduskeag, within the Corinth town line.

Directions: In Kenduskeag, at the junction of ME 15 and Stetson Road, go north on ME 15 for 2.4 miles to Cushman Road on the left (west), turn left onto Cushman Road, and go 1.1 miles to a T (unmarked); turn left and go 0.05 mile to Covered Bridge Road on the right (west), turn right onto Covered Bridge Road, and go 0.2 mile to the bridge.

GPS: 44° 56.615N 068° 58.118W

Year: 1876 **Truss:** Long **Waterway:** Kenduskeag Stream **In Use:** Yes
Number of Spans: 1 **Owner:** State **Builder:** Royal A. Sweet
Length: 97 ft. 1 in. **Width:** 14 ft. $3\frac{1}{2}$ in. **Condition:** Good
Number: ME-10-02 **Register:** Feb. 16, 1970

There is some variation in the recorded dates of origin for the Robyville Bridge. They range from 1870 to 1876. However, the date recorded by the Maine Department of Transportation and the *World Guide to Covered Bridges* is 1876. Royal A. Sweet is credited with having built the structure at a cost of $1,375.06. A unique feature of this bridge is its covering. After having visited 206 covered bridges in New England, this is the only one we saw that is completely covered with wooden shingles on both the sides and portals, including approximately twelve feet of the inside of the portal opening. According to a bronze plaque mounted at the bridge site, this is the oldest surviving example of a Long truss system in the state of Maine. State records indicate that the bridge load-bearing capacity was increased in 1984 with the addition of four steel I beams. This may be the point at which the original cut stone abutments were reinforced with concrete. The bridge, however, retains its original nineteenth-century appearance. In addition to being listed on the National Register of Historic Places, it was also designated a Maine Historic Engineering Landmark on January 17, 2002.

Low/New Low/Lowe's Bridge

Location: Approximately 2 miles east of the locality of Gilford, between the town lines of Gilford and Sangerville.

Directions: In Guilford, at the junction of ME 6/ME 15/ME 16 and ME 23, go east on ME 6/ME 15/ME 16 for 2.3 miles to Lowe's Bridge Road on the right (south); turn right to cross the bridge. Parking is available on the south side of the bridge or at the roadside rest on the north side.

GPS: 45° 10.528N 069° 18.902W

Year: 1857, rebuilt 1990   **Truss:** Long   **Waterway:** Piscataquis River
In Use: Yes   **Number of Spans:** 1   **Owner:** Towns of Gilford and Sangerville
Builder: Isaac Wharff and Leonard Knowlton   **Length:** 146 ft. 3 in.
Width: 13 ft. 10¾ in.   **Condition:** Excellent   **Number:** ME-11-01 (2)
Register: Does not qualify

Records show that there have been several bridges spanning the Piscataquis River built at this location between Guilford and Sangerville. The first one, built in 1830, was destroyed by floodwaters in 1843. In 1857 Isaac Wharff was paid $500.00 to provide the abutments for a new span, and Leonard Knowlton $250.00 for lumber and labor. That second bridge stood for 130 years until the flood of April 1, 1987, completely destroyed the span. According to a report prepared by Ryan-Biggs Associates (RBA): "Loss of this treasured landmark, a

link to the forefathers of engineering, generated much local support for replacement with another covered bridge." Consequently, the Maine Department of Transportation, which has total responsibility for maintenance and rehabilitation of the state's historic bridges, contracted RBA "to replicate the original as closely as possible but with additional live-load capacity and in compliance with current codes and standards. RBA prepared the design and construction documents for the new bridge. It was assembled off-site, rolled into place, and lowered onto the original stone-masonry abutments that had been raised almost 3 feet to reduce the potential for future flood damage. RBA received a National Honor Award for Engineering Excellence from the American Consulting Engineers Council for work on this project." The replicated span was dedicated and reopened to traffic on August 23, 1990, at a total cost of $640,000. It is an extremely substantial structure. Even the insides of the portal entrances are double-sided with overlapped, unpainted, one-by-eight-inch, vertical board siding for the first seventeen feet five inches. The sides on the 146-foot long span are similarly treated. The roof is covered with wooden shakes, which are laid in unusually close courses. The deck consists of contemporary glulam panels covered with a single lengthwise plank runner in the traffic area. This new structure is destined to last through the present century and beyond.

WALDO COUNTY

Field of Dreams Bridge

Location: On the Field of Dreams, a recreation park, in the locality of Unity, within the Unity town line.

Directions: In Unity, at the junction of US 202/ME 9 and ME 139 East, go east on US 202/ME 9 for 0.4 mile to the park on the left (northwest). The bridge is located next to the first parking area.

GPS: 44° 37.126N 069° 19.655W (coordinates recorded in parking lot close to the bridge)

Year: 2000   **Truss:** Paddleford   **Waterway:** Drainage depression in field
In Use: Foot and bicycles   **Number of Spans:** 1   **Owner:** Town of Unity
Builder: William Dunton   **Length:** 41 ft. 7 in.   **Width:** 10 ft. 6 in.
Condition: Excellent   **Number:** ME-14-02   **Register:** Does not qualify

When one drives through the Town of Unity on US Route 202 and Main Route 9, one is sure to see the large sign on the north side of the highway: FIELD OF DREAMS . . . *Everyone Welcome* . . . BERT AND CORAL CLIFFORD. Several years ago, Bert and Coral Clifford, two philatropic citizens, spearheaded a project

to provide a twenty-seven-acre park for Unity. The park includes a picnic area, a playground for young children, three ball fields, tennis courts, a basketball court, a one-mile walking path, and, as a finishing touch, a covered bridge. When Bert and Coral visited the Town of Bethel and saw the Paddleford truss replica of the Sunday River Bridge that Bill Dunton had built on his Big Adventure Center miniature golf course, they immediately asked if he would build a similar bridge for them at the Field of Dreams Park. In 2000, Bill built his second covered bridge spanning a depression near the highway. It is built in the same, nineteenth-century fashion as his Artist's Bridge replica using hand-made trunnels and timber joinery. This bridge, too, is covered with unpainted, regular-width, vertical board siding on the sides and with random-width, vertical board siding on the portals; it, too, has a deck of lengthwise planks and a roof of wooden shakes. There are no windows in the structure, but the upper half of each side is open, exposing the intricate Paddleford truss timbers. When visiting the central Maine area, be sure to stop in to see this twenty-first-century reproduction of a nineteenth-century historic span.

MASSACHUSETTS

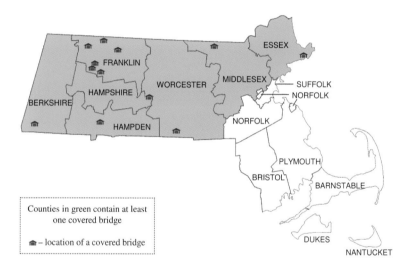

ESSEX

FRANKLIN

WORCESTER   MIDDLESEX

HAMPSHIRE   SUFFOLK
                            NORFOLK
BERKSHIRE

HAMPDEN   NORFOLK

                           PLYMOUTH

                  BRISTOL
                           BARNSTABLE

Counties in green contain at least
one covered bridge

🏠 – location of a covered bridge

DUKES

NANTUCKET

Massachusetts

"The Bay State"

In his book *Covered Bridges of the Northeast*, Richard Sanders Allen refers to Massachusetts as the "cradle of covered bridge building in America." Timothy Palmer, a resident of Rowley, Massachusetts, and builder of the first wooden bridges in the New World, built great wooden arch bridges across the Merrimack River in the northeast corner of the state as early as 1792. These were the first of many uncovered wooden bridges he built in the Bay State. It is thought by some that he certainly must have read an English translation of Palladio's *Treatise on Architecture*, because Palmer's humpback-style arch bridges resembled one of the plans sketched by Palladio. Then, after being convinced by Judge Peters of Philadelphia that covering the Permanent Bridge, which he had built over the Schuylkill River in 1805, would preserve the truss structure and extend the life of the bridge, Palmer covered the shorter of the two spans crossing the Merrimack in 1810. Therefore, it is claimed by some that since its truss structure was built in 1792, it should really be considered the first and oldest covered bridge built in America.

It was not long before Palmer's bridge-building skills became known throughout the entire northeastern part of the country. He was soon joined by Captain Isaac Damon of Northampton, Massachusetts. It was Damon who became one of the leading promoters of the Town lattice truss bridge. These men were soon joined by designers like William Howe of Spencer, Massachusetts, who patented the Howe truss in 1840. Howe had the good fortune of marrying into the Stone family, who could see the value in Howe's patent and went on to promote the building of bridges in a number of states using his design. Amasa Stone, Jr., together with brothers Joseph and Daniel and a railroad man, Auriah Boody, bought the patent from Howe and promoted its use throughout New England, Pennsylvania, and New Jersey. Other names such as George B. Boomer and his older brother Lucius, and Richard Hawkins, also loom large among the early covered bridge builders of Massachusetts.

In all, at one time, Massachusetts could lay claim to over one hundred covered bridges that spanned the numerous waterways in the state. At least eight of them stood in the Connecticut River Valley, and a number of them were concentrated in the Greenfield area, north of Springfield, which itself had become one of the hubs of covered bridge building activity. Today only seven historic covered bridges still stand in the Bay State. The normal ravages of time and nature—floods, ice, and wear—account for many of the loses; others have been lost to arson and neglect. Yet among the seven surviving historic spans, the fate of at least five is in question. This seems to be largely due to a lack of concern, possibly at the state level, for a serious program of covered bridge rehabilitation. More about this situation will be mentioned in the discussions regarding specific bridges.

In addition to the seven historic bridges, five other covered spans are documented in this guide. Two of them were erected in the last twenty years on private property in Franklin County, both designed and built by Dwight Scott. The others are a footbridge built in Stanley Park, Westfield; the Dummerston Bridge that was moved from Vermont to Old Sturbridge Village in 1951; and a bridge built in 1983 by Frank Sawyer in Essex County. This makes a total of twelve covered spans that existed within the Massachusetts borders at the time this guide was researched and documented, in late 2002 and early 2003.

Upper Sheffield/Sheffield Bridge

Location: In the north end of Sheffield, a locality within the Sheffield town line.

Directions: In the locality of Sheffield, travel north on US 7. Watch for a sign on the right (east) side of the road pointing to Sheffield Covered Bridge. It is just south of the First Baptist Church, also on the right side of US 7.

GPS: 42° 07.413N 073° 21.292W

Year: 1854, rebuilt 1998   **Truss:** Town   **Waterway:** Housatonic River
In Use: Foot traffic only   **Number of Spans:** 1   **Owner:** Town of Sheffield
Builder: Unknown   **Length:** 93 ft. 1 in.   **Width:** 11 ft. $10\frac{1}{2}$ in.
Condition: Excellent, new   **Number:** MA-02-01 (2)
Register: Does not qualify; old bridge listed Nov. 24, 1978

The original covered bridge built on this site was erected in 1854 after the Sheffield selectmen were directed to advertise for building proposals. After approximately one hundred years of use, some of the timbers and framework were replaced, and completely new siding was put on the north side. In 1967 the capacity of the bridge was limited to three tons. The bridge carried vehicular traffic until 1974, when it was closed to all vehicular traffic. In the early morning of August 13, 1994, "the venerable bridge was burned to the ground!" It has been beautifully reconstructed on the original site since 1994 using whatever

material could be salvaged from the original bridge. However, it appears that is was rebuilt with primarily new material.

The deck is covered with wide lengthwise planks, the roof with cedar shakes, the sides with vertical boards, and the portals with horizontal boards on the gable ends and vertical boards on the legs. The entire structure is painted gray. The bridge rests on marble slab abutments on the east end and stone and mortar abutments on the west end. It has a long, stone and mortar, road-level wingwall on the northeast end and a moderately long one on the southeast end. Wingwalls on the west end are rather obscure; there are only large boulders laid dry to retain the roadbed. The marble used for the east abutment is the same kind used in the lower part of the Washington Monument located in our nation's capital.

ESSEX COUNTY

Sawyer Pond Bridge

Location: In Magnolia, a locality within the Gloucester city line.

Directions: From MA 128 North, exit 14, go east on MA 133 for 1 mile, turn right onto Magnolia Ave. (no road name was visible on our 2002 visit), and go 1.7 miles to 138 Magnolia Ave., on the right. The bridge is over Sawyer Pond adjacent to the private home.

GPS: 42° 35.483N 070° 43.126W

Year: 1983   **Truss:** Town   **Waterway:** Sawyer Pond   **In Use:** Yes, private
Number of Spans: 1   **Owner:** Scott Sawyer   **Builder:** Frank Sawyer
Length: 40 ft.   **Width:** 9 ft. 4¾ in.   **Condition:** Very good   **Number:** MA-05-01
Register: Does not qualify

A carved wooden plaque located inside this lovely covered span says:

1980 1983 . . . FRANK SAWYER . . . BUILT ALL ALONE . . . AT AGE 73–76

An article by Jack Harrington, also posted inside the bridge, explains:

As a long time bridger and reader of TOPICS I have grown used to seeing many small backyard stringer bridges. These usually have some sort of false work that try to make them look like a covered bridge. I mentally tip my hat to the owner for being that much interested in covered bridges and then I go on my way.

This summer I found an exception to my rule. I was driving through Magnolia Ave., in the Magnolia section of Gloucester (Essex Co., MA) when

I suddenly had a feeling that I had just passed a real covered bridge. I turned around, went back, and there it was! This was a beautiful Town lattice bridge that was big enough to drive through! It was in the back yard of Frank Sawyer at 138 Magnolia Ave. Frank is a retired contractor and needed access to the back of his pond.

He started his planning with a stringer bridge in mind. As he researched it by visiting many covered bridges in the Connecticut River Valley area, he changed his plans to a covered bridge with load bearing trusses. . . .

The bridge is made of spruce and fir with oak treenails that he turned on his lathe. There are 315 sixteen inch "trunnels" and 104 eight inch ones lubricated with linseed oil. Frank decided to call it Cape Ann CB over Sawyer Pond. He does not want to call it Sawyer CB.

On our visit to the bridge in January 2003, Priscilla Sawyer, widow of the nephew to whom Frank willed the property upon his death, explained that Frank built the bridge without help from anyone. He wanted to do it alone. He built it in memory of his first wife. The splendid workmanship in the Town truss does not show in the photo, because the side openings had been closed for the winter. Visitors are always welcome but must understand that they enter the property at their own risk.

Arthur A. Smith Bridge

Location: Just west of Colrain, a locality within the Colrain town line.

Directions: Just north of Shellburne Falls, at the junction of MA 2 and MA 112 North, go north on MA 112 for 4.8 miles to Lyonsville Road on the left (west); turn left onto Lyonsville Road and go 0.1 mile to the bridge.

GPS: 42° 40.188N 072° 43.093W (coordinates recorded at parking area near the bridge)

Year: 1870   **Truss:** Burr   **Waterway:** North River (now dry land)
In Use: Closed   **Number of Spans:** 1   **Owner:** Town of Colrain
Builder: Unknown   **Length:** 98 ft.   **Width:** 14 ft. 7 in.
Condition: Very poor   **Number:** MA-06-03   **Register:** Feb. 3, 1983

This bridge, it appears, "does not have a friend in the world." It has been resting on cribbing along the banks of the North River since September 1991, when it was moved to this location by Arnold Graton. Using three pair of oxen working in shifts, Graton made the move as an attempt to preserve the bridge temporarily. More than a decade later, a newspaper article in the *Boston Globe* (November 25, 2002) claimed that it "has been propped up on wood cribbing awaiting repair for so long that the cribbing is starting to rot away."

The bridge was named for Arthur Alan Smith, a Civil War army captain and

local resident who lived near the bridge at the time it was erected. The bridge is now over 133 years old. In 1920 it was strengthened with the addition of an arch. This may be the time that some accounts indicate that the original Burr arch was beginning to separate and was strengthened with an eleven-ply arch tied to the bottom chord with metal rods at each vertical, multiple kingpost member. With this timely reinforcement, it survived the floods of 1936, 1938, 1948, and 1950. In 1956, additional general repairs were made. On February 3, 1983, the bridge was accepted in the National Register of Historic Places. It certainly does not deserve the lack of preservation that it has suffered in the past twelve years, and this is not the fault of the town selectmen, who have been seeking assistance for years. State Senator Stephen Brewer, when informed of the plight of this and other Massachusetts bridges that have been closed, pledged his support. He was quoted in the newspaper article mentioned above: "I love these bridges. They are a link to our heritage and a tourist attraction. We need to find out the extent of the problem and get these bridges open again." His expectation was that state highway aid or funds available through the National Historic Covered Bridge Preservation Program (NHCBPP) may help put the project back on track. According to the listing of the NHCBPP for 2002, $461,830 was awarded to Colrain, Massachusetts, for rehabilitation work on its covered bridge. At the time of this writing, additional information was not available.

Bissell Bridge

Location: 0.2 mile north of Charlemont, a locality within the Charlemont town line.

Directions: In the locality of Charlemont, from the junction of MA 2 and MA 8A North, go north on MA 8A for 0.2 mile to the bypassed bridge on the left (west) side of the highway.

GPS: 42° 37.892N 072° 52.121W

Year: 1951   **Truss:** Long variation   **Waterway:** Mill Brook   **In Use:** Closed
Number of Spans: 1   **Owner:** Town of Charlemont
Builder: T. J. Harvey and Sons   **Length:** 94 ft. 5$\frac{1}{2}$ in.   **Width:** 24 ft. 11 in.
Condition: Fair   **Number:** MA-06-04   **Register:** Does not qualify

Unfortunately, four of the covered bridges in Massachusetts that are "endangered species" are located in Franklin County. The Bissell Bridge is one, but this is not the first time that the town selectmen of Charlemont have had difficulty in getting action on their covered spans. In 1940, the first bridge built near the home of Adam Bissel, in 1880, was in serious trouble. Iron and sulphur from the Davis mines had crossed the bridge for many years since 1882,

when the mine opened. In 1940, the bridge was condemned. According to Richard Sanders Allen in *Covered Bridges of the Northeast,* the town selectmen penned a poem to the state public works commissioner, William F. Callahan, with these sentiments:

> The Bissel Bridge is falling down,
> Right in the middle of our town,
> Please view the matter with alarm
> And do vote "Yes" unto our plan.

The commissioner went along with their request, and a muse in his department replied with:

> Struck by the setting's natural beauty
> The Commissioner said 'twas the state's duty
> To save that lovely rustic view
> And save the state some money, too.
> For it seems the wood bridge can compete
> And still be cheaper than concrete
> The Town of course will pay its part
> To gladden every tourist's heart.

Consequently, in 1951 the present bridge was built, but once again the Bissel Bridge is in need of restoration. It was closed in 1995, and presently the town selectmen of Charlemont are again looking to the state for assistance. Perhaps they need another poet to help convey the unfortunate plight of this worthy crossing. As the interior photograph shows, it is an excellent example of a Long truss with some variation.

The Long truss of the Bissell Bridge.

Burkeville Bridge

Location: Just west of Conway, a locality within the Conway town line.

Directions: From I-91 North, exit 24, at the end of the ramp junction with US 5 North/MA 10 North/MA 116 North, go north for 1.0 mile; 116 North turns left. Follow MA 116 North through Conway. After an additional 6.6 miles, watch for the covered bridge on the left (south) side of the highway. Or from I-91 South, exit 25, at the end of the exit ramp, go north on MA 116 for 6.3 miles, then watch for the covered bridge on the left (south) side of the highway.

GPS: 42° 30.474N 072° 42.642W

Year: 1870   **Truss:** Howe variation   **Waterway:** South River
In Use: Closed   **Number of Spans:** 1   **Owner:** Town of Conway
Builder: Unknown   **Length:** 106 ft.   **Width:** 13 ft. 10 in.
Condition: Very poor   **Number:** MA-06-01   **Register:** Sept. 9, 1988

An article in the *Boston Globe* (November 25, 2002) captioned "State's covered bridges languish in disrepair," by reporter Ryan Slattery, starts with this paragraph:

> Residents of the small Berkshire town of Conway will soon be celebrating an anniversary, but don't expect a party. There will be no parade, no balloons, and no marching band, just anger and frustration because, yes, the Burkeville Bridge is still closed.

Built in 1869 or 1870, this historic landmark was in danger of closing in 1939 when it was considered unsafe for regular, heavy traffic because of hurricane and flood damage. Heavy traffic was routed a different direction, however, and use of the bridge for light traffic continued. Finally, in 1983, after the state highway department found that it was no longer safe, the bridge was closed to all traffic. State officials then decided to restore it as a pedestrian-only bridge. However, that plan, too, ran into a problem when the contractor hired to do the job simply walked away sometime during 2000. The president of the Conway Historical Society stated to the *Globe* reporter: "We're coming up on the 20th smash anniversary of nonactivity. . . . They say they'll have it done by next fall, but they've been saying that since 1983."

The bridge now stands completely closed off with chain-link fence, Jersey barriers, and plastic orange construction barrels with blinking yellow lights, awaiting some kind of action from the state Department of Transportation.

Creamery Bridge

Location: 1.6 miles west of Ashfield, a locality within the Ashfield town line.

Directions: From the junction of MA 112 and MA 116, west of the village of Ashfield, go east on MA 116 for 2.4 miles to Creamery Road, turn right (southwest) onto Creamery Road, and go 1.6 miles to a driveway on the left. (A sign at the driveway reads: "Creamery Bridge Sugar House Maple Syrup $30.00 gal.") Visitors are welcome.

GPS: 42° 31.181N 072° 48.046W

Year: 1985   **Truss:** Queenpost   **Waterway:** Creamery Brook
In Use: Yes, private   **Number of Spans:** 1   **Owner:** Dwight and Debra Scott
Builder: Dwight Scott   **Length:** 40 ft.   **Width:** 12 ft. 8 in.
Condition: Excellent   **Number:** MA-06-11   **Register:** Does not qualify

This is the only full-size, vehicular covered bridge in Franklin County that is in regular use today. Although not a historic bridge, it is an authentic queenpost truss structure, built and maintained by its owner, Dwight Scott. Mr. Scott is a private building contractor who erected this bridge in 1985 to provide access to his home and sugarhouse. When asked why the bridge was named Creamery Bridge, he explained that it was just off Creamery Road, crossing Creamery Brook to the home of the contractor, who operates Creamery Construction Company. It is a lovely, forty-foot span covered with unpainted, random-width, vertical boards on both the sides and with portals that have been left to weather naturally. It rests on concrete abutments, has a deck of random-width, lengthwise planks with crosswise planks at each entrance, and has a roof of wooden shakes. It sits in an extremely picturesque setting. We found it a delightful spot to visit both in the fall of 2002 and the winter of 2003. Dwight and Debra Scott, owners of the property and the bridge, welcome visitors any time.

Grays Sugarhouse Bridge

Location: 2.6 miles north of the locality of Ashfield, within the Ashfield town line.

Directions: From the junction of MA 112 and MA 116, just west of the locality of Ashfield, go south (it actually appears to be east) on MA 116 South for

0.9 mile to Baptist Cor. Rd. on the left (north); turn left onto Baptist Cor. Rd. and go 2.5 miles to Barnes Rd. on the left; turn left onto Barnes Road and go 0.1 mile to Grays Sugarhouse. The bridge is to the right.

GPS: 42° 32.723N 072° 46.835W (coordinates recorded on Barnes Road near the bridge)

Year: 1994   **Truss:** Kingpost   **Waterway:** Tributary of Bear River
In Use: Foot traffic only   **Number of Spans:** 1
Owner: William and Marian Gray   **Builder:** Dwight Scott and Boy Scouts
Length: 20 ft. $\frac{1}{4}$ in.   **Width:** 6 ft.   **Condition:** Good   **Number:** MA-06-12
Register: Does not qualify

This small footbridge is another covered span designed by Dwight Scott. In 1994, when William Gray needed a footbridge to cross a tributary of the Bear River, which ran through his property between the farmhouse and his sugarhouse, he contacted Mr. Scott. At the time, Dwight was working with the Boy Scouts of the area and considered it an excellent project for the scouts. Having built his own full-size covered bridge just nine years earlier, he had the expertise and engineering skill necessary to create the proper structure for the terrain. The truss style he chose, because of the short, twenty-foot span, was a kingpost truss. The supporting truss members of the bridge and the deck were built entirely of locust cut and milled on the Gray farm. Both the sides, which are covered only on the bottom half, and the portal gable ends are covered with natural, random-width, vertical pine boards, and the roof is covered with slate shingles. On our first visit to the bridge in September 2002, a young couple was getting ready to have their wedding ceremony performed at the bridge the next day. Visitors are always welcome at the Gray sugarhouse and farm; however, it might be a good idea to let them know they have visitors.

Green River Pumping Station/ Eunice Williams Bridge

Location: Approximately 5 miles north-northwest of Greenfield, a locality within the Greenfield town line.

Directions: From I-91, exit 26, go east on MA 2A for 0.8 mile to Conway St.; turn left (north) onto Conway St. for 1.5 miles to Nashs Mill Road; turn left onto Nashs Mill Road for 0.65 mile to Colrain Road; turn right and go 0.1 mile to Plain Road; bear right on Plain Road and go 2.9 miles to an unmarked road on the right (referred to as Eunice Williams Road); turn right and go 0.2 mile to the bridge.

GPS: 42° 38.782N 072° 37.218W

Year: 1972   **Truss:** Howe   **Waterway:** Green River   **In Use:** Closed 2003
Number of Spans: 1   **Owner:** State   **Builder:** Unknown   **Length:** 93 ft. $8\frac{1}{2}$ in.
Width: 13 ft. $8\frac{1}{2}$ in.   **Condition:** Good but damaged   **Number:** MA-06-02 (2)
Register: Does not qualify

This is the fourth of the Franklin County covered bridges that have been closed in recent years because of need for repairs. On our first visit to the bridge in September 2002, we felt that it was in good condition, and so we were quite surprised to find it closed when we returned in January 2003. A newspaper article that we read a short time later confirmed that the bridge had been closed "after inspectors discovered that it was warping and the structure was slowly being torn apart, possibly the result of large commercial trucks ignoring posted weight limits." There is no information available regarding plans for repair.

The bridge was only thirty years old, having been built and dedicated in 1972 to replace an older covered span destroyed by arson three years earlier. The older bridge had been there since 1870. The people of the area were devastated by the fire but determined that the bridge should be replaced. The town selectmen decided that an exact replica of the original Howe truss bridge should be built with slight modification to improve safety. The 1972 span is covered with unpainted, board and batten siding on both the sides and the portals, the deck is covered with lengthwise planks with runners in the traffic area, and the roof is covered with wooden shakes. The name of the road on which the bridge is located and the second name of the bridge, given above, is attributed to Eunice Williams, wife of an early-eighteenth-century minister, who was slain near this spot while a captive of Mohawk Indians on a march to Canada after a raid on Deerfield, Massachusetts.

HAMPDEN COUNTY

Goodrich Bridge

Location: In Stanley Park, Westfield, a locality within the Westfield town line.

Directions: From I-90, exit 3, at the end of the exit ramp, turn right on N. Elm St. and go south 1.8 miles to the circle in midtown; bear right on Court St. and go 0.6 mile; bear right onto Western Ave. and go 0.9 mile to Kensington Ave.; turn left onto Kensington Ave. and go 0.1 mile to Stanley Park entrance on the right side. Turn right into the park and go 0.1 mile; turn left into the parking area. Park at the far end of parking area near the carillon tower. Follow the paved drive to the right, behind the tower, to the flagstone steps descending to the ponds and the covered bridge area.

GPS: 42° 07.363N 072° 47.174W (coordinates recorded at top of flagstone steps leading to the bridge)

Year: 1965 **Truss:** Town **Waterway:** Pond **In Use:** Foot traffic only
Number of Spans: 1 **Owner:** Stanley Park, Westfield **Builder:** Unknown
Length: 40 ft. 3½ in. **Width:** 8 ft. 1 in. **Condition:** Very good
Number: MA-07-01 **Register:** Does not qualify

This is another lovely little footbridge that is really not an authentic covered bridge designed to carry vehicular traffic. We have included it in our guide primarily because it has been documented and given an "official" number in one other source of covered bridge information—the *World Guide to Covered Bridges* (*WGCB*).

While it is not possible to determine if this is only a stringer bridge with a simulated authentic truss, the Goodrich Bridge, together with other early

American structures, certainly does add a great amount of charm to Stanley Park in the village of Westfield. However, the bridge has been documented in *WGCB* as a Town truss structure. It has a deck of lengthwise planks, a roof of cedar shakes, and is covered with vertical boards on the sides, horizontal boards on the portal gable ends, and vertical boards on the legs of the gable ends. The entire structure is painted brown and rests on stone and mortar abutments. It has five windows on each side.

Gilbertville / Ware Bridge

Location: In Gilbertville, a locality within the Hardwick town line.

Directions: In Ware, at the junction of MA 32 North and MA 9 East, go east on MA 9/MA 32 for 1.6 miles; turn left (north) on MA 32 and go 3 miles to Bridge St. in Gilbertville; turn left (west) on Bridge St. and go 0.1 mile to the bridge.

GPS: 42° 18.603N 072° 12.711W

Year: 1886   **Truss:** Town   **Waterway:** Ware River   **In Use:** Closed
Number of Spans: 1   **Owner:** Towns of Ware and Hardwick
Builder: Unknown   **Length:** 137 ft.   **Width:** 19 ft. 10 in.
Condition: Awaiting restoration   **Number:** MA-08-04/MA-14-01
Register: May 8, 1986

In August 2002, when we visited the Gilbertville Bridge, it had just recently been closed to traffic. To the naked eye, the bridge appeared to be in very good condition; however, several local residents indicated that it had been weakened by reckless driving over the span. They specifically referred to drivers rapidly accelerating as they crossed the bridge in an effort to "lay rubber" on the bridge deck. A young couple living in an apartment adjacent to the bridge were serving as its "overseers" and the young man and an associate indicated that they expected to be working on the crew that will rehabilitate the bridge. They claimed that there were plans to restore and reopen the span; however, no definite time line had been established.

At the time of our visit, the bridge had a deck of lengthwise planks with a number of depressed, burnt tire marks, a roof of cedar shakes, sides covered with wide, vertical boards, and portals covered with wide, horizontal boards on the gables and vertical boards on the legs. The entire structure was unpainted on the sides but painted barn red with white trim on the portals. A lengthwise opening in the sides extended for nearly the entire length of the structure. Resting on stone and mortar abutments capped with concrete, it had a posted six-ton limit, and there was no additional supporting metal superstructure. The extensive amount of graffiti on the bridge and the damage that has led to its closing cause us to feel that some visitors have little appreciation for this historic structure.

Chester H. Waterous/Charles H. Waterous/Nehemiah Jewett's Bridge

Location: In East Pepperell, within the Pepperell town line.

Directions: Just west of East Pepperell, at the junction of MA 111 and MA 113, go east on MA 113 for 0.8 mile to an intersection where MA 113 bears right; turn left and go 0.2 mile to the bridge.

GPS: 42° 40.170N 071° 34.503W

Year: 1848, rebuilt 1962   **Truss:** Pratt variation   **Waterway:** Nashua River
In Use: Yes   **Number of Spans:** 1+   **Owner:** Town of Pepperell
Builder: Abel Jewett/Daniel D'Onfro's Sons, Inc.   **Length:** 108 ft. $2\frac{1}{2}$ in.
Width: 26 ft. $3\frac{1}{2}$ in.   **Condition:** Good   **Number:** MA-09-01 (2)
Register: Does not qualify

At the time of this writing, the Chester H. Waterous Bridge was the only authentic, historic covered bridge in use on a public road in the entire state of Massachusetts. This is rather unfortunate, when one realizes that a total of six authentic, historic bridges could still be in use. According to *Covered Bridges of Massachusetts, a Guide,* 1996 edition, written by Andrew R. Howard, the original covered span that once stood at this site was built in 1842 by Abel Jewett; however, a carving on a piece of the original bridge mounted on the present

Pratt truss of the Chester H. Waterous Bridge.

bridge states: "THIS PLAQUE IS MADE OF WOOD FROM THE ORIGINAL COVERED BRIDGE ERECTED IN THE YEAR 1848 . . . REPLACED BY THE PRESENT BRIDGE IN 1962." Additional information contributed by Howard indicates that the cost of the new bridge was $233,000 and implies that it was built by Daniel D'Onfro's Sons, Inc., of Leominster. The truss structure is a variation of the Pratt truss (see the interior photo) and, from all the information available, it is probably built on a superstructure of steel. Howard claims that forty tons of steel were used in the construction. The deck of the new structure originally was two-by-six-inch Douglas fir planks treated to withstand rot, but the entire deck is now covered with macadam. The sides and portals are covered with vertical board siding, also Douglas fir, painted gray. The entire structure rests on stone and mortar abutments capped with concrete, and it is covered with a wooden shake roof. There is a pedestrian walkway on each side of the bridge; they are quite necessary for this two-lane bridge, which carries quite a volume of vehicular traffic.

Dummerston/Vermont Bridge

Location: In Old Sturbridge Village, within the Sturbridge town line.

Directions: The entrance to Old Sturbridge Village is located at the west end of Sturbridge along US 20.

GPS: 42° 06.503N 072° 05.920W (coordinates recorded at entrance to village visitors center)

Year: 1951   **Truss:** Town   **Waterway:** Arm of Quinebaug River
In Use: Foot traffic and horse-drawn tour wagons   **Number of Spans:** 1
Owner: Old Sturbridge Village   **Builder:** Unknown   **Length:** 55 ft. $3\frac{1}{2}$ in.
Width: 19 ft. $11\frac{1}{2}$ in.   **Condition:** Very good   **Number:** MA-21-03
Register: Does not qualify

This covered bridge, which adds greatly to the nineteenth-century setting of Old Sturbridge Village, became part of the village setting when it was moved from Dummerston, Vermont, in 1951. In 1955, as a result of the great hurricane and flood, it broke from its abutments and floated in the Quinebaug River. Prior to the flood, it had been located further upstream. After being retrieved, it was placed in its present location. Currently the only vehicular traffic that the bridge carries is that of the horse-drawn wagon that transports visitors through the village. Otherwise, it carries a variety of foot traffic, both two-legged and four-legged.

The bridge is a very substantial Town truss structure rebuilt in this location on cut stone abutments laid dry, which are extended to relatively short road-level wingwalls. The deck consists of random-width crosswise planks, and the roof is covered with cedar shakes. The sides and portals are covered with unpainted, random-width vertical boards. The portal legs have an interesting decorative curved arch at the top, which extends outward to support the nearly twenty-foot-wide portal gable. There are no openings in the sides. The bridge certainly adds a lovely, rustic charm to this reconstruction of a typical village that might have existed in Massachusetts over one hundred years ago. Payment of an admission fee is required to enter Old Sturbridge Village to view the bridge. The village is closed weekdays from January until Presidents' Day Weekend.

NEW HAMPSHIRE

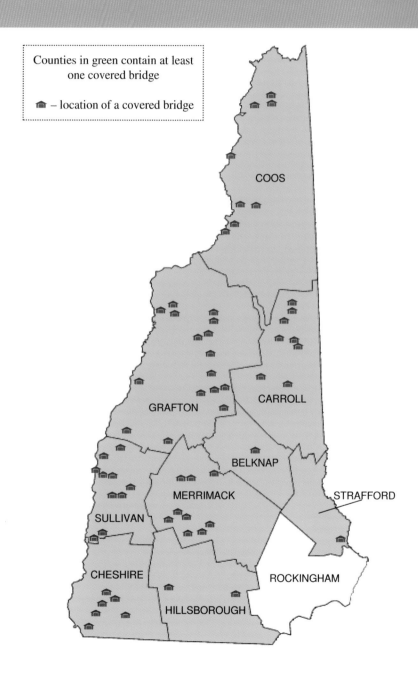

Counties in green contain at least
one covered bridge

🏠 – location of a covered bridge

COOS

GRAFTON

CARROLL

BELKNAP

MERRIMACK

STRAFFORD

SULLIVAN

CHESHIRE

ROCKINGHAM

HILLSBOROUGH

New Hampshire

"The Granite State"

I t was not until the 1820s that the first covered bridge appeared in the Granite State. One of the earliest was the Haverhill-Bath Bridge, a Town lattice truss structure, built in 1829. That bridge is still standing today.

According to the 1994 publication *New Hampshire Covered Bridges, "A Link with Our Past,"* prepared by the New Hampshire Department of Transportation, nearly four hundred covered bridges stood in the state at one time. However, as in every other state, that number gradually dwindled, and today only fifty-four historic structures can still be located—from the Ashuelot Bridge in the southwest corner of Cheshire County to the Happy Corner Bridge in the northern tip of Coos County. Again, the ravages of time, floodwaters, lack of maintenance, and the destructive nature of thoughtless individuals account for the diminished number.

Fortunately, in recent years, much has been done to preserve the covered spans that remain, not only in New Hampshire, but across the entire nation. The Surface Transportation and Uniform Relocation Assistance Act of 1987, passed by the federal government, states: "Congress hereby finds and declares it to be in the national interest to encourage the rehabilitation, reuse and preservation of bridges significant in American history, architecture, engineering and culture. Historic bridges are important links to our past, serve as safe and vital transportation routes in the present, and can represent significant resources for the future." Acting on this legislation, the state of New Hampshire, with considerable assistance by local authorities, has done much to preserve and rehabilitate many of its covered spans. It also has, under the guidance of the state's fire marshal, a committee exploring various ways to circumvent the problem of arson, which has been one of the major causes of bridge destruction. In some towns, the rehabilitated structures already benefit from one or several of the fire prevention recommendations—a fire suppression system, use of fire retardation materials, electronic alarms, neighborhood surveillance organizations, and programs of public education.

Today, in addition to the fifty-three historic covered bridges that are still standing in the state, there are eight that have been built in the later part of the twentieth century. These are the Tannery Hill Footbridge in Gilford, Belknap County; the Wentworth Golf Club Bridge in Jackson, Carroll County; the Cocheco River Pedestrian Bridge in Dover, Strafford County; the Stowell Road/Baboosic Brook Bridge, a "nontraditional" truss bridge, in Merrimack, Hillsborough County; and the last four, all in Grafton County: the Sentinel Pine Bridge in the Flume Gorge at Franconia Notch State Park, the Allen Hollis Footbridge at Kinsman Notch, the Jack O' Lantern Bridge just south of Woodstock, and the Brundage Bridge on private property several miles north of Grafton.

It should also be noted that three of the bridges counted among the fifty-three historic, authentic bridges are interstate bridges linking New Hampshire and Vermont—the Columbia Bridge and the Mount Orne Bridge in Coos County, and the Cornish-Windsor Bridge in Grafton County. However, while these are interstate bridges because they connect the two states, the bridges technically belong to the state of New Hampshire, since New Hampshire's western boundary extends to the west shoreline of the Connecticut River. Another interesting fact is that these interstate bridges, like a number of other covered bridges, operated originally as toll bridges. Little by little this practice, considered by many to be "an interstate holdup," was discontinued as the towns and the state of New Hampshire bought out the bridge companies assessing the toll. Finally, on June 1, 1943, the Cornish-Windsor Bridge was opened with great ceremony and without cost to all those who wanted to cross to the other side. Although these three interstate bridges are primarily the responsibility of New Hampshire, the state of Vermont does pay a small percentage toward their preservation. These bridges also have a two-part number—one for the state of New Hampshire, the other for the state of Vermont. Consequently, these three bridges are documented in a separate section of the guide titled New Hampshire/Vermont.

Tannery Hill Footbridge

Location: In the locality of Gilford, within the Gilford town line.

Directions: Take the US 3 North/NH 11 East bypass around Laconia. Exit at the NH 11A exit. At the end of the exit ramp go east (right) to Gilford on NH 11A for 2.4 miles to signs on the south (right) side of the highway for Town Hall . . . Police Dept. Turn right and right again to the parking area. The bridge can be seen straight ahead.

GPS: 43° 32.998N 071° 24.312W (coordinates recorded in parking lot close to the bridge)

Year: 1995   **Truss:** Town   **Waterway:** Gunstock Brook
In Use: Foot traffic only   **Number of Spans:** 1   **Owner:** Town of Gilford
Builder: Tim Andrews   **Length:** 42 ft. $7\frac{1}{4}$ in.   **Width:** 6 ft. $5\frac{1}{2}$ in.
Condition: Excellent   **Number:** NH-01-02   **Register:** Does not qualify

This is a late-twentieth-century, authentic covered bridge in every respect except its size. It was not designed or built to accommodate vehicular traffic; consequently it will not be found in *New Hampshire Covered Bridges,* an excellent book displaying all fifty-three of New Hampshire's authentic vehicular bridges. In the 1990s, there was a need to span the Gunstock Brook, which flows through a rather deep gorge between the village of Gilford and the Town Hall and Police Department complex. Realizing the need, the Gilford Rotary Club contracted Tim Andrews, a local bridge builder, to construct a footbridge to

permit easier access to the municipal buildings. The site chosen for the bridge was one where a historic covered bridge had stood about fifty years ago. The truss chosen for the span was the nineteenth-century Town lattice truss, and the material used was all local lumber—spruce, pine, and hemlock. In 1995, the bridge was completed and, according to a bronze plaque located at the site of the bridge, presented to the community of Gilford.

The bridge is a lovely structure covered with unpainted, natural, vertical, random-width boards on its sides and portals; it has a deck of lengthwise planks and a roof of silver, standing rib sheet metal. The sides of the span are completely open in the central half of the bridge, allowing a side view of the latticework from the outside, as well as an excellent view of the tumbling waters of Gunstock Brook from the inside. If you happen to be in the Lakes Region of New Hampshire, be sure to visit this gem in its spectacular rustic setting.

CARROLL COUNTY

Albany Bridge

Location: 7 miles west of the locality of Conway, within the Albany town line.

Directions: In Conway, at the junction of NH 113 West and NH 16 South, go west on NH 113 for 0.8 mile to NH 112 (Kancamagus Highway) on the right (north), turn right onto NH 112, and go 6.25 miles to Passaconaway Road on the right (north); turn right and go 0.05 mile to the covered bridge parking area to the right. A parking permit is required. During the camping season, the bridge is open to the campground.

GPS: 44° 00.345N 071° 14.463W (coordinates recorded in parking lot near the bridge)

Year: 1858   **Truss:** Paddleford   **Waterway:** Swift River   **In Use:** Yes
Number of Spans: 1   **Owner:** Town of Albany
Builder: Amzi Russell and Leander Morton   **Length:** 125 ft. 10 in.
Width: 18 ft. 9 in.   **Condition:** Good   **Number:** NH-02-06
Register: Eligible but not listed

This lovely covered bridge is located just a short distance from the Kancamagus Highway, one of the most scenic highways in the world. It provides an appropriate entrance to the Covered Bridge Campground, one of many campgrounds located in the White Mountain National Forest. The bridge presently standing at this site is a replacement for the original bridge built there in 1857. (The first bridge was destroyed by a windstorm in 1858.) The builders, Amzi Russell and Leander Morton, agreed with the Town of Albany to rebuild the

structure for $1,300 minus the price paid for the original bridge. The Paddleford truss structure, nearly 126 feet long, is reinforced with a shallow laminated arch, consisting of sixteen layers of two-by-eight-inch planks attached to the inside of each truss. Several accounts indicate that the wooden substructure of the deck was replaced in 1981–82 by steel stringers. However, the deck itself is still covered with two-by-six-inch lengthwise planks.

The entire structure rests on cut stone abutments that extend to road-level wingwalls. The center portion of the bridge siding is open for the entire length of the span. The side covering consists of random-width, vertical boards, the portal covering of horizontal clapboard, all of which is unpainted, left to weather naturally. The roof is covered with corrugated metal, possibly a twentieth-century alteration, to help shed the heavy winter snows. This bridge, one of the first we encountered on our travels through the White Mountains a number of years ago, has always been one of our favorites, probably because of its brightly colored roof and its spectacular setting over the Swift River.

Bartlett Bridge

Location: 1.8 miles west of the locality of Glen, within the Bartlett town line.

Directions: In Glen, at the junction of NH 16 and NH 302, go west on NH 302 for 1.8 miles to the bypassed bridge on the north side of the highway.

GPS: 44° 05.686N 071° 12.197W (coordinates recorded in parking lot next to the bridge)

Year: 1851   **Truss:** Paddleford with arch   **Waterway:** Saco River
In Use: As a gift shop   **Number of Spans:** 1   **Owner:** Dan and Nancy Wanek
Builder: Unknown, restored by Milton Graton in 1966   **Length:** 170 ft. 7 in.
Width: 16 ft. 5 in.   **Condition:** Good   **Number:** NH-02-02
Register: Eligible but not listed

One of the recorded dates for the construction of the Bartlett Bridge is 1851. Milton Graton, who did major repair work on the bridge in 1966, indicated that the origin of the bridge was sometime before 1870. In any event, the bridge served as a major artery for traffic between Portland, Maine, and Montreal in Quebec, Canada. In 1939 the bridge was abandoned and closed to all traffic. For a period of time it was used to store town equipment, and its condition deteriorated considerably. During the 1950s it was also used to store rolls of snow fence during the warm-weather months. Finally, in 1966 Mrs. Cassinelli, a teacher of needlework, purchased the bridge from the Town of Bartlett for one dollar. Realizing its deplorable condition, she contracted Milton Graton to repair the bridge to a sound, safe condition; and, wanting a place to market her fine fabric items, she had Mr. Graton build a gift shop and move it into the northern end of the bridge.

Later, in 1990, Marc and Mary Ellen Frydman, new owners of the bridge and gift shop, had additional renovations made to the structure. The twelve-ply, laminated arches that reinforce the Paddleford truss were strengthened, and one layer of the bridge's decking was removed. This reduced the weight of the bridge by twenty-five tons. The cost of this renovation was $38,000. The most recent owners of the bridge, Dan and Nancy Wanek, also operate a bed-and-breakfast establishment in the Covered Bridge House, an old country home located on the property immediately next to the bridge. They still operate the 1966 shop located on the bridge from Memorial Day weekend through October.

Durgin Bridge

Location: Approximately 3 miles northeast of the locality of North Sandwich, within the Sandwich town line.

Directions: In Bennett Corners, at the junction of NH 25 and NH 113, go northwest on NH 113 (Jackson Pond Road) for 1.6 miles to an unmarked crossroad, turn right, and go 1.6 miles to Durgin Bridge Road; turn right to cross the bridge. Or, in North Sandwich, at the junction of NH 113 and NH 113A, go north on NH 113A (Whiteface Road) for 0.8 mile to Fellows Hill Road on the right (east), turn right, and go 1.4 miles to Durgin Bridge Road; turn left to cross the bridge. Parking is available on the north side of the bridge.

GPS: 43° 51.347N 071° 21.863W

Year: 1869   **Truss:** Paddleford with arch   **Waterway:** Cold River
In Use: Yes   **Number of Spans:** 1   **Owner:** Town of Sandwich
Builder: Jacob Berry   **Length:** 99 ft. 6 in.   **Width:** 16 ft. 10½ in.
Condition: Good   **Number:** NH-02-07   **Register:** Sept. 22, 1983

This bridge is one among several of Jacob Berry's covered bridges built in Carroll County. It is the fourth bridge to be constructed at this crossing. Three earlier bridges were washed away in 1844, 1865, and 1869. The date 1828, on the portal name plaque, may be the date at which the first bridge was built in this location. According to the publication *New Hampshire Covered Bridges,* Jacob Berry claimed that this bridge was so well built that it could be filled with wood and it would still stand. No one has ever tried to prove that claim. It is, however, a very substantial, Paddleford truss structure reinforced with a large, high, Burr-type arch consisting of two-by-twelve-inch laminated planks. The cover-

ing of the bridge sides is rather different, a treatment we have seen on very few covered bridges. They are covered with vertical board and battens, but the battens, which are usually on the outside, are placed on the inside of the bridge. The portal gables, which extend well over the bridge deck, are covered with horizontal boards. All the siding is unpainted and has naturally weathered to a dark, rustic appearance. The bridge is completely closed with the exception of narrow openings directly below the eaves and two long, narrow windows on each side.

Records indicate that Milton Graton and his son, Arnold, repaired and strengthened the bridge in 1967–68 and that it was rehabilitated again in 1983 at a cost of $48,000. The bridge was named for James Holmes Durgin, who operated a gristmill nearby. Today, the road that crosses through the bridge is named Durgin Bridge Road. Several accounts also indicate that the area around the bridge played a large part in the operation of the Underground Railroad, which reached its peak of operation between 1830 and 1865.

Jackson/Honeymoon Bridge

Location: In the locality of Jackson, within the Jackson town line.

Directions: In Jackson, at the junction of NH 16 North and NH 16A, go east on NH 16A to the bridge.

GPS: 44° 08.491N 071° 11.193W

Year: 1876   **Truss:** Paddleford with arch   **Waterway:** Ellis River
In Use: Yes   **Number of Spans:** 1   **Owner:** State
Builder: Charles Broughton and son, Frank   **Length:** 124 ft. 8 in.
Width: 19 ft. $4\frac{1}{2}$ in.   **Condition:** Fair   **Number:** NH-02-01
Register: Eligible but not listed

According to information contained on the Carter Notch Inn website: "As you enter Jackson through its historic covered bridge built in 1876, you realize why it was nicknamed 'The Honeymoon Bridge.' As you pass through the bridge, you realize that you are entering a special place where the quality of life is unchallenged, the beauty of the area is breathtaking, and your appreciation of it increases every day that you relax amid its natural beauty." Although this does not explain how the bridge became known as the "Honeymoon Bridge," even today the early tradition of newlyweds having their photograph taken at the bridge continues.

This is truly a most photogenic bridge, located at the entrance to a quaint New England town. The builder of the bridge, Charles Broughton, assisted by his son Frank, was a sergeant in the Eighteenth Regiment of the New Hampshire Volunteers during the Civil War. It is also reported that he was a "finish carpenter, an avid fiddler, and a skillful bear hunter." Town records indicate

that the pedestrian walkway on the north side of the bridge was added in 1930. This bridge is another excellent example of a Paddleford truss bridge reinforced with a Burr-type arch. The arch, like many others in Carroll County, is a multi-ply, laminated arch containing twelve layers of two-by-eight-inch planks. The trusses at one time were more open than they are presently. Today, even the lower portion of the inside of the truss is covered with vertical boards.

In 2001, the Jackson/Honeymoon Bridge was the beneficiary of a $64,000 grant made available through the National Historic Covered Bridge Preservation Program. These funds were used for the installation of a Protectowire fire detection system and a dry sprinkler system. According to the proprietor of the Wentworth Golf Resort, located a short distance north of the bridge, rehabilitation of the Jackson span is scheduled for sometime in the immediate future; the work may even be completed by the time this guide comes off the press.

Saco River Bridge

Location: In the locality of Conway, within the Conway town line.

Directions: In Conway, at the junction of NH 16 and NH 113, go west on NH 16/NH 113 to the next intersection, 0.05 mile (there is a traffic light at the intersection), turn right, and go 0.25 mile to a fork; take the right fork (straight ahead) and go 0.05 mile; turn right to cross the bridge. Or, from the junction of NH 16 and NH 113, go north on NH 16 for 0.7 mile to East Side Road on the left (west), turn left onto East Side Road, and go 0.4 mile to the bridge.

GPS: 43° 58.989N 071° 06.994W

Year: 1890   **Truss:** Paddleford with arch   **Waterway:** Saco River
In Use: Yes   **Number of Spans:** 2   **Owner:** State
Builder: Charles Broughton and son, Frank   **Length:** 228 ft. 8 in.
Width: 20 ft. 4 in.   **Condition:** Good   **Number:** NH-02-03
Register: Eligible but not listed

The first covered bridge built on this site was erected by Jacob Berry and Peter Paddleford in 1850. It was a replacement for a crudely framed log structure that had collapsed. That bridge survived until it was destroyed by the Swift River Bridge, which crashed into it in 1869 after being swept from its abutments. After the second loss, the bridge was replaced by Allen and Warren of Conway, but it, too, was destroyed by a tannery fire in 1890. The present bridge was built by Charles Broughton and his son, Frank, the same year. On our visit to the bridge in January 2003, we found it in good condition, giving us the impression that relatively recent restoration work had been done on the structure. The only record we could find was a reference to a 1989 restoration by the New Hampshire Department of Transportation and a 2001 grant from the National Historic Covered Bridge Preservation Program, mentioned below.

The bridge is a two-lane, two-span, Paddleford truss structure with substantial reinforcing—laminated, Burr-type arches—each one nineteen layers of two-by-eight-inch planks. The bridge has a pedestrian walkway on each side, both of which are covered with vertical boards on the lower third only. The south side is unpainted, but the north side is painted gray to match the clapboard siding of the portal gable ends, which are trimmed in white. The deck consists of wide lengthwise planks, and the roof is covered with red, ribbed sheet metal. The entire structure rests on cut stone abutments, which are extended to road-level wingwalls, and on a center pier, also of cut stone.

In 2001, the Saco River Bridge was the beneficiary of a $140,000 grant made available through the National Historic Covered Bridge Preservation Program. These funds were used for the installation of a Protectowire fire detection system and a dry sprinkler system.

Swift River Bridge

Location: In the locality of Conway, within the Conway town line.

Directions: In Conway, at the junction of NH 16 and NH 113, go west on NH 16/NH 113 to the first intersection (there is a traffic light at the intersection), turn right (north), and go 0.4 mile to the bypassed bridge on the right (east). (Bear left at the fork 0.2 mile after the turn north at the intersection.)

GPS: 43° 59.082N 071° 07.169W

Year: 1869, restored 1991   **Truss:** Paddleford with arch
Waterway: Swift River   **In Use:** Foot traffic only   **Number of Spans:** 1
Owner: Town of Conway   **Builder:** Jacob Berry and son, Jacob Jr.
Length: 133 ft. 10 in.   **Width:** 18 ft. 6 in.   **Condition:** Very good
Number: NH-02-05   **Register:** Eligible but not listed

Records indicate that the first bridge built on this site was erected by John Douglas in 1850. That structure served the community quite well until the spring thaw of 1869, when the bridge was swept from its abutments by the raging waters of the Swift River, which sent it downstream into the Saco River, where it crashed into the Saco River Bridge. The parts of both bridges flowed

rapidly downstream, where much of the lumber was salvaged and utilized in the construction of the new Swift River Bridge. Jacob Berry and his son, Jacob Jr., started building the new bridge the same year. That structure was used until it was bypassed in 1974 with a new concrete and steel bridge built in the vicinity. Even though the covered bridge was no longer used for vehicular traffic, there was sufficient interest among the townspeople to save it for future generations. A bronze plaque located near the bridge states:

SWIFT RIVER COVERED BRIDGE

1869

RESTORED IN

1991

THROUGH THE GENEROUS DONATIONS

OF MANY PRIVATE CITIZENS

AND THE TOWN OF CONWAY

UNITING TO PRESERVE A SYMBOL

OF OUR COMMUNITY HERITAGE

The interior photo shows an excellent example of a Paddleford truss, which has been reinforced with a multi-ply, laminated, Burr-type arch. The arch in this case consists of nineteen layers of two-by-eight-inch planks. The 1991 restoration has put the bridge in excellent condition, but it is used only for pedestrian traffic. It is a very attractive span, with its horizontal clapboard por-

The Paddleford truss of the Swift River Bridge with multi-ply, laminated, Burr-type arch.

tals painted white with barn-red trim and its barn-red, vertical board sides—open approximately one-third in the middle for the entire length of the bridge, making the truss structure quite visible. The gray, seamed, sheet metal roof readily sheds the heavy winter snows. The entire structure rests on cut stone abutments, which are extended to road-level wingwalls, one of which is capped with concrete.

Wentworth Golf Club Bridge

Location: In the locality of Jackson, within the Jackson town line.

Directions: In Glen, at the junction of NH 16 and US 302, go north on NH 16 for 2.26 miles to NH 16A on the right (east); turn right onto NH 16A into the village of Jackson. The entrance to the golf course is left (west) of 16A in Jackson.

GPS: 44° 08.799N 071° 11.106W (coordinates recorded in parking lot of the golf course)

Year: 1990   **Truss:** Warren   **Waterway:** Ellis River
In Use: Seasonal, golfers and skiers   **Number of Spans:** 1
Owner: Michael Mallett   **Builder:** Mallett Co.   **Length:** 115 ft.
Width: 11 ft. 8 in.   **Condition:** Excellent   **Number:** NH-02-13
Register: Does not qualify

When there was a need to span the Ellis River, which flows through the Wentworth Golf Club in Jackson, New Hampshire, the owner and builder of the

course, Michael Mallet, chose to bridge the waterway with an authentic, Warren truss covered bridge. The structure was built by the Mallet Company in 1990. Its picturesque form can readily be seen from NH Route 16, which bypasses the village. It is a very attractive span, with noticeable camber, adjacent to the number nine tee box. It is painted barn red with sparkling white trim. Its sides are covered with vertical, tongue-and-groove siding, the portal gable ends with horizontal clapboard, the roof with green shingles, and the deck with crosswise planks. Because of its position on the golf course, the players have the pleasure of passing through this span several times while playing a round of golf. During the winter months, when the golf course is converted into a cross-country ski area, skiers also have the pleasure of traversing this lovely span. If visiting during the golf season, it is best to stop at the pro shop for permission before venturing onto the golf course. It is possible to view or photograph this span any time during the year from NH Route 16.

Whittier/Bearcamp Crossing Bridge

Location: 0.5 mile west of the locality of West Ossipee, within the Ossipee town line.

Directions: In West Ossipee, at the junction of NH 16 and NH 25, go west on NH 25 for 0.5 mile to a road on the right (north), turn right, and go 0.2 mile to the bypassed bridge.

GPS: 43° 49.323N 071° 12.716W

Year: 1870s   **Truss:** Paddleford with arch   **Waterway:** Bearcamp River
In Use: Foot and snowmobile   **Number of Spans:** 1
Owner: Town of Ossipee   **Builder:** Jacob Berry   **Length:** 136 ft. 7 in.
Width: 18 ft. $1\frac{1}{2}$ in.   **Condition:** Very good   **Number:** NH-02-08
Register: Mar. 15, 1984

Records of the Town of Ossipee indicate that several bridges have been built at this location. A crude timber bridge built in 1791 had been repaired three times—1803, 1811, and 1820. A new bridge was built by Wentworth Lord in 1820 at a cost of $133. It was rebuilt in 1832. A third bridge was built by John Brown in 1849 at a cost of $234. The fourth bridge, the present bridge, is credited to Jacob Berry, who also built two other bridges in Carroll County. A bronze plaque located at the bridge site lists "circa 1870" as the date of that construction. Improvements were made in 1958 when "steel telltales" were erected to protect the upper knee braces and stringers; however, these were removed at the time of the 1982–83 restoration, which was done by Milton Graton and Sons at a cost of $85,000. A large portion of the funds came from a summer resident, Gordon Pope, and the remainder from the state. The plaque, mentioned above, states: "Restoration completed—1983 and dedicated to

the memory of NANCY SHELDON POPE . . . May 14, 1916–June 20, 1982 . . . by Gordon A. Pope . . . family and friends . . . and The State of New Hampshire . . . August 20, 1983." On March 15, 1989, the bridge was closed to vehicular traffic. On our visit to the bridge in January 2003, it was being used for snowmobile traffic as well as a pedestrian crossing.

Records indicate that the sides of the original bridge were completely closed with the exception of tiny windows. The Graton restoration left the upper portion of the bridge open approximately a third of the way from each end. The sides of the bridge are covered with vertical boards and the gable ends of the portals with horizontal boards, all of which have weathered naturally. The Paddleford trusses are reinforced with very substantial, high, Burr-type arches, which consist of fifteen two-by-ten-inch laminated planks. Since the roof was completely snow covered on our visit, we were only able to assume that it was covered with wooden shakes. The bridge has a very rustic appearance in a lovely rural setting.

Ashuelot/Upper Village/Village/ Village Station Bridge

Location: In the locality of Ashuelot, within the Winchester town line

Directions: In Hinsdale, at the junction of NH 119 and NH 63 North, go southeast on NH 119 for 3.6 miles to the road on the right in the village of Ashuelot; the bridge is just to the right.

GPS: 42° 46.645N 072° 25.404W

Year: ca.1853–58   **Truss:** Town   **Waterway:** Ashuelot River
In Use: Yes   **Number of Spans:** 2   **Owner:** Town of Winchester
Builder: Nicholas Powers   **Length:** 173 ft. $6\frac{1}{2}$ in.   **Width:** 16 ft. 10 in.
Condition: Very good   **Number:** NH-03-02   **Register:** Feb. 20, 1981

This lovely bridge, according to some recorded information, was built by Nicholas Powers in 1864. The bridge was originally constructed to transport lumber across the Ashuelot River for use by the Ashuelot Railroad. A plaque placed at the side of the north portal of the bridge indicates that the bridge was built "circa 1853–1858"; however, some other documented sources indicate that it was built in 1864. The bridge was completely rehabilitated in 1999 by the Town of Winchester with major funding provided by the New Hampshire Department of Transportation. The restored structure has highly decorated portals covered with white, vertical board and batten siding, trimmed with red. It

rests on cut stone abutments placed on a concrete foundation, has a deck of wide, lengthwise planks, and has a roof of red, seamed sheet metal that is extended on either side of the roadway to cover walkways. It is a most striking structure in a beautiful rustic setting.

Carlton/Carleton/Whitcomb Bridge

Location: 1.5 miles south of the locality of Swanzey, within the Swanzey town line.

Directions: In Keene, at the junction of NH 101 East and NH 12 South, go south on NH 12 for 0.8 mile to the junction with NH 32 on the right (south), turn right onto NH 32, and go 4.4 miles to Carlton Road on the left (east); turn left onto Carlton Road and go 0.2 mile to the bridge.

GPS: 42° 51.285N 027° 16.473W

Year: 1869   **Truss:** Queenpost with kingpost
Waterway: South Branch of Ashuelot River   **In Use:** Yes
Number of Spans: 1   **Owner:** Town of Swanzey
Builder: Local barn builders   **Length:** 67 ft. $8\frac{1}{4}$ in.   **Width:** 14 ft. $3\frac{1}{2}$ in.
Condition: Very good   **Number:** NH-03-07   **Register:** June 10, 1975

The earliest crossing in the location of the Carlton Bridge is recorded as having been built around 1789. However, it was not a covered bridge. The first covered bridge on this site was built in 1869 by local barn builders. Compared to the other bridges in the area, it is a relatively short span and could be built using a

truss structure familiar to the builders because it was similar to trusses used in barns in the vicinity. Because of needed repairs, the bridge was closed in 1974. Estimates by the state Department of Transportation in 1979 indicated that $487,000 would be needed to completely rehabilitate the bridge. In 1996 the bridge was completely rebuilt and finished with a new, seamed metal roof. The refurbished structure is covered with barn-red, vertical, random-width siding on both the sides and the portals. The portals are trimmed with white. The portal legs and the portal entrances are painted white on the bottom half. The span rests on cut stone abutments, which are extended to road-level wingwalls. It has two windows on the upstream side. After being completely restored, this lovely bridge should remain standing for a considerable length of time.

Coombs Bridge

Location: Approximately 5 miles north of the locality of Winchester, within the Winchester town line

Directions: In Winchester, at the junction of NH 119 East and NH 10 North, go north on NH 10 for 4.8 miles to Coombs Bridge Road on the left (west), turn left, and go 0.3 mile to the bridge.

GPS: 42° 50.280N 072° 21.642W

Year: 1837   **Truss:** Town   **Waterway:** Ashuelot River   **In Use:** Yes
Number of Spans: 1   **Owner:** Town of Winchester
Builder: Anthony Coombs   **Length:** 114 ft. 8 in.   **Width:** 14 ft. $\frac{1}{2}$ in.
Condition: Very good   **Number:** NH-03-03   **Register:** Nov. 21, 1976

The 1989 edition of the *World Guide to Covered Bridges* indicates that the Coombs Bridge was built in 1830. Documentation on the "New Hampshire Bridges" internet site lists 1837 as the date of construction. It also indicates that the bridge was named for its builder, Anthony Coombs. Repairs were made to the bridge in 1964, and it was completely rehabilitated in 1971 at a cost of $13,340. Records of 1994 indicate that the bridge was in need of major repairs. When we visited the bridge in 2002, however, it appeared to be in good shape. The list of covered bridges distributed by the state's welcome centers indicates that traffic on the bridge is now restricted to passenger cars only. The covered bridge is bypassed by a road to the north for truck traffic.

Cresson/Sawyer's Crossing Bridge

Location: Approximately 3 miles south of the locality of Keene or approximately 10.6 miles northeast of the locality of Winchester, within the Swanzey town line.

Directions: In Winchester, at the junction of NH 119 East and NH 10 North, go north on NH 10 for 8.6 miles to Sawyers Crossing Road, turn right (east) onto Sawyers Crossing Road, and go 2 miles to a T, turn right, and go 0.1 mile to the bridge. Or, in Keene, at the junction of NH 12/101 and NH 10 South, go south on NH 10 for 0.6 mile to Matthews Road on the left (east), turn left onto Matthews Road, and go 2 miles to a stop sign; the bridge is just ahead to the left.

GPS: 42° 53.183N 072° 17.209W

Year: 1859   **Truss:** Town   **Waterway:** Ashuelot River   **In Use:** Yes
Number of Spans: 2   **Owner:** Town of Swanzey   **Builder:** Unknown
Length: 159 ft. 2½ in.   **Width:** 16 ft. 3¾ in.   **Condition:** Excellent
Number: NH-03-05   **Register:** Nov. 14, 1978

The first bridge in this location was an uncovered crossing built prior to the Revolutionary War for 53 pounds, 6 shillings. In 1859 the first covered span was built to replace the original bridge at a cost of $1,735.94. As stated on the "New Hampshire Bridges" internet site: "The event was celebrated with a big dance held right on the bridge. Lanterns were hung from the rafters, a four piece orchestra played, lunch was served at midnight, and the dance continued all night." In 1983 repairs were made to the bridge at a cost of $61,028.15. The town of Swanzey contributed $16,446.22, and the balance came from the state. A more recent report indicates that the bridge was completely restored in 1996 by Wright Construction Co., Inc., Mt. Holly, Vermont. The contractor's documentation states the "project consisted of major truss component replacement, floor system replacement, and a new roofing system." The report continues: "This wooden bridge was reconstructed to maintain the historical appearance

and much of the historical joinery of the original construction, including turning our own wooden pegs on site."

On our visit to the bridge in October 2002, we found it in excellent condition. The barn-red structure rests proudly on cut stone abutments that extend to road-level wingwalls. It has a deck of lengthwise planks and a roof of dark gray seamed sheet metal. Barring unforseen circumstances, the bridge should serve the area for many years to come.

Slate Bridge

Location: Approximately 6 miles north-northeast of the locality of Winchester, within the Swanzey town line.

Directions: In Winchester, at the junction of NH 119 East and NH 10 North, go north on NH 10 for 5.1 miles to Westport Village Road on the right (east), turn right onto Westport Village Road, and go 0.7 mile to an unnamed road; turn left and go 0.15 mile to the bridge.

GPS: 42° 50.830N 072° 20.425W

Year: 1862, rebuilt 2001   **Truss:** Town   **Waterway:** Ashuelot River
In Use: Yes   **Number of Spans:** 1   **Owner:** Town of Swanzey
Builder: Unknown   **Length:** 142 ft. $6\frac{1}{2}$ in.   **Width:** 14 ft. $\frac{1}{2}$ in.
Condition: Excellent   **Number:** NH-03-06 (2)   **Register:** Nov. 14, 1978

The first covered bridge was built on this site in 1862 to replace an uncovered span dating back to the early 1800s. *New Hampshire Covered Bridges: "A Link*

with Our Past" tells the story of William Wheelock, who "was halfway across the earlier bridge with a span of four oxen when the bridge collapsed dropping both driver and animals into the river." There is no record of the builder for the new covered span. There is a record, however, that the bridge was damaged by a snowplow in 1987, which required repairs amounting to $2,000. The 1862 bridge was completely destroyed by fire on March 8, 1993. But it was not until 2001 that a restoration of the nineteenth-century span was erected, much to the delight of the local townspeople.

The present bridge is a substantial, nearly 143-foot, Town lattice truss structure. It rests on cut stone abutments, capped with concrete, which are extended to road-level wingwalls. The deck consists of lengthwise planks; the roof is gray, seamed sheet metal; the sides are completely covered with natural, vertical board siding and the portals with barn-red, clapboard siding with white trim. The present structure is maintained by the New Hampshire Department of Transportation. The replicated bridge has been equipped with a fire alarm and sprinkler system as well as lighting.

Thompson/West Swanzey Bridge

Location: In the locality of West Swanzey, within the Swanzey town line.

Directions: In Winchester, at the junction of NH 119 East and NH 10 North, go north on NH 10 for 7.7 miles to California Street on the right (east), turn right onto California Street, and go 0.2 mile to the bridge.

GPS: 42° 52.320N 072°19.694W

Year: 1832   **Truss:** Town   **Waterway:** Ashuelot River   **In Use:** Yes
Number of Spans: 2   **Owner:** Town of Swanzey   **Builder:** Zadoc Taft
Length: 151 ft. 2 in.   **Width:** 16 ft.$\frac{1}{2}$ in.   **Condition:** Good
Number: NH-03-04   **Register:** Feb. 29, 1980

Data on this bridge presented on the "New England Bridges" internet site indicates that it was built by Zadoc Taft in 1832 at a cost of $523.27. In 1973, when the bridge had a posted limit of six tons, school buses were allowed to cross but only if the passengers unloaded first and the bus crossed empty. The students would walk across the bridge and board the bus on the other side. In 1976, a contemporary, steel and concrete bridge was built nearby to accommodate heavy vehicles. In the fall of 1990, a report by state inspectors indicated that the bridge was unsafe, and therefore it was closed. A highway committee was formed to develop proposals for the rehabiltation of the four covered bridges in the town of Swanzey. An engraved stone at the side of the bridge says: "THOMPSON COVERED BRIDGE   ORIGINALLY CONSTRUCTED IN 1832 BY ZADOC TAFT   RECONSTRUCTED IN 1993 AND DEDICATED ON AUGUST 14, 1993 WITH THE COOPERATION OF THE CITIZENS OF SWANZEY . . . WRIGHT CONSTRUCTION, MT. HOLLY, VT. DION ENGINEERING, MARLBOROUGH, N.H. DION AND STEVENS ENGINEERING, BRATTLEBORO, VT." The bridge has an interesting portal shape covered with barn-red vertical siding trimmed in white. It also has a pedestrian walkway on the north side of the bridge. Both this and the Slate Bridge are equipped with fire alarm and sprinkler systems.

Groveton Bridge

Location: In the locality of Groveton, within the Northumberland town line.

Directions: The bypassed bridge is just northeast of the junction of US 3 and NH 110 in Groveton.

GPS: 44° 35.720N 071° 30.585W

Year: 1852 **Truss:** Paddleford with arch
Waterway: Upper Ammonoosuc River **In Use:** Foot and snowmobile
Number of Spans: 1 **Owner:** Town of Northumberland
Builder: Capt. Charles Richardson and Son **Length:** 128 ft. 4 in.
Width: 18 ft. 1¾ in. **Condition:** Fairly good **Number:** NH-04-04
Register: Eligible but not listed

The Groveton Bridge, credited to Captain Charles Richardson and his son, while not quite as ornate as the Stark Bridge, a few miles to the east, is a lovely Paddleford truss span with gracefully arched portals. Unfortunately, because of the reconstruction of US Route 3 in 1939, the span has been bypassed. However, the Town of Northumberland is proud of its one remaining covered bridge and has made efforts to keep it in usable condition if only for pedestrian and snowmobile traffic. In 1964, noted covered bridge builder and author of *The Last of the Covered Bridge Builders* Milton Graton, while passing through Groveton on the way to a rigging job, stopped to sympathize with townspeople on the condition of their covered bridge. He observed that "it needed prayer as

well." The town selectmen, also aware of the deteriorating state of the span, sought Graton's assistance. In the spring of 1965, he, his son Arnold, and supporting crew set out to correct the weaknesses in the bridge. Milton records a lengthy, enlightening account of this restoration in his book. The Paddleford trusses, which Graton claims are "the most difficult of all trusses to frame" had started to fail, having acquired a negative camber through the years. These were completely rebuilt; new arches were installed with proper seats in the vertical portion of the abutments; a water pipe, which had carried part of the town's water supply through the bridge, was hidden beneath the deck; and, although his account does not indicate it, we are sure that attention was given to the siding, deck, and roof as well. When we visited the bridge in May 2003, we found it to be still in fairly good condition. It is one of the few New England bridges that are painted both inside and out. It is a brilliant white.

Happy Corner Bridge

Location: In the locality of Happy Corner, 5.7 miles east-northeast of the locality of Pittsburg, within the Pittsburg town line.

Directions: In Pittsburg, at the junction of US 3 and NH 145, go north on US 3 for 5.6 miles to Hill Road on the right (south), turn right onto Hill Road, and go 0.1 mile to the bridge.

GPS: 45° 05.062N 071° 18.797W

Year: 1869   **Truss:** Paddleford with arch   **Waterway:** Perry Stream
In Use: Yes   **Number of Spans:** 1+   **Owner:** Town of Pittsburg
Builder: Unknown   **Length:** 81 ft. 3 in.   **Width:** 17 ft. $1\frac{3}{4}$ in.
Condition: Fairly good   **Number:** NH-04-01
Register: Eligible but not listed

The little settlement in which this bridge is located was a bustling community in the mid-1800s. At Perry Stream, which the bridge spans, there was a sawmill, a starch mill, a store with a post office, a barbershop, the Temperance Hall, and, not too far away, the Danforth School. Stories are told about an elderly gentleman who lived at the house that still stands at the crossroads who liked to sing and dance. He also owned a Victrola, which he played frequently, encouraging the local folks to assemble at his home. Those were "happy" times. Consequently, the settlement became known as Happy Corner, and, of course, the covered bridge was known by the same name. There is no record of the exact date on which the bridge was built, although it is thought to be one of the oldest in the northern part of the state, but the design of the portal gable is identical to that of the River Road Bridge, suggesting that both bridges may have been built by the same builder. The major difference between the two

bridges is the truss system. Happy Corner Bridge, because of its greater length, required a truss that could carry a longer span than the queenpost used in the River Road Bridge; consequently, its builder used the Paddleford truss. Today the truss is reinforced with a six-ply laminated arch consisting of two-by-six-inch planks. The only record of restoration work having been done on the span is published in the state's book *New Hampshire Covered Bridges,* which indicates that it was repaired in the mid-1960s by the state at a cost of $12,000, shared by the state and the Town of Pittsburg. The pier, which lends support to the deck near the southern shore of Perry Stream, may have been added at the time of that restoration. We considered the condition of the bridge to be fairly good when we visited it in May 2003.

Mechanic Street/Israel River Bridge

Location: In the locality of Lancaster, within the Lancaster town line.

Directions: In Lancaster, just north of the junction of US 2 West and US 3 South, NH 135 goes south and Mechanic Street goes east. Go east on Mechanic Street for 0.2 mile to the bridge.

GPS: 44° 29.216N 071° 33.868W

Year: 1862   **Truss:** Paddleford   **Waterway:** Israel River   **In Use:** Yes
Number of Spans: 1   **Owner:** Town of Lancaster   **Builder:** Unknown
Length: 97 ft. 4 in.   **Width:** 20 ft. 2 in.   **Condition:** Good
Number: NH-04-06   **Register:** Eligible but not listed

This covered span is one of five Paddleford truss bridges built in Coos County. There is no record of either the builder or the original cost. It is an exceptionally wide bridge and could comfortably accommodate two-way traffic. There is no record of any work having been done on the bridge during its first one hundred years. However, in 1962, exactly one hundred years after it was erected, the Town of Lancaster requested that the state provide an estimate for rehabilitation of the structure. The estimate provided was $18,000, $10,800 was to be provided by the town, and the state would furnish the rest. At ensuing town meetings, no action was taken, but in 1967 the state did repair the abutments. On our visit to the bridge in May 2003, we found a well-maintained span resting on concrete abutments with no indication of steel substructure. The span supports a six-ton live load. It has a corrugated metal roof with a rather wide overhang that helps to protect the upper part of the truss structure, which is open for the upper half. The lower portions of the sides are covered with unpainted, well-weathered, vertical board siding, and the gracefully curved, portal gable ends, which extend several feet beyond the bridge deck, are covered with barn-red, clapboard siding trimmed with white. According to Richard Sanders Allen in *Covered Bridges of the Northeast,* published in 1985: "the portals . . . were the only places for the builder of a covered bridge to show his originality where it could be admired by all comers." The portal of this bridge is certainly one that gives the unknown builder a mark of distinction.

Pittsburg-Clarksville Bridge

Location: Just west-southwest of the locality of Pittsburg, between the town lines of Pittsburg and Clarksville.

Directions: In Pittsburg, at the junction of US 3 and NH 145, go south on US 3 for 0.8 mile to Fletcher Road on the left (south), turn left onto Fletcher Road, and go 0.1 mile to the closed bridge.

GPS: 45° 03.282N 071° 24.409W

Year: ca. 1876   **Truss:** Paddleford with arch   **Waterway:** Connecticut River
In Use: Foot only   **Number of Spans:** 1+
Owner: Towns of Pittsburg and Clarksville   **Builder:** Unknown
Length: 89 ft. 9 in.   **Width:** 17 ft. $\frac{1}{2}$ in.   **Condition:** Fair
Number: NH-04-03   **Register:** Eligible but not listed

There are several accounts of negotiations between Pittsburg and Clarksville that took place during the latter part of the 1870s. The town officials of Pittsburg had raised funds to "build a bridge at Fletcher's Mill." Ebeneezer Fletcher had owned a sawmill near the bridge site since 1825. The bridge built at this site, the northernmost location of a covered bridge crossing the Connecticut River between the villages of Pittsburg and Clarksville, consequently became known as the Pittsburg-Clarksville Bridge. After the bridge was built, around 1876, the town selectmen of Pittsburg asked their neighbors across the river if they would pay two-thirds of the cost of the bridge. The Clarksville officials voted "not to pay anything." Evidently, relations between the two towns improved, because in 1974, when there was a need to rehabilitate the bridge at a cost of $6,700, both towns and the state provided the required funds. In 1981,

the bridge was closed to vehicular traffic, possibly when a modern bridge was built to carry US Route 3 across the river. On our visit to the bridge in May of 2003 we found the bridge to be in fair condition and agree with Glenn Knobloch in his 2002 edition of *Images of America: New Hampshire Covered Bridges* where he says: "funds will be needed soon for further renovation if the bridge is to survive." We noticed that the bridge is leaning upstream.

River Road Bridge

Location: 7.6 miles east-northeast of the locality of Pittsburg, within the Pittsburg town line.

Directions: In Pittsburg, at the junction of US 3 and NH 145, go north on US 3 for 6.4 miles to River Road on the right (south), turn right onto River Road, and go 1.2 miles to the bridge.

GPS: 45° 04.349N 071° 18.346W

Year: 1858   **Truss:** Queenpost   **Waterway:** Perry Stream
In Use: Foot only   **Number of Spans:** 1   **Owner:** Town of Pittsburg
Builder: Unknown   **Length:** 52 ft. 9 in.   **Width:** 14 ft. 11½ in.
Condition: Fair   **Number:** NH-04-02   **Register:** Eligible but not listed

There are few accounts about this bridge. While it is in one of the most remote and seemingly less traveled parts of New Hampshire, one hesitates to say that it is a forgotten bridge. Glenn Knobloch in his book *Images of America: New Hampshire Covered Bridges* writes: "Now bypassed and in a state of slow de-

cay, this bridge is located in an out-of-the-way spot that is both peaceful and beautiful. . . . It has a simple barnlike facade that is found in the other remaining bridges in the area, suggesting a common builder." The state's publication *New Hampshire Covered Bridges* indicates that the bridge was built in 1858. There is no indication concerning the time it was bypassed by a simple, steel-supported span that carries the unpaved road past the original covered one. The original is a relatively short queenpost truss structure whose sides and portals are covered with unpainted, random-width, vertical boards; its roof is covered with seamed sheet metal that is beginning to show the signs of age, and its deck is covered with lengthwise planks. The deck has never been reinforced with steel but does have simple wooden gates on each end to prevent vehicular traffic. The portal gable ends extend several feet beyond the deck, and the eaves also extend beyond the sides, which are open to the elements on the upper half. These extensions may help to prolong the life of the bridge.

Stark Bridge

Location: In the locality of Stark, within the Stark town line.

Directions: In Groveton, at the junction of US 3 and NH 110, go east on NH 110 for 6.7 miles to Northside Road on the left (north); turn left onto Northside Road to cross the bridge.

GPS: 44° 36.051N 071° 24.478W

Year: 1862 **Truss:** Paddleford **Waterway:** Upper Ammonoosuc River
In Use: Yes **Number of Spans:** 1+ **Owner:** Town of Stark
Builder: Capt. Charles Richardson or son **Length:** 139 ft. 8 in.
Width: 17 ft. 5½ in. **Condition:** Good **Number:** NH-04-05
Register: Dec. 1, 1980

This covered bridge has a typical New England village setting. It is a white bridge next to a white church on one end and a cottage with a white picket fence on the other, with the wooded mountainside of Dickey Hill in the background. Documented sources differ on the date of Stark's origin: the *World Guide to Covered Bridges* places it at 1853, but two books on New Hampshire covered bridges, one written by Glenn A. Knoblock and the other published by the state, both place it at 1862. Only one of our sources lists a possible builder of this span. Knoblock says that it may have been Captain Charles Richardson or his son. He was responsible for the Groveton Bridge just a few miles to the west of Stark, and both bridges were built in the same decade. According to the state's account, the bridge was originally a single Paddleford truss structure with a central pier, but during the 1890s the pier and the bridge were washed away by floodwaters. With the assistance of a team of oxen, the bridge was brought back and set onto the original cut stone and mortar abutments along

with a new stone pier, and arches were added to strengthen the span. Once again, by the 1940s, the bridge needed repairs. In 1954 it was rehabilitated by removing the arch, adding steel to the substructure, and rebuilding the central pier. Later in the 1950s the residents of Stark voted to replace the bridge with a steel structure, but the outcry from artists and covered bridge enthusiasts was so great that the span was restored with the aid of financial support from the state. In 1982, the roof was replaced at a cost of $18,750, and in 1983 the state refurbished the substructure at an additional cost of $35,500. The walkways on either side of the bridge with overhanging eaves and the portal gable ends, which extend well beyond the bridge deck, should certainly help to preserve the truss structure of this bridge for quite some time into the future.

GRAFTON COUNTY

Allen Hollis Footbridge

Location: In Lost River Gorge, Kinsman Notch, 5.6 miles west of the locality of North Woodstock, within the Woodstock town line.

Directions: In North Woodstock, at the junction of US 3 and NH 112, go west on NH 112 for 5.6 miles to the entrance of Lost River Gorge. This attraction is closed from mid-October to early May. All gorge identification is removed for the off-season closure.

GPS: 44° 02.268N 071° 47.094W (coordinates recorded in parking lot of Lost River Gorge)

Year: 1981   **Truss:** Multiple kingpost   **Waterway:** Lost River
In Use: Foot only   **Number of Spans:** 1
Owner: Society for the Protection of N.H. Forests
Builder: Society for the Protection of N.H. Forests   **Length:** 30 ft. 10 in.
Width: 7 ft. 6¼ in.   **Condition:** Very good   **Number:** NH-05-113
Register: Does not qualify

This thirty-foot-long, multiple kingpost footbridge is located along the foot trail through Lost River Gorge. It was built there in 1981 in memory of Allen Hollis, who served as a ranger in the gorge for a number of years. It was built "in-house" by his coworkers, staff members of the Society for the Protection of New Hampshire Forests. It is accessible only by going into the gorge; however, if one is interested only in seeing the bridge, it is just a short walk down into the gorge from the exit. We approached it in this manner on our visit to the gorge in May 2003 with the assistance of the manager of the attraction, who was most accommodating. The gorge is a natural wonder that we want to visit someday, but the weather, on the day we were there, was a little too wet for a trip through the entire gorge. The structure is a true, authentic multiple kingpost truss, but built to accommodate only pedestrian traffic. It is covered with unpainted, random-width, vertical board siding on both the sides and the portal gable ends; the roof is covered with wooden shakes and the deck with crosswise planks, which are actually a continuation of the planks used throughout the gorge walkways. Keep in mind that if you want to see this span, you will have to visit the gorge during its open season from early May to mid-October.

Bath Bridge

Location: In the locality of Bath, within the Bath town line.

Directions: In Bath, where US 302/NH 10 makes a hard turn to the northeast, an unmarked street/road goes west over the bridge. (Some accounts identify this street/road as Pettyboro Road.)

GPS: 44° 10.017N 071° 57.988W

Year: 1832 **Truss:** Burr, mutiple kingpost, and supplementary arches
Waterway: Ammonoosuc River **In Use:** Yes **Number of Spans:** 4
Owner: Town of Bath **Builder:** Unknown **Length:** 375 ft. 3 in.
Width: 22 ft. 4¾ in. **Condition:** Good **Number:** NH-05-03
Register: Sept. 1, 1976

Other than the Cornish-Windsor Bridge, an interstate span, this is the longest covered bridge still standing within the borders of New Hampshire. It is a four-span combination of Burr trusses and multiple kingpost trusses with arches added in the early twentieth century. There has always been a need for a crossing at this location. The first bridge, an uncovered structure, was built here in 1794 at a cost of $366.66. It lasted only until 1806, when it was destroyed by floodwaters. The cost of the replacement bridge, also uncovered, was $1,000. It and the third bridge were also destroyed by floods and rebuilt in 1820 and 1824 respectively. The fourth bridge lasted only until 1830, when it too was lost, this time by fire. In 1831, efforts began to erect a new crossing, this time a covered bridge. $1,400 was allocated for the construction of two stone abutments, piers, and other materials. In March 1832, an additional $1,500 was provided to complete the spans. It appears that the original bridge consisted of a Burr

truss structure on each end with multiple kingspost trusses in the center spans. When the bridge was raised over the railroad in 1920, additional arches may have been added to the three eastern spans. According to *New Hampshire Covered Bridges*, the bridge is posted as a one-lane bridge with a load limit of six tons, for passenger cars only.

Blair Bridge

Location: In the locality of Blair, just east of US 3, within the Campton town line.

Directions: In Campton Hollow, at the junction of NH 175 and Perch Pond Road, go south on NH 175 for 1.3 miles to Blair Road on the right (west), turn right onto Blair Road, and go 0.6 mile to the bridge. Or, from I-93, exit 26, just north of Plymouth, go north on US 3 for approximately 3 miles to Blair; at the blinking light at the intersection with Blair Road on the right (east), turn right onto Blair Road and go 0.05 mile to the bridge.

GPS: 43° 48.615N 071° 39.986W

Year: 1869   **Truss:** Long with Burr-type arch   **Waterway:** Pemigewasset River
In Use: Yes   **Number of Spans:** 2   **Owner:** Town of Campton
Builder: Original unknown, 1977 restoration by Milton Graton and son, Arnold
Length: 295 ft. 5 in.   **Width:** 16 ft. 5$\frac{3}{4}$ in.   **Condition:** Very good
Number: NH-05-09   **Register:** Eligible but not listed

In his book *The Last of the Covered Bridge Builders*, Milton Graton indicates that prior to 1828 there had been a fording place in the Pemigewasset River

near the location of the present Blair Bridge. In 1828, during a storm, the local doctor who was trying to ford the river found the current too strong and lost his horse. The doctor survived, but this incident prompted the immediate building of a bridge. Records show that the bridge was completed in 1829 at a cost of $1,000. That bridge survived until 1868, when it was completely destroyed by an arsonist. In his trial, the arsonist, Lem Parker, confessed and claimed that "God told him to do it." Unfortunately, there were no witnesses, so he was found not guilty. A replacement, Long truss bridge, was completed by 1869.

In 1977 Milton Graton and his son, Arnold, were contracted to rebuild the 1869 two-span structure. In the restoration process Mr. Graton found only one timber that had survived from the original 1829 structure. The bridge, as it stands today, is a substantial, two-span, Long truss structure that has been reinforced with Burr-type arches consisting of nine layers of three-by-eight-inch planks. The random-width, vertical board siding has been left unpainted and has weathered naturally, and the gable ends of the portals are covered with white, horizontal clapboard siding. The entire bridge rests on cut stone abutments reinforced with concrete and a cut stone center pier.

Brundage Bridge

Location: 2.5 miles north of the locality of East Grafton, within the Grafton town line.

Directions: At the junction of US 4 and Turnpike Road, 3.1 miles east of Grafton Center Cemetery along US 4 in Grafton, go north on Turnpike Road for 1.4 miles to Mill Brook Road on the right (north), turn right onto Mill Brook Road, and go 1.8 miles to a hidden, overgrown lane on the left (west). Walk in the lane several hundred feet to the bridge. (Note: Mill Brook Road bears right after 1.4 miles.) Do not attempt to drive in the lane; motor vehicles are not permitted on the road to the bridge.

GPS: 43° 36.390N 071° 56.270W (coordinates recorded along Mill Brook Road at beginning of lane to the bridge)

Year: 1957   **Truss:** Town   **Waterway:** Mill Brook   **In Use:** Private
Number of Spans: 1   **Owner:** Brundage-Cater Family Trust
Builder: William Cady   **Length:** 30 ft. 10 in.   **Width:** 11 ft. $7\frac{3}{4}$ in.
Condition: Good   **Number:** NH-05-15   **Register:** Does not qualify

In 1946, Charles Brundage purchased a 130-acre tract of land, including a saltbox house and a barn, in the rural area north of East Grafton. Shortly thereafter, he acquired additional acreage that eventually totaled five hundred acres. Access to his property was along an unimproved road that crossed Mill Brook. Charles was planning on purchasing a Bailey bridge to span the brook, but William

Cady, who had assisted Brundage on other repairs on his recently acquired home, indicated that, "he could build a much better bridge." After looking at a number of covered bridges in the area, Bill Cady settled on the Town lattice truss structure as the one he would use to construct the span. In 1957, Bill erected a most substantial structure. The bridge is still standing today, well maintained by descendants of Charles Brundage who now manage the original acreage as the Brundage-Cater Family Trust. The bridge is a relatively short span, covered with barn-red, vertical board and batten siding on both the sides and the portals; the roof is covered with regular roofing shingles, and the deck with lengthwise planks. The entire structure rests on stone abutments. The road to the bridge, which had at one time been used as a shortcut by the Brundage neighbors between two of the unpaved roads in the area, is now obscure. The entrance to the bridge itself is closed with a locked cable to discourage vandalism. Mr. Brundage's daughter has indicated disappointment in the amount of thoughtless damage that has been done. She informed us that there was even a fire on the bridge at one time caused by persons trying to cook on it. It is really a lovely structure, which we are sure will be treated with great respect by fellow "bridgers" who happen to locate this lovely covered gem. Visitors are requested not to enter the access road with vehicles.

Bump/Webber Bridge

Location: 1.2 miles southeast of the locality of Campton Hollow, within the Campton town line.

Directions: In Campton Hollow, at the junction of NH 175 and Perch Pond Road, go east on Perch Pond Road for 0.4 mile to the intersection of Page Road on the left (north) and Eastern Corner on the right (south), turn right onto Eastern Corner Road, and go 0.9 mile (continue to bear left) to Bump's Intervale on the left; turn left to cross the bridge.

GPS: 43° 48.866N 071° 37.313W

Year: 1972   **Truss:** Queenpost   **Waterway:** Beebe River   **In Use:** Yes
Number of Spans: 1   **Owner:** Town of Campton   **Builder:** Arnold Graton
Length: 68 ft. 3 in.   **Width:** 14 ft. 9½ in.   **Condition:** Good
Number: NH-05-08 (2)   **Register:** Does not qualify

The first bridge built on the site of the Bump Bridge was also a queenpost truss span. In 1972, when Milton Graton was contracted to "keep it going for a few more years," he discovered that the main truss timbers were so badly decayed that nothing could be salvaged. Consequently, as a result of a "deal" that he reached with the town selectmen, he agreed to rebuild the Bump Bridge for $2,500 if he would be allowed to enter a competitive bid for restoration of the Blair Bridge, also located in Campton. The Blair Bridge was a much larger restoration and would make up for any loss Graton suffered on the rebuilding of the Bump Bridge. As a result, the Town of Campton had a new bridge built over the Beebe River at Campton Hollow in 1972 and an outstanding restoration of the Blair Bridge, just a few miles away over the Pemigewasset.

An interesting feature of the Bump Bridge is that it does not rest on abutments on either end of the bridge. Instead it rests on timber bents. There are two ramps that lead to the bridge on either end, one of which is eleven feet six inches and the other six feet four inches. The bridge is limited to passenger cars only, with a three-ton limit.

Clark's/Clark's Trading Post Railroad Bridge

Location: On the property of Clark's Trading Post, in the locality of North Woodstock, within the Lincoln town line.

Directions: In North Woodstock, at the junction of US 3 and NH 112, go north on US 3 for 1.4 miles to a gravel road on the right (east). This road provides access to the trading post grounds closest to the railroad covered bridge. Admission to the trading post is not required to visit and/or photograph the bridge.

GPS: 44° 03.061N 071° 41.309W (coordinates recorded in parking area close to the bridge)

Year: 1904   **Truss:** Howe   **Waterway:** Pemigewasset River
In Use: Concession operation only   **Number of Spans:** 1
Owner: Clark's Trading Post   **Builder:** Unknown   **Length:** 116 ft.
Width: 14 ft. 8 in.   **Condition:** Good   **Number:** NH-05-14
Register: Eligible but not listed

This railroad bridge was originally part of the railroad transportation system on a short stretch of track than ran between Montpelier and Barre, Vermont. The span was built in 1904 and provided passage across the Winooski River. In 1960 the railroad line ceased operations, and consequently the bridge was no longer needed. In the early 1960s, Ed Clark and his brother Murray became aware of the abandoned covered bridge and realized that it would be an excellent addition to their roadside attraction, Clark's Trading Post. The trading post, a roadside enterprise started by Edward and Florence Clark in 1928, had been operating under that name since 1949. Ed and Murray traveled to Vermont, disassembled the covered span, and hauled it back to New Hampshire. They also acquired granite blocks from an abandoned Maine Central Railroad bridge that crossed the Connecticut River in Coos County, New Hampshire. These they used to build the abutments on either bank of the Pemigewasset River, which flows through the trading post property. On those abutments, with the assistance of Ed's two sons and other workmen of the enterprise, they reconstructed the covered railroad bridge brought back from Vermont. The steam engines of the White Mt. Central Railroad have been traveling across that span ever since 1965, taking trading post visitors on a two-and-one-half-mile journey into the foothills of the White Mountains of New Hampshire. As mentioned in the directions above, a visit to the trading post is not required to visit and photograph the railroad bridge, but it might be an interesting diversion in a trip planned exclusively for "bridging." The bridge can be seen any time of the year; however, the trading post is open only during the usual tourist season, beginning Memorial Day weekend and continuing through mid-October. The schedule is subject to change. Check before visiting.

Edgell Bridge

Location: 2.5 miles south-southwest of the locality of Orford, within the Lyme town line.

Directions: Just southwest of Orford, at the junction of NH 10 and NH 25A East, go south on NH 10 for 1.6 miles to River Road on the right (west); go right onto River Road and continue for 0.9 mile to the bridge.

GPS: 43° 52.076N 072° 09.865W

Year: 1885   **Truss:** Town   **Waterway:** Clay Brook   **In Use:** Yes
Number of Spans: 1+   **Owner:** Town of Lyme   **Builder:** Walter Piper
Length: 149 ft. 7½ in.   **Width:** 15 ft. 10 in.   **Condition:** Good
Number: NH-05-11   **Register:** Eligible but not listed

When built in 1885, the total cost of this bridge was $1,825.27. It was built by Walter Piper when he was only eighteen years old. There are records of its having been rebuilt or restored three times during the twentieth century. The first

time, in 1936, it had to be returned to its abutments when floodwaters carried it off its northern abutment. This led to its being tied down with cables. Two of these guy wires are still in place where they are anchored to pillars in Clay Brook. The second time, in 1971, it was necessary to make repairs to the abutments, replace the floor, and realign the structure. The cost for this project was $23,829. The third time occurred in February 1982, when the roof collapsed under a heavy load of snow. In July of that year it was repaired at a cost of $30,000. It appears that the replaced roof is one of ribbed sheet metal. On our visit to the bridge in April 2003, the span appeared to be in good condition. It does, however, have one unusual feature. There is a concrete pier, shaped like an inverted U, that is placed several feet from each of the abutments, providing additional support to the total structure. The bridge sides are covered with vertical board, which appears to be relatively new and unpainted on the south side and painted gray, but well weathered, on the north side; the portals are covered with weathered, gray, clapboard siding. The deck consists of wide, lengthwise planks. There is a narrow, lengthwise opening under the eave on the south side; on the north side, in addition to the narrow eave opening, there are four window-like openings. This span should continue to serve the towns of Lyme and Orford well into the twenty-first century.

Flume Bridge

Location: In the Flume Gorge, Franconia Notch State Park, within the Lincoln town line.

Directions: In North Woodstock, at the junction of NH 112 and US 7, go north on US 7 for approximately 5 miles to the entrance to the Flume Gorge parking area on the right (east). Access to the bridge is only through admission to the Flume Gorge. A map to the gorge trail shows the location of the bridge. Admission is charged.

GPS: 44° 05.814N 071° 40.839W (coordinates recorded in parking lot of the Flume Gorge)

Year: 1871   **Truss:** Paddleford   **Waterway:** Pemigewasset River
In Use: Yes, park bus only   **Number of Spans:** 1   **Owner:** State
Builder: Unknown   **Length:** 51 ft. 6 in.   **Width:** 17 ft. 4¼ in.
Condition: Very good   **Number:** NH-05-05   **Register:** Eligible but not listed

This is one of our favorite covered bridges, possibly because it was the first one we photographed in the early years of our married life. It spans the Pemigewasset River in a quiet picturesque valley with the White Mountains in the distance. Our references provide us with two different years of origin. The date given in the *World Guide to Covered Bridges* is 1866, and the date given in *New Hampshire Covered Bridges* (*NHCB*) is 1871. There is also discussion among some covered bridge historians regarding the original location of this bridge. Some think it was built elsewhere and moved to the Flume; others believe it was built in its present location. According to *NHCB:* "many believe it was built for its present location in 1871 when the Lincoln Turnpike Company,

created by an act of the Legislature, obtained the right to build the road from the main highway, U.S. Route 3, to a point near the foot of the Flume." The Paddleford truss members of this bridge, unlike many, are covered both inside and outside for approximately one-half of their height with vertical tongue-and-groove boards. The inside portions are painted gray, the upstream side is painted brown, and the downstream side is unpainted and naturally weathered. The attractively shaped portal gable ends are covered with horizontal clapboard siding painted barn red with sparkling white trim. In 1951, the original, half-inch-thick, thirty-inch-long roof boards, applied like shingles, were replaced with twentieth-century, machine-split wooden shingles. Visitors to the Flume Gorge are required to pay an admission fee and should be aware that the gorge is open only from early May through late October, from 9:00 A.M. to 5:00 P.M., except for July and August, when closing time is extended to 5:30 P.M.

Haverhill-Bath/Bath-Haverhill Bridge

Location: In the locality of Woodsville, between the town lines of Bath and Haverhill.

Directions: In Woodsville, at the junction of US 302 and NH 135, go north on NH 135, turn right immediately onto Oak Hill, then left immediately onto North Court, and left again to the bridge.

GPS: 44˚ 09.263N 072˚ 02.169W

Year: 1829 **Truss:** Town with 2 arches **Waterway:** Ammonoosuc River
In Use: No, closed **Number of Spans:** 2 **Owner:** Towns of Bath and Haverhill
Builder: Unknown **Length:** 277 ft. 1 in. **Width:** 19 ft. $4\frac{1}{2}$ in.
Condition: Damaged, awaiting restoration **Number:** NH-05-04
Register: Apr. 18, 1977

A plaque posted near the portal of the bridge states: "This bridge was planned in 1827 and completed in 1829. It was built in accordance with Ithiel Town's lattice truss patent at a cost of approximately $2,400.00. It is the first and only bridge on this site and was in continuous use until 1999, when it was closed to vehicular traffic." The completion date of 1829 makes this the oldest remaining covered bridge in New Hampshire, and all of New England. It would be the oldest covered bridge in the United States except that the Hassenplug Bridge in Union County, Pennsylvania, holds that honor with the date of 1825.

The bridge has suffered severe damage from floodwaters, especially the flood of 1927, when a large tree floated down the river and pierced a portion of the lattice truss. After its closure in 1999, the Haverhill-Bath Covered Bridge Committee was formed. By the year 2000, the committee turned over $45,302.04 to the Town of Haverhill to create an expendable trust for restoration of the bridge. This money was privately raised and will be supplemented with a Fed-

eral Enhancement Grant of $200,000 and an additional $152,000 available from the state of New Hampshire. Thus approximately $400,000 is available to begin restoration.

On August 14, 2002, an attempted arson on the bridge did some minor damage, but the Protectowire fire detection system that was installed on the bridge notified the fire department, which responded quickly to extinguish the fire. Hoyle, Tanner & Associates, Inc., of Manchester, New Hampshire, have already completed the engineering phase of the project and are now in the design phase. It is possible that by the time this guide is in circulation, the restoration work on this exceptionally fine historic bridge will have begun or will even be completed.

Jack O' Lantern Bridge

Location: On the Jack O' Lantern Resort Golf Course, within the Woodstock town line.

Directions: In North Woodstock, at the junction of US 3 and NH 112, go south on US 3 for 6 miles to the Jack O' Lantern Resort and Golf Course on the left (east) side of the road. The covered bridge is visible from the parking area. It is located between the eighth green and the ninth tee box.

GPS: 43° 56.982N 071° 40.744W (coordinates recorded in parking lot of the golf course)

Year: 1986   **Truss:** Town   **Waterway:** Pond on the Jack O' Lantern Golf Course
In Use: Yes, foot and golf carts   **Number of Spans:** 1

Owner: Jack O' Lantern Resort (Keating Family)　**Builder:** Milton Graton
Length: 80 ft. 6 in.　**Width:** 6 ft. $7\frac{1}{2}$ in.　**Condition:** Excellent
Number: NH-05-18　**Register:** Does not qualify

This lovely golf course pathway bridge has a very interesting history. In 1878, a Town lattice truss covered bridge was built in the village of Woodstock spanning the Pemigewasset River. It connected East Side Road, which is now NH Route 175, with lower Woodstock Village. It was a single-span bridge built with local timbers planed at the John Emmons Lumber Co. located at nearby Mirror Lake. That Woodstock Bridge, the last of four built in the town, was destroyed by fire in 1971. Rebuilding the bridge proved to be too difficult, so the Keating family, owners of the Jack O' Lantern Resort, decided to build a replica on the resort's golf course. In 1986, the family contracted Milton Graton, known among covered bridge enthusiasts as the "Last of the Covered Bridge Builders," to replicate the Woodstock Bridge for use over a pond between the number eight green and the number nine tee box on the golf course. Graton built the bridge at a railhead near his home, and in October 1986 it was brought north by special train and put in place on the golf course. It is a truly authentic covered bridge in every respect, except that it cannot accommodate regular automobile traffic. It is also a perfect reproduction of the original Woodstock Bridge except for size: its dimensions are reduced by approximately 50 percent. When you're in the Woodstock area, be sure to look for this reproduction. It is easily seen from US Route 3 in any season of the year.

Packard Hill Bridge

Location: Approximately 2 miles east-southeast of the locality of Lebanon, within the Lebanon city limits.

Directions: East of Lebanon, at the junction of I-89 South exit 17 ramp and US 4, go east (right) on US 4 for 0.2 mile to Riverside Road on the north (left), turn left onto Riverside Road, and go 0.8 mile to the bridge. Or from the junction of I-89 North exit 17 ramp and US 4, go east (right) on US 4 for 0.35 mile to Riverside Road on the north (left), turn left onto Riverside Road, and go 0.8 mile to the bridge.

GPS: 43° 38.313N 072° 13.334W

Year: 1991   **Truss:** Howe   **Waterway:** Mascoma River   **In Use:** Yes
Number of Spans: 1   **Owner:** City of Lebanon
Builder: Milton Graton and Associates   **Length:** 76 ft. 3¾ in.
Width: 15 ft. 6 in.   **Condition:** Very good   **Number:** NH-05-50 (2)
Register: Does not qualify

Sometime between 1780 and 1790 an open wooden bridge spanned the Mascoma River to reach the home of Ichabod Packard on the north side of the river. Packard also had a combination sawmill and gristmill on the south side of the river. According to town records, that bridge was either repaired or replaced in the early 1800s with an open queenpost truss bridge. That span was replaced in 1878 with a Howe truss covered bridge. Records show that the 1878 bridge cost $456.02. It served the area until 1952, when it was removed and re-

placed with a Bailey bridge. That bridge was removed, in turn, in 1991, when the Milton Graton Associates firm was hired to build a new covered span. The bridge that Graton erected was a replica of the nineteenth-century Howe truss structure. It was built in the usual Graton fashion with all materials and joinery typical of his covered bridge builder forerunners. The dedication ceremonies for that new structure were held on September 4, 1991. The present structure is covered with unpainted, vertical boards on both the sides and the portals; the deck is covered with lengthwise planks; and the roof is covered with wooden shakes. It rests on a combination of stone and mortar abutments on the north end and large granite slabs on the south end. Both abutments extend to moderate-length, road-level wingwalls. There is a pedestrian walkway on the upstream side of the span. It is a heavily traveled span serving quite a busy residential section of suburban Lebanon. The Howe truss can be seen easily in the photo.

Sentinel Pine Bridge

Location: In the Flume Gorge, Franconia Notch State Park, within the Lincoln town line.

Directions: In North Woodstock, at the junction of NH 112 and US 7, go north on US 7 for approximately 5 miles to the entrance to the Flume Gorge parking area on the right (east). Access to the bridge is only through admission to the Flume Gorge. A map to the gorge trail shows the location of the bridge. Admission is charged.

GPS: 44° 05.814N 071° 40.839W (coordinates recorded in parking lot of the Flume Gorge)

Year: 1939   **Truss:** Stringer with multiple kingpost
Waterway: Pool in Flume Gorge   **In Use:** Foot traffic only
Number of Spans: 1   **Owner:** State
Builder: Society for the Protection of N.H. Forests   **Length:** 61 ft. 2 in.
Width: 5 ft. 1 in.   **Condition:** Very good
Number: NH-05-d   **Register:** Eligible but not listed

This is one of the bridges mentioned in the beginning of this section on New Hampshire covered bridges that cannot be considered an authentic, historic bridge. It is classified as a "stringer" bridge. However, because of its popularity in the Flume Gorge, it certainly should be included in this guide.

For more than a century before September 21, 1938, a white pine, 175 feet tall, measuring sixteen feet in circumference, stood overlooking the pool in the upper part of the Pemigewasset River Gorge. It was known as the Sentinel Pine because it seemed to stand watch over the pool and the surrounding terrain. It

is estimated that if it were still standing today, it would be over 265 years old. On that September day in 1938, the Great Hurricane struck this part of the White Mountains and uprooted many of its trees. Unfortunately, the Sentinel Pine was one of them. The following year, the Society for the Protection of New Hampshire Forests used approximately ninety feet of that massive tree to span the river gorge above the pool, which the tree had guarded for many years. With it as the "stringer" base and using lumber from some of the other trees that were blown down, workmen constructed a multiple kingpost covered footbridge across the gorge. The truss timbers of the bridge were held together in nineteenth-century fashion with wooden pegs. The roof was covered with handmade shingles by John G. Welch and Old Joe Poloquin, an American Indian, affectionately known by the locals as Indian Joe. With the exception of improved steps and walkways approaching the bridge, the span remains nearly the same as it was constructed in 1939.

Smith Millennium/Smith Bridge

Location: West-northwest of the locality of Plymouth and east-northeast of the locality of West Plymouth, within the Plymouth town line.

Directions: In West Plymouth, at the junction of NH 3A South and NH 25 West, go east on NH 3A/NH 25 for 1.5 miles to Smith Bridge Road on the left (north), turn left onto Smith Bridge Road, and go 0.5 mile to the bridge. Or, just northwest of Plymouth, at the junction of NH 3A/NH 25 and

Highland St., go west on NH 3A/NH 25 for 0.4 mile to Smith Bridge Road on the right (north), turn right onto Smith Bridge Road, and go 0.5 mile to the bridge.

GPS: 43° 46.527N 071° 44.356W

Year: 2001   **Truss:** Long with arch   **Waterway:** Baker River   **In Use:** Yes
Number of Spans: 1   **Owner:** Town of Plymouth
Builder: Stan Graton (bridge) and Hayden Hillsgrove (stone masonry)
Length: 167 ft. 4 in.   **Width:** 25 ft. $\frac{1}{2}$ in.   **Condition:** Excellent
Number: NH-05-10 (2)   **Register:** Does not qualify

The bridge that preceded the present bridge on this site dated back to 1850, when Herman Marcy of Littleton, New Hampshire, was hired "to frame, raise, and finish a covered bridge across the Baker River for the Town of Plymouth." He was to build a bridge on the same plan and style as the one located on Pont Fayette, which crossed the Pemigewasset River between Plymouth and Holderness. The truss design used by Marcy was one created and patented by Colonel Stephen H. Long of Hopkinton, New Hampshire. A state historic marker located near the bridge site indicates that the 1850 bridge cost approximately $2,700. According to *New Hampshire Covered Bridges,* Marcy's 1850 bridge was a replacement for one built in the early 1800s by a Captain Charles Richardson.

The 1850 span was used continuously, with repairs being made in 1940, 1949, and 1958. In 1971 it was completely rehabilitated at a cost of $7,876. After its restoration, signs posted on the bridge included: "One Lane Bridge," "One Car at a Time on Bridge," and "Speed Limit 15 MPH." It remained in use until April 16, 1993, when it was destroyed by fire. The state rebuilt the span between 2000

The extremely substantial Long truss with arch of the Smith Millennium Bridge.

and 2001, when it was renamed the Smith Millennium Bridge. The new structure is a two-lane bridge using the same Long truss design reinforced with substantial twenty-two ply laminated arches—all of which are constructed using contemporary glue-laminated timbers. The interior photo clearly shows the details of the truss structure. This new span is designed to carry loads equivalent to those of interstate highway bridges. It was built at a cost of $3.3 million and dedicated in 2001.

Squam River Bridge

Location: Between the localities of Holderness and Ashland, within the Ashland town line.

Directions: In Holderness, at the junction of NH 113 and US 3/NH 25, go southeast on US 3/NH 25 for 1.8 miles to River Road on the left (south), turn left, and go 0.1 mile to the bridge. Or, from I-93 North, exit 24, follow US 3/NH 25 through Ashland for 2.6 miles to River Road on the right (south), turn right, and go 0.1 mile to the bridge.

GPS: 43° 43.125N 071° 37.123W

Year: 1990   **Truss:** Town   **Waterway:** Squam River   **In Use:** Yes
Number of Spans: 1   **Owner:** Town of Ashland
Builder: Milton Graton and Sons   **Length:** 63 ft. 10 in.   **Width:** 14 ft.
Condition: Excellent   **Number:** NH-05-112   **Register:** Does not qualify

When a steel and concrete bridge over Squam River was condemned by the state in the 1980s, the state proposed a new, two-lane, steel bridge for this site. However, the citizens of the Town of Ashland preferred a one-lane covered bridge. Consequently, at a 1988 town meeting they voted to place $35,000 in a fund specifically for the building of a new covered bridge. Since additional funds would be required, the Squam River Covered Bridge Society of the Ashland Historical Society organized special events such as dinners and bake sales, but the majority of the contributions came from over five hundred donors. According to a bronze plaque mounted on the bridge, Milton Graton and Sons were contracted to erect the new structure, which was dedicated on July 1, 1990, to its builder, Milton Graton.

The single-span is a lovely, Town lattice truss structure, built by the Gratons in the traditional nineteenth-century fashion. The entire structure is covered with unpainted, random-width vertical board siding—the sides are covered only on the lower portion, exposing the intricate lattice truss work, and the portal entrances are covered both inside and outside. A pedestrian walkway provided on one side of the bridge was being used as part of a snowmobile trail on our visit to the bridge in January 2003. The entire structure rests on cut stone abutments that are extended to long, road-level wingwalls. It has been finished with a wooden shake roof. The residents of Ashland can be very proud of their covered bridge, for which they worked so hard and contributed so much.

Swiftwater Bridge

Location: In the locality of Swiftwater, within the Bath town line.

Directions: Southeast of Swiftwater, at the junction of NH 116 South and NH 112 West, go west on NH 112 for 6.5 miles to Porter Road on the right (north); turn right onto Porter Road to the bridge. Or, approximately 1 mile south of Bath, at the junction of US 302/NH 10 and NH 112, go east on NH 112 for 2.1 miles to Porter Road on the left (north), turn left onto Porter Road, and go 0.1 mile to the bridge.

GPS: 44° 08.022N 071° 57.058W

Year: 1849   **Truss:** Paddleford   **Waterway:** Wild Ammonoosuc River
In Use: Yes   **Number of Spans:** 2   **Owner:** Town of Bath
Builder: Unknown   **Length:** 162 ft. 10 in.   **Width:** 18 ft. 8½ in.
Condition: Excellent   **Number:** NH-05-02   **Register:** Nov. 21, 1976

This is the fourth bridge to span the Wild Ammonoosuc River in this location. Three earlier structures were destroyed by floods. The first bridge, built in 1810, was destroyed in 1818 and replaced the same year; the second was destroyed in 1828 and replaced in 1829; that bridge remained until it was replaced by the present span. The present bridge, a covered span built in 1849, was rebuilt by the state in 1947 with the costs being shared by the state and the Town of Bath. A bronze plaque mounted at the bridge site indicates that the bridge was rehabilitated once again in 1998–99 by the Town of Bath with major funding provided by the New Hampshire Department of Transportation. The engineer for this project was Hoyle, Tanner & Associates, Manchester, New Hampshire, and the contractor was Wright Construction Co., Inc., Mt. Holly, Vermont. The re-

The Paddleford truss system of the Swiftwater Bridge.

habilitation project consisted of major structural renovations to the existing Paddleford truss system, improvements to the floor and deck system, erosion control, new siding, new roofing, fireproofing, and a fire alarm system. The interior photo is a good view of the Paddleford truss.

Turkey Jim Bridge

Location: On the property of Branch Brook Campground, within the Campton town line.

Directions: In West Campton, at the junction of US 3 and NH 49, go east on NH 49 for 0.1 mile to Branch Brook Road on the left (north), turn left onto Branch Brook Road to the gated campground entrance. The owners of the campground are preparing a parking area next to the entrance where visitors to the bridge can park. We have been told that directions to locate the bridge will be posted at the campground entrance.

GPS: 43° 50.998N 071° 39.667W (coordinates recorded at entrance gate to the campground)

Year: 1958   **Truss:** Queenpost   **Waterway:** West Branch Brook
In Use: Foot and snowmobile   **Number of Spans:** 1
Owner: Branch Brook Campground   **Builder:** Milton Graton
Length: 60 ft. 6$\frac{3}{4}$ in.   **Width:** 13 ft. 3 in.   **Condition:** Fair
Number: NH-05-07 (2)   **Register:** Does not qualify

The first covered bridge built in this location dates back to 1874. At that time it provided access across West Branch Brook to the property of Jim Cummings, a farmer who raised turkeys. In the local area he was popularly known as Turkey Jim. Consequently, the bridge, providing passage to his property, became known by the same name. Through the years the bridge deteriorated quite extensively, and when Milton Graton was asked to repair the bridge in the 1950s, he discovered that it was beyond repair. As a result, the bridge was rebuilt in 1958 in the typical Graton fashion with a total replication of the origi-

The unusual queenpost truss system of the Turkey Jim Bridge.

nal. Even the name was retained. Unfortunately, floodwaters carried the bridge downstream in 1964, but it was retrieved and placed back on its abutments. Today, the bridge is surrounded by the Branch Brook Campground, whose owners have been maintaining the bridge in recent years. It is presently closed to all vehicular traffic but is still used for pedestrian traffic during the camping season and snowmobile traffic during the winter. There are two rather different features of this bridge that should be highlighted. The exterior photo shows that there are two buttress timbers placed at equal thirds along the side of the bridge; very few New England bridges have this feature. And, in the interior photo, the truss consists of a primary queenpost truss with another, smaller queenpost truss inside, unusual in any queenpost truss.

HILLSBOROUGH COUNTY

County/County Farm Bridge

Location: 2.6 miles east-southeast of the locality of Hancock, on the town lines of Greenfield and Hancock.

Directions: In Hancock, where NH 137 goes north and NH 123 goes south, a road goes east-southeast (at the next intersection it is identified as Duncan Road); go east-southeast on Duncan Road for 1 mile until it meets an improved road. Continue straight on the improved road for 0.4 mile to the junction with US 202. Cross over US 202 (Duncan Road becomes Forest Road); continue on Forest Road for 1.2 miles to the bridge.

GPS: 42° 57.414N 071° 56.104W

Year: 1937 **Truss:** Pratt modified **Waterway:** Contoocook River
In Use: Yes **Number of Spans:** 1 **Owner:** State **Builder:** Henry Pratt
Length: 86 ft. 8 in. **Width:** 21 ft. $\frac{1}{2}$ in. **Condition:** Good
Number: NH-06-02 **Register:** May 21, 1975

The first bridge built on this site was a Long truss bridge erected by Charles Gray of Hancock in 1852. However, in 1936 that structure was damaged beyond repair by floodwaters. The present structure, which has a modified Pratt truss, was designed by Henry Pratt of Antrim and built in 1937 as a Federal Emergency Relief Administration project. The company in charge of the construction was Hagan-Thibodeau Construction Company of Wolfeboro, New Hampshire. The new structure was placed on stone and mortar abutments reinforced with concrete, which extend to wingwalls a little below road level. It is covered with tongue-and-groove vertical siding on both the sides and the portals, all of which are left unpainted. It has a paved macadam deck and a shingled roof. The bridge is wide enough to accommodate two lanes of traffic. The center post of the truss is clearly identified with the names of the two towns that the bridge connects—Greenfield and Hancock. The interior photo displays the modified Pratt truss of this span.

In 2001, the County Bridge was the beneficiary of a $36,000 grant made available through the National Historic Covered Bridge Preservation Program. These funds were used for the installation of a Protectowire fire detection system and a dry sprinkler system.

The modified Pratt truss system of the County Bridge.

Stowell Road/Baboosic Brook Bridge

Location: Approximately 5.8 miles northeast of the locality of Amherst, within the Merrimack town line.

Directions: Along the NH 101 bypass of Milford, at the junction of the ramp to Amherst, NH 122, go east on NH 101 for 4.8 miles to Stowell Road on the right (south), turn right onto Stowell Road, and go 1.0 mile to the bridge.

GPS: 42° 53.767N 071° 33.801W

Year: 1990   **Truss:** Nontraditional   **Waterway:** Baboosic Brook
In Use: Yes   **Number of Spans:** 1   **Owner:** Town of Merrimack
Builder: Merrimack Highway Dept.   **Length:** 32 ft. $4\frac{1}{4}$ in.   **Width:** 17 ft. $9\frac{1}{2}$ in.
Condition: Good   **Number:** NH-06-S   **Register:** Does not qualify

In 1990, the Town of Merrimack erected a wooden covered bridge to replace a town bridge that had existed on Stowell Road over the Baboosic Brook. Estimates for a modern concrete bridge replacement ranged around about $100,000. The current structure is a pre-engineered bridge system manufactured by Wheeler Consolidated, Inc., St. Louis Park, Minnesota, which was provided in kit form by the Krenn Bridge Company of Flint City, Michigan, through its New England distributor, Construction Dynamics Company of New Boston, New Hampshire. The bridge deck was supplied in three panelized sections consisting of dowel-laminated solid Douglas fir lumber. The deck panels were spliced together by means of shiplap joints. The bridge kit also included an interior guardrail, wall framing, and a roof. The fir deck timbers

were creosote treated prior to lamination to seal the wood and prevent decay, and the entire deck area was surfaced with asphalt. The framing materials for the walls and roof were coated with a fire-retardant paint. The entire bridge kit cost the Town of Merrimack $33,000, with most of the labor and equipment being provided by the Merrimack Highway Department. The bridge does not have a conventional truss design; consequently it has not been given a standard covered bridge number but a number that is part of the "modern shelter" numbering system. It does, however, give the appearance of a covered bridge in a very lovely, suburban setting.

MERRIMACK COUNTY

Bement Bridge

Location: On the south edge of the locality of Bradford, within the Bradford town line.

Directions: Southeast of Bradford, at the junction of NH 114 and NH 103, go east on NH 103 for 0.2 mile to Center Street on the left (south); turn left onto Center Street to the bridge.

GPS: 43° 15.850N 071° 57.185W

Year: 1854 **Truss:** Long **Waterway:** West Branch of Warren River
In Use: Yes **Number of Spans:** 1 **Owner:** Town of Bradford
Builder: Stephen H. Long **Length:** 65 ft. **Width:** 17 ft. $\frac{1}{2}$ in.
Condition: Good **Number:** NH-07-03 **Register:** Nov. 21, 1976

Although other bridge structures were erected on this site as early as 1799–1800, the first covered bridge was built here by the engineer and designer of the bridge's truss, Stephen H. Long of Hopkinton, New Hampshire. Mr. Long was formerly an engineer with the U.S. Army and designed his bridge truss while working with the Baltimore and Ohio Railroad. Long originally patented his truss design in 1830 with further patent improvements in 1835 and 1837. It was unusual for a bridge to actually be built by its truss designer. Usually the designer was paid a royalty for the use of his patent by a bridge builder hired for the project. Reports regarding the original covered bridge construction indicate that Long made the unusual choice of using only hemlock to build the bridge. It was named for Samual Bement, whose property was near the site.

Since the bridge was built on a slight elevation above the floodplain, there is little report of its having been damaged by floodwaters. However, it was repaired by the Town of Bradford in 1947 and closed in March 1968 awaiting

repairs, which were done by the state in 1969 at a cost of $24,478.14. One-third of that cost was paid by the town. Additional repairs were necessitated in 1987, when it was damaged by a vehicle, and once again during the winter of 1989–90, when a cracked floor beam was repaired by the town. On our visit to the bridge in October 2002 we found it in fine condition.

Cilleyville/Bog Bridge

Location: On the north edge of the locality of Cilleyville, within the Andover town line.

Directions: In Cilleyville, where NH 4A goes north off NH 11, the bridge is located just southeast of the junction.

GPS: 43° 25.825N 071° 52.146W

Year: 1887   **Truss:** Town   **Waterway:** Pleasant Brook   **In Use:** Being restored
Number of Spans: 1   **Owner:** Town of Andover
Builder: Print Atwood, Al Emerson, and Charles Wilson
Length: 54 ft. 2½ in.   **Width:** 11 ft. 4¼ in.
Condition: Being restored as footbridge   **Number:** NH-07-01   **Register:** 1989

According to *New Hampshire Covered Bridges,* published by the New Hampshire Department of Transportation, this was the last covered bridge to be built in the Town of Andover. It was built by Print Atwood, who was assisted by Al Emerson and Charles Wilson, at a cost of $522.63. The Department of Trans-

portation account tells the local tale that "during construction, Emerson and Wilson became upset and cut some of the timbers short, causing the bridge to tilt. On the other hand, engineers might suggest that the tilt is caused by the very nature of the Town lattice design." However, we have not found that to be the case in other Town truss structures, and if there ever was a tilt in the Cilleyville Bridge, there was none when we visited it in April 2003. At that time the bridge was in the process of being completely restored by Barnes and Bridges of New England, a bridge restoration company of Gilford, New Hampshire. The abutments had been repaired with the original blocks of granite, some of which had fallen into the brook; defective timbers of the lattice truss had been replaced; the siding and portals had been replaced with new, unpainted, random-width, vertical board siding; and the wooden shakes on the roof had been replaced. A craftsman of the restoration company informed us that when their work is completed, the bridge will be reopened as a pedestrian footbridge. The total cost of this project is reported to be $156,000. A grant of $72,000 was awarded to the Town of Andover through the Land and Community Heritage Investment Program made possible by Citizens for New Hampshire Land and Community Heritage. The balance of the funds were raised through local efforts—largely contributions of $5 to $50. This is another example of citizens working together to preserve an important part of our historical heritage.

When the bridge was first built here, there was another covered bridge in Cilleyville spanning the Blackwood River called the Cilleyville Bridge, and the bridge at the present site was called the Bog Bridge. However, in 1908, after the original Cilleyville Bridge was torn down, the bridge at this site assumed its name. Another interesting bit of information about this span is that it was the model for the Shattuck murals of typical New Hampshire scenes that were on the walls of the State House in Concord.

Dalton/Joppa Road Bridge

Location: Just southeast of the locality of Warner, within the Warner town line.

Directions: Southeast of Warner, at the junction of I-89, exit 8, and NH 103, go west on NH 103 for 0.9 mile to Joppa West Road on the left (south) side of the highway, turn left onto Joppa West Road, and go 0.15 mile to the bridge.

GPS: 43° 16.617N 071° 48.677W

Year: 1853 **Truss:** Long modified with queenpost **Waterway:** Warner River
In Use: Yes **Number of Spans:** 1 **Owner:** Town of Warner
Builder: Joshua Sanborn with abutments by George Sawyer and Walter Davis
Length: 78 ft. 9 in. **Width:** 14 ft. 3 in. **Condition:** Good
Number: NH-07-05 **Register:** Nov. 21, 1976

The recorded date of construction of the Dalton, sometimes called Joppa Road, Bridge is 1853. Joshua Sanborn is listed as the builder, with George Sawyer and Walter Davis laying the abutments. There is some discrepancy as to the actual classification of the truss system. The *World Guide to Covered Bridges* lists it as a kingpost and queenpost, the Warner Historical Society in its 1974 publication *Warner, N.H., 1880–1974* classifies it as a Haupt-type truss, the nomination form for the National Register of Historic Places calls it a Long truss with an auxiliary queenpost, and the New Hampshire Department of Transportation classifies it as a "Long truss with an auxiliary queenpost system." Our visit to the bridge led us to the conclusion that the truss structure is a modified Long truss sandwiched between two queenpost trusses. Look carefully at the interior photo to see if you agree. In any event, it is definitely quite a substantial structure, which is being well maintained in a lovely setting.

Modified Long truss sandwiched between two queenpost trusses of the Dalton Bridge.

Keniston Bridge

Location: Just west-southwest of the locality of Andover, within the Andover town line.

Directions: Just east of Andover, where US 4 from the southeast joins NH 11, go west on US 4/NH 11 for 1.5 miles to Bridge Road on the south (left); go south on Bridge Road for 0.1 mile to the bridge.

GPS: 43° 26.105N 071° 50.162W

Year: 1882 **Truss:** Town **Waterway:** Blackwater River **In Use:** Yes
Number of Spans: 1 **Owner:** Town of Andover **Builder:** Albert R. Hamilton
Length: 64 ft. 10 in. **Width:** 16 ft. 6 in. **Condition:** Fairly good
Number: NH-07-02 **Register:** 1989

This bridge is one of two covered bridges proudly owned by the Town of Andover. However, it is the only one that still carries vehicular traffic. The Keniston span was built in 1882 by Albert R. Hamilton, the same craftsman who built the Andover Town Hall in 1879. The cost of the entire bridge was $745.56. In its just over 121-year history it has been refurbished several times, always by the town. According to information on an Andover website, "Andover Master Plan . . . VI. Conservation and Preservation . . . A. Historic Preservation": "In 1949 the bridge was jacked up, the roof was reshingled and defective lattice work was spliced or replaced. In 1981 major repairs included the reconstruction of the upper abutments, the addition of steel girders under the floorboards, and

the renewal of the floor. The granite abutments were also partially replaced with concrete at some point. Most of the repairs to the Keniston Bridge are not noticeable, so it retains most of its original appearance and charm." Other than these repairs, the bridge has been damaged only once by a natural disaster when, in 1972, ice tore off several planks. These, too, were repaired by the town. On our visit to the bridge in April 2003, we found that reroofing of the wooden shakes was in progress on the east side of the bridge. Two guy rods, which appear to be a permanent arrangement, run from each end of the eaves on the west side of the bridge to anchors along the banks of the Blackwater River. We assumed that these were installed to provide additional support to the bridge against the prevailing winds, which sweep through the river valley. Otherwise, the town has this relatively short Town lattice structure in fairly good condition.

New England College/Henniker Bridge

Location: On the campus of New England College in the locality of Henniker, within the Henniker town line.

Directions: Just north of Henniker, at the junction of the US 202/NH 9 exit ramp and NH 114, go south on NH 114 for 0.5 mile to an intersection, turn right, and go 0.2 mile to a dirt driveway on the left leading to the college athletic fields. Turn left, pass the soccer field on the right, bear left at the gated road, and continue to the bridge. Do not drive on the bridge. It is barricaded on the east end.

GPS: 43° 10.665N 071° 49.476W

Year: 1972   **Truss:** Town   **Waterway:** Contoocook River
In Use: Foot traffic only   **Number of Spans:** 1   **Owner:** New England College
Builder: Milton and Arnold Graton   **Length:** 140 ft. 1 in.   **Width:** 14 ft. 4 in.
Condition: Good   **Number:** NH-07-12   **Register:** Does not qualify

The New England College Bridge is a relatively recent covered bridge built by an exacting twentieth-century bridge builder, Milton Graton, and his son Arnold. It was erected in 1972 using the same techniques as its Town lattice truss counterparts of the nineteenth century. The truss members are all held together with the time-tested trunnel fasteners and after assembly were drawn across the Contoocook River in nineteenth-century fashion with a team of oxen. The bridge was erected in a most picturesque setting where it joins the main campus of New England College to the quaint village of Henniker. Although built of sufficient width to accommodate vehicular traffic, it serves only as a footbridge. It provides a very convenient shortcut to many of the college athletic fields, which are located across the river from the main college campus. The bridge was built at a cost of $80,000.

Railroad/Contoocook/Old Contoocook Railroad/Hopkinton Railroad Bridge

Location: In the locality of Contoocook, within the Hopkinton town line.

Directions: In the village of Contoocook, at the junction of NH 127 North and NH 103 West (at the circle, center of the community), go north-northwest on NH 127/NH 103. The bridge is just to the right (east).

GPS: 43° 13.389N 071° 42.843W

Year: 1889   **Truss:** Town (double)   **Waterway:** Contoocook River
In Use: Foot traffic only   **Number of Spans:** 2
Owner: N.H. Division of Historic Resources
Builder: Joseph Barnard or Dutton Woods   **Length:** 157 ft. $5\frac{1}{2}$ in.
Width: 15 ft.   **Condition:** Fair, starting to lean   **Number:** NH-07-07
Register: Jan. 11, 1980

According to information submitted on the nomination form to the National Register of Historic Places, this bridge is the oldest covered railroad bridge still standing in the United States. There is some uncertainty concerning the original builder, but it is believed to have been built betwen 1849 and 1850 by either Joseph Barnard of Contoocook or Dutton Woods of Henniker. It was originally built to serve the Concord and Claremont Railroad but had major reconstruction in 1889 when it was part of the Claremont Branch of the Boston and Maine Concord Division. In 1936 and again in 1938 the bridge was washed from its abutments by floodwater, but each time it was brought back and restored. In 1952 new owners of the railroad line curtailed some of their services, and by 1962 the line was completely abandoned and the tracks were removed. From 1962 to 1990 the bridge was used as a warehouse by a local merchant. In 1990 the bridge was turned over to the New Hampshire Division of Historic Resources. The stone highway bridge that crosses the Contoocook River right next to the Railroad Bridge was also a covered bridge at one time. At that time the highway and railroad bridge openings were only twenty feet apart without any crossing gates to warn road users of oncoming train traffic, but there was apparently never a problem. Take the time to walk through the bridge, and you will soon be transported to the days of long ago when the big locomotives with their huge smokestacks hurtled through this dark passageway.

Rowell's/Rowell Bridge

Location: On the western edge of the locality of West Hopkinton, within the Hopkinton town line.

Directions: Approximately 4 miles east of Henniker, at the junction of US 202/NH9 and NH 127, go north on NH 127 for 1.0 mile. The bridge is straight ahead where NH 127 bears right.

GPS: 43° 11.545N 071° 44.908W

Year: 1853   **Truss:** Long with Burr-type arch   **Waterway:** Contoocook River
In Use: Yes   **Number of Spans:** 1   **Owner:** Town of Hopkinton
Builder: Horace Childs with brothers Enoch and Warren   **Length:** 167 ft. 7 in.
Width: 15 ft. 2 in.   **Condition:** Very good   **Number:** NH-07-08
Register: Nov. 21, 1976

This bridge was named for the Rowell family, who owned the adjacent property. It was built at a cost of $300.25 by Horace Childs of Henniker with the help of his brothers, Enoch and Warren. That cost included a fee of $2.00 paid to Isaac Rowell for two days' labor and $2.50 for the use of his oxen and plow. The truss used by the Childs brothers was designed by Stephen H. Long of Hopkinton, uncle of the brothers. Look carefully at the interior photo of the truss structure. The typical Burr-type arch sandwiched between members of the Long truss was made of solid timbers rather than planks laminated together.

Shortly after it was built, the bridge was vibrated off its abutments by a herd of cattle being driven through it too fast. It was promptly moved back in place. In 1930 a concrete pier was erected in the center of the river in hopes of adding stability to the bridge. However, the pier caused the bridge to wobble slightly

The Burr-type arch sandwiched between members of the Long truss of Rowell's Bridge.

under the load of traffic and, consequently, the top of the pier was removed. The bridge continued to function well without the extra support. In 1965, age and use started to take their toll, and the bridge was rebuilt at a cost of $9,521. In 1982 it was rehabilitated again, this time at a cost of $9,000. From 1993 to 1996 the bridge was closed again for major repairs. The illustrated map and guide *New Hampshire Covered Bridges* states: "Much of the original wood, particularly on the bottom half of the bridge, had rotted so badly it had to be replaced." Original wood was used where possible. Douglas fir from the Northwest was used for other truss member replacements. However, local woods were used for the outside coverings. The roof was also replaced with green, seamed sheet metal. Notice, too, the extremely wide overhang of the roof. This helps to provide extra protection to the open truss members in the upper half of the bridge.

Sulphite Railroad / Upside-Down Bridge

Location: On the southern edge of the locality of Franklin, within the Franklin urban limits.

Directions: In Franklin, at the junction of US 3 North/NH 11 East and NH 127 North, go east on US 3/NH 11 for 1.4 miles to Cross Mill Road on the right (southwest), turn right onto Cross Mill Road, and go 0.3 mile to the beginning of the trail to the bridge at a gated entrance to the old railroad track bed. The bridge is a brisk 16-minute walk from here. Be sure to follow the old track bed toward the north. Remnants of the track are still visible at some places along the path.

GPS: 43° 26.533N 071° 37.297W (coordinates recorded at beginning of the old track bed trail)

Year: 1896   **Truss:** Pratt   **Waterway:** Winnipesaukee River
In Use: Foot traffic only   **Number of Spans:** 3   **Owner:** State
Builder: Bridge and Building Dept. of Boston and Maine Railroad
Length: 231 ft.   **Width:** Unable to measure
Condition: Only skeleton truss remains   **Number:** NH-07-09
Register: June 11, 1975

Most "bridgers" claim that half the fun of "bridging" is finding the bridge. That is certainly true of this one, but hopefully the directions we have provided above will make that task a little easier. All that remains of this covered bridge is the skeleton of the Pratt truss that provided the support for the span and its cover when the bridge was first constructed. The covering was destroyed by fire in 1980, presumed to be the work of arsonists. The skeleton of the railroad bridge that is still standing is one that replaced the original bridge built by the Franklin and Tilton Railroad around 1891 or 1892. It is a most unusual covered bridge because, whereas most covered bridges cover the roadway of the span, this bridge carried its roadway on the top of the structure. Consequently, some of the locals refer to it as the "Upside-Down Bridge." The railroad ties and the rails, which were warped by the fire, are still in place. Train traffic over the bridge ceased in 1973, when the railroad suspended operations. The bridge's primary name is derived from the large amounts of sulphur that were transported over the rail lines to the large pulp and paper mills near the railroad. The New Hampshire Department of Transportation has estimated that it would cost $500,000 to restore this bridge to its original state as a covered bridge; however, since railroad use has been suspended, the only reason for that

restoration would be to preserve the historic integrity of the structure. In 1997, the Department of Transportation prepared a ten-year plan that the governor submitted to the legislature for construction of and improvements to rail trails that exist throughout the state. The rail trail across the Sulphite Railroad Bridge is one of those scheduled for work between 1998 and 2003. There is no indication, however, if that proposal will affect the bridge in any way.

Waterloo Bridge

Location: In the locality of Waterloo, within the Warner town line.

Directions: Just east of Waterloo, at the junction of the I-89 exit 9 ramp and NH 103 West, go west on NH 103 for 0.9 mile to New Market Road on the left (south), turn left onto New Market Road, and go 0.2 mile to the bridge (cross over an intersection after 0.1 mile).

GPS: 43° 17.294N 071° 51.363W

Year: 1857   **Truss:** Town   **Waterway:** Warner River   **In Use:** Yes
Number of Spans: 1   **Owner:** Town of Warner   **Builder:** Dutton Woods
Length: 76 ft. 4 in.   **Width:** 13 ft. $10\frac{1}{2}$ in.   **Condition:** Good
Number: NH-07-04   **Register:** Nov. 21, 1976

According to some sources, the earliest date for the construction of a covered bridge on the site of the Waterloo Bridge is 1840. Other sources list it as 1857, the year in which the bridge was completely rebuilt by Dutton Woods of Con-

toocook. The original cost of construction in 1840 and the builder are unknown. In 1970, as part of the Town Bridge Aid Program, the bridge was rebuilt again at a cost of $16,300. In 1987, further rehabilitation was done by the state at a cost of $3,000. On our visit in October 2002, we found the bridge in good condition. The sturdy Town lattice truss structure is covered with vertical board siding left to weather naturally, and it has a roof of red, seamed sheet metal. The red roof was one of the improvements made during the 1987 rehabilitation. The structure rests on concrete abutments poured on top of cut stone and fieldstone laid dry. These in turn extend to road-level wingwalls.

STRAFFORD COUNTY

Cocheco River Pedestrian/Cocheco River Foot/Dover Pedestrian Bridge

Location: In the locality of Dover.

Directions: In Dover, at the junction of NH 4/NH 9 and NH 108, go east on Washington St. (NH 4) for 0.2 mile to the bridge. (NH 4 turns left; continue straight on Washington St.)

GPS: 43° 11.712N 070° 52.232W (coordinates recorded at parking area near the bridge)

The Warren truss of the Cocheco River Pedestrian Bridge.

Year: 1996   **Truss:** Warren   **Waterway:** Cocheco River
In Use: Foot traffic only   **Number of Spans:** 1   **Owner:** City of Dover
Builder: Moores Marine Construction Corp.   **Length:** 153 ft.
Width: 9 ft. 1 in.   **Condition:** Excellent   **Number:** NH-09-08
Register: Does not qualify

In the late twentieth century, a major Portsmouth employer, located in the downtown Dover area, had been busing its employees from a remote parking lot on the far side of the Cocheco River. The city of Dover decided to resolve the problem and hired H. E. Bergeron Engineers (HEB) to design a bridge that would provide direct access from the parking area, across the Cocheco River, to the downtown business district. The solution designed by HEB was a 153-foot, Warren truss footbridge that was erected in 1996 between Washington and River Streets. In addition to pedestrian traffic, the bridge supports service vehicles or light trucks equipped with snowplows. An interesting aspect of the actual construction was that the entire bridge was erected in a clearing on land approximately two hundred yards upriver. The completed structure was lifted onto a barge and floated downstream to the bridge site. Since the Cocheco River flows into a tidewater area, at high tide the next day the barge was rotated, and two cranes lifted the completed span onto its abutments.

Moores Marine Construction Corporation of Dover was the builder. The cost of the project was $200,000. The completed structure was covered with vertical tongue-and-groove boards on the sides and horizontal clapboard siding on the portals, all of which are painted barn red with white trim. At the time of our visit in January 2003, the bridge was completely snow covered, but it appeared that the roof consists of wooden shakes. The entire structure rests on concrete abutments poured on cut stone bases. Dover can be quite proud of this, the only covered bridge in Strafford County. The interior photo clearly shows the Warren truss.

Blacksmith Shop/Kenyon Hill Bridge

Location: 2.3 miles south of the Cornish-Windsor Covered Bridge, within the Cornish town line.

Directions: At the New Hampshire end of the Cornish-Windsor Covered Bridge, go south on NH 12A for 0.3 mile to Town House Road, which is straight ahead (NH 12A bears to the right); continue on Town House Road for 2 miles to the bridge on the right, closed to traffic. (On our 2003 visit, Town House Road was not identified at the NH 12A junction.)

GPS: 43° 27.781N 072° 21.236W (coordinates recorded at parking area near the bridge)

Year: 1881   **Truss:** Multiple kingpost   **Waterway:** Mill Brook
In Use: Foot traffic only   **Number of Spans:** 1   **Owner:** Town of Cornish
Builder: James Tasker   **Length:** 91 ft.   **Width:** 11 ft. $11\frac{1}{4}$ in.
Condition: Fairly good   **Number:** NH-10-01   **Register:** May 22, 1978

This bridge is one of the eleven or more covered bridges built in this area by James Tasker. The cost of this bridge when it was built in 1881 was $873. It was built to serve one family that lived on the east side of Mill Brook. It derived its most familiar name from a blacksmith shop that was located nearby in an area known as Slab City. Its second name is derived from the name of the hill on the eastern side of the bridge. The bridge is nestled in a quiet valley between Kenyon Hill and Dingleton Hill. According to *New Hampshire Covered Bridges,* published by the New Hampshire Department of Transportation, the bridge was repaired by Milton Graton in 1963, at which time he raised the southern end two feet and the northern end one foot and replaced the floor and sheathing. The restoration of this and the Dingleton Hill Bridge, both done by Graton at a combined cost of $30,000, were made possible through a Federal Historic Preservation Fund matching grant from the National Park Service of the U.S. Department of the Interior through the New Hampshire Division of Historical Resources, the Putnam Foundation, the Cecil Howard Charitable Trust, the Eva Gebhart-Gourgaud Foundation, and the Town of Cornish. The bridge was rededicated on October 23, 1983. Hyland Tasker, a great-grandnephew of the builder, was present for the festivities. When the bridge was reopened, it was for foot traffic only. When we visited the bridge in May 2003, it was still in fairly good condition.

Blow-Me-Down/Bayliss Bridge

Location: 4.3 miles north of the Cornish-Windsor Bridge, or approximately 1.8 miles south of the locality of Plainfield, near the town lines of Cornish and Plainfield.

Directions: At the New Hampshire end of the Cornish-Windsor Covered Bridge, go north on NH 12A for 4 miles to Mill Road on the right (southeast), turn right onto Mill Road, and go 0.3 mile to the bridge. (On our visit in 2003, Mill Road identification was visible only after making the turn onto it from NH 12A.)

GPS: 43˚ 31.040N 072˚ 22.452W

Year: 1877   **Truss:** Multiple kingpost   **Waterway:** Blow-Me-Down Brook
In Use: Yes   **Number of Spans:** 1   **Owner:** Town of Cornish
Builder: James Tasker   **Length:** 85 ft. 1 in.   **Width:** 14 ft. 2$\frac{1}{4}$ in.
Condition: Good   **Number:** NH-10-10   **Register:** May 19, 1978

As can be seen in the photo, this bridge spans a rather deep gorge across the Blow-Me-Down Brook, quite a picturesque setting. It was built in 1877 by James Tasker at a cost of $528. There's a record of only one restoration. That was done by Milton Graton and his son Arnold in 1980. Funds for that project were provided by a Federal Historic Preservation Fund matching grant from the

National Park Service of the U.S. Department of the Interior acquired through the New Hampshire Division of Historical Resources, as well as by the Town of Cornish, the Cornish Historical Society, and private contributions. It appears, also, that some of the knee braces may have been replaced in more recent years. The sides of the bridge, which have narrow, window-like openings on each side—two on the upstream side and one on the downstream side—are covered with unpainted, random-width, vertical boards that have been left to weather naturally; the portal is covered with brown, random-width, vertical boards; the deck is covered with lengthwise planks; and the roof with green, standing-seam sheet metal. The portal gable ends project several feet over each end of the deck, providing additional protection from the elements. This bridge is a lovely structure in a rustic rural location.

Corbin Bridge

Location: 2.4 miles north-northeast of the locality of Newport, within the Newport town line.

Directions: In Newport, at the junction of NH 10 North and NH 11 East/NH 103 East, go north on NH 10 for 1.7 miles to Corbin Road on the left (west), turn left onto Corbin Road, and go 0.7 mile to the bridge.

GPS: 43° 23.465N 072° 11.706W

Year: ca. 1845, rebuilt 1994   **Truss:** Town
Waterway : Croydon Branch of Sugar River   **In Use:** Yes
Number of Spans: 1   **Owner:** Town of Newport

Builder: Arnold Graton and Associates   **Length:** 102 ft. 6 in.
Width: 13 ft. 11 in.   **Condition:** Excellent   **Number:** NH-10-05 (2)
Register: Does not qualify

Records indicate that the original covered bridge on this site was built around 1845. The original builder is not known. The bridge was built on the Corbin property owned by Austin Corbin, a well-known banker, railroad president, and real estate developer. When the state suggested closing the bridge in 1979, the town reduced the posted weight limit from six tons to three tons. In 1980 the bridge was completely rehabilitated by the state at a cost of $43,000. A portion of this amount was funded by a federal Historic Preservation Fund matching grant from the National Park Service of the U.S. Department of the Interior acquired through the New Hampshire Division of Historical Resources. After this reconstruction the bridge was opened again with a six-ton limit. On May 25, 1993, the bridge was completely destroyed by fire, one of three covered bridges destroyed within a three-month period. All three fires were believed to be the work of arsonists. Covered bridge enthusiasts inspired the town residents to such an extent that fund-raising efforts were started to rebuild the bridge. Twelve hundred trunnels were sold by the Newport Historical Society at a cost of $25 each to supplement the replacement insurance coverage. Arnold Graton and Associates did an extremely exacting job of replicating the original structure even to the extent of having a team of oxen pull the bridge from the site of construction to the bridge site. The trip required three days, which turned into a townwide festival that attracted about ten thousand people, some of them descendants of the original Corbin family.

Dingleton Hill Bridge

Location: 1.2 miles south of the Cornish-Windsor Covered Bridge, within the Cornish town line.

Directions: At the New Hampshire end of the Cornish-Windsor Covered Bridge, go south on NH 12A for 0.3 mile to Town House Road, which is straight ahead (NH 12A bears to the right); continue on Town House Road for 0.9 mile to the bridge on the right, on Root Hill Road. (On our 2003 visit, Town House Road was not identified at the NH 12A junction.)

GPS: 43˚ 27.871N 072˚ 22.155W

Year: 1882   **Truss:** Multiple kingpost   **Waterway:** Mill Brook   **In Use:** Yes
Number of Spans: 1   **Owner:** Town of Cornish   **Builder:** James Tasker
Length: 77 ft. 2 in.   **Width:** 14 ft.   **Condition:** Fairly good
Number: NH-10-02   **Register:** Nov. 8, 1978

This is another of James Tasker's eleven or more covered bridges built in this part of New Hampshire. This one he built in 1882 at a cost of $812. Between the time it was built and the latter part of the twentieth century, the bridge was largely maintained by the farmers who used the bridge on a regular basis. By 1983, it was in need of more extensive repairs. Consequently, Milton Graton was contracted to do work on both this bridge and the Blacksmith Shop Bridge, which is located about a mile away. The cost of the combined restorations was $30,000. Funds were acquired through a Federal Historic Preservation Fund matching grant from the National Park Service of the U.S. Department of the Interior through the New Hampshire Division of Historical Resources, the Putnam Foundation, the Cecil Howard Charitable Trust, the Eva Gebhart-

The multiple kingpost truss of the Dingleton Hill Bridge.

Gourgaud Foundation, and the Town of Cornish. The bridge was rededicated on October 23, 1983. Hyland Tasker, a great-grandnephew of the builder, was present for the festivities. The sides of the bridge are covered with unpainted, random-width, vertical board siding on the lower half only; the portals are covered with brown, random-width, vertical board siding; the deck with lengthwise planks; and the roof with standing-seam sheet metal. This is another lovely, multiple kingpost span, located in a quiet rural valley at the base of Dingleton Hill. The interior photo shows an excellent example of the multiple kingpost truss.

McDermott/Cold River Bridge

Location: 2 miles north-northeast of the locality of Alstead, within the Langdon town line.

Directions: In Alstead, at the junction of NH 12A and NH 123, go east on NH 123 for 0.7 mile to the junction with NH 123A on the left (north), turn left onto NH 123A, and go 1.2 miles to Crane Brook Road on the left (west); turn left onto Crane Brook Road and go 0.1 mile to the bypassed bridge.

GPS: 43° 10.198N 072° 20.745W

Year: 1869   **Truss:** Town with arch   **Waterway:** Cold River
In Use: Foot traffic only   **Number of Spans:** 1   **Owner:** Town of Langdon
Builder: Albert S. Granger   **Length:** 85 ft. $3\frac{1}{2}$ in.   **Width:** 13 ft. $6\frac{1}{2}$ in.
Condition: Poor   **Number:** NH-10-06   **Register:** May 17, 1973

This is the second of two bridges scheduled for rehabilitation by the Langdon Covered Bridge Association, which was formed in 1997. The efforts of this society have already completely restored the other covered bridge located in the Town of Langdon, the Prentiss/Drewsville Bridge. There are records of three other bridges having been built in the location of the McDermott Bridge, all of them of the pole and plank variety. None were covered; hence the need for more frequent replacement. In 1869 a covered bridge was built on this site by Albert Granger using a truss system designed and patented by his father, Sanford Granger. The New Hampshire Department of Transportation has called this truss system a Town lattice truss with light arches. In 1961 it was anticipated that the aged covered structure could be restored at a cost of $7,000—$2,100 to be paid by the town and $4,900 by the state. However, in 1964 the town decided to bypass the covered bridge with a modern structure, which was built downstream under the Town Bridge Aid Program. Consequently, the covered bridge was closed to vehicular traffic and retained by the town for historic reasons. Hopefully, visitors to the bridge site in the near future will find a completely rehabilitated structure through the efforts of the local covered bridge association.

Meriden/Mill Hollow/Mill Bridge

Location: In the locality of Mill Hollow, within the Plainfield town line.

Directions: In Meriden, at the junction of NH 120 and Main St., go northwest on Main St. for 0.8 mile to the bridge on Colby Hill Road, on the southwest (left) side of the road.

GPS: 43° 33.200N 072° 15.938W

Year: 1880   **Truss:** Multiple kingpost   **Waterway:** Bloods Brook
In Use: Yes   **Number of Spans:** 1+   **Owner:** Town of Plainfield
Builder: James Tasker   **Length:** 79 ft. 5½ in.   **Width:** 14 ft. 6 in.
Condition: Fairly good   **Number:** NH-10-08   **Register:** Aug. 27, 1980

The bridge that is standing in this location today is the third one to span this deep gorge. The previous structures were open-timber bridges. This bridge was built by James Tasker in 1880 for the sum of $465. The abutments were prepared by Levi Sanderson for $220. According to information recorded by the New Hampshire Department of Transportation in *New Hampshire Covered Bridges,* the present span has been altered at least four times in its 123-year life span. The first time was after Hurricane Carol damaged the span on August 20, 1954. The repairs cost $3,000. The second time was in 1963, when it was necessary to increase the load limit of the then 83-year-old structure. This was done by reinforcing the deck with steel beams, which increased its carrying capacity to fifteen tons. (It is thought by some that this was the first bridge to benefit from the state's Town Bridge Aid Program.) The third time was after the collapse of the roof under an exceptionally heavy snowfall in 1977. Those repairs cost $8,296. And the last recorded restructuring was the improvement to the substructure of the bridge in 1985 at a cost of $57,000. Today the multiple kingpost truss span is supported in the center with five long, vertical columns that rest on a concrete base on the east bank of Bloods Brook and support a transverse beam under the deck of the span. Notice, in the photograph, the relatively narrow width of each of the eleven panels on either side of the center kingpost. This truss structure can be seen quite clearly because the sides are open for approximately the upper half. At the present time, the bridge appears to be in fairly good condition and continues to be maintained by the Town of Plainfield.

Pier/Chandler Station Railroad Bridge

Location: 1 mile west-southwest of the locality of Kelleyville, within the Newport town line.

Directions: In Newport, at the junction of NH 10 and NH 11/NH 103, go west on NH 11/NH 103 for 2.9 miles to Chandler Road on the left (south), turn left onto Chandler Road, and go 1 mile to a parking area near the old railroad right-of-way on the right (north). Walk northeast along the right-of-way to the bridge. (The bridge is visible from Chandler Road after approximately 0.9 mile.)

GPS: 43° 21.732N 072° 14.532W (coordinates recorded at beginning of old track bed trail to the bridge)

Year: 1896   **Truss:** Town (double)   **Waterway:** Sugar River
In Use: As a trail   **Number of Spans:** 2   **Owner:** State
Builder: Bridge and Building Dept. of Boston and Maine Railroad
Length: 228 ft. 7½ in.   **Width:** 15 ft. ¾ in.   **Condition:** Good
Number: NH-10-03   **Register:** June 10, 1975

This bridge is located along a railroad trail that is part of a statewide system being maintained by the New Hampshire Department of Highways. The original railroad tracks that once crossed the bridge have been replaced with lengthwise planks, making the bridge deck easier to traverse. Facts that we were able to acquire about this bridge vary. The *World Guide to Covered Bridges* (*WGCB*), published by the National Society for the Preservation of Covered Bridges, lists its date of origin as 1896; *New Hampshire Covered Bridges* (*NHCB*), published by the New Hampshire Department of Transportation, indicates that the bridge

The double Town truss of the Pier Railroad Bridge.

was built in 1907 by the Boston and Maine Railroad to replace an older wooden bridge built by the Sugar River Railroad in 1871 or 1872. Another variation exists in the identification of the truss—the *WGCB* identifies the truss structure as a double Town truss, and *NHCB* identifies it as a Town-Pratt truss. On our visit to the bridge in May 2003, our opinion of the truss agrees with that of the *WGCB*. We found a two-span, double Town lattice truss constructed with very substantial lattice web timbers (see the interior photo). At least one hundred spans of this type were used along the Boston and Maine Railroad system, some of them built by the Pratt Construction Company. This may be where the Town-Pratt truss name was derived. For more information on the Town-Pratt truss we refer the reader to the page in this guide on the Fisher Railroad Bridge, Lamoille County, Vermont. Notice, in the exterior photo, the substantial pier positioned in midstream. This may be where the bridge name Pier originates. The bridge has also been known as Chandler Station; the locality of Chandlers Mills is a short distance from the bridge.

Prentiss/Drewsville Bridge

Location: 1.5 miles north of the locality of Drewsville, within the Langdon town line.

Directions: Just past Drewsville, traveling east on NH 123, where NH 123 makes a 90-degree turn to the east, the road to the Prentiss/Drewsville Bridge goes north. Follow this unmarked road for 1.4 miles to the bypassed bridge. The DeLorme *Atlas* identifies this road as Cheshire Turnpike.

GPS: 43° 09.193N 072° 23.605W

Year: ca. 1874   **Truss:** Town   **Waterway:** Great Brook
In Use: Foot traffic only   **Number of Spans:** 1   **Owner:** Town of Langdon
Builder: Albert S. Granger   **Length:** 36 ft. 3 in.   **Width:** 15 ft. 11 in.
Condition: Very good   **Number:** NH-10-07   **Register:** May 24, 1973

Records indicate that bridges stood on this site before the date of construction listed above for the covered bridge. The earliest date on record, 1791, is for the second bridge, which was built on land cleared and settled by John Prentiss in 1785. The Cheshire Turnpike Company acquired the bridge in 1805 as part of its turnpike, which ran from Canada to Boston. According to the "New Hampshire Bridges" internet site, "On March 10, 1874, the town voted to raise $1,000 to replace the old structure with a thirty foot Granger covered bridge." Consequently, shortly thereafter Albert Granger erected the first covered bridge on this site. The bridge he built was based on a truss design created and patented by Albert's father, Sanford Granger. It was a variation of the Town lattice truss. That structure served the community well until 1954, when it was bypassed by a modern bridge. In 2000 the bypassed bridge was completely restored by the Langdon Covered Bridge Association and is now open to foot traffic in a clearing just to the east of the "Cheshire Turnpike" as identified in the DeLorme *New Hampshire Atlas & Gazeteer*. Although one of the shortest covered bridges in New Hampshire, Prentiss Bridge stands quite proudly in its restored state in a lovely rural setting.

Wright Railroad Bridge

Location: 1.8 miles west-southwest of the locality of Kelleyville, within the Newport town line.

Directions: In Newport, at the junction of NH 10 and NH 11/NH 103, go west on NH 11/NH 103 for 2.9 miles to Chandler Road on the left (south), turn left onto Chandler Road, and go 1.8 miles to a parking area near the old railroad right-of-way on the right (north). Walk west along the right-of-way for approximately 0.25 mile to the bridge.

GPS: 43° 21.512N 072° 15.232W (coordinates recorded at beginning of old track bed trail to the bridge)

Year: 1896   **Truss:** Town (double) with arch   **Waterway:** Sugar River
In Use: As a trail   **Number of Spans:** 1   **Owner:** State
Builder: Bridge and Building Dept. of Boston and Maine Railroad
Length: 135 ft. 11$\frac{1}{2}$ in.   **Width:** 14 ft. 10$\frac{1}{2}$ in.   **Condition:** Fairly good
Number: NH-10-04   **Register:** June 10, 1975

This bridge is located along a well-maintained rail trail that is part of a state-wide system being maintained by the New Hampshire Department of Highways. The original railroad tracks that once crossed the bridge have been replaced with lengthwise planks, making the bridge deck easier to traverse. Facts that we were able to acquire about this bridge vary. The *World Guide to Covered Bridges* (*WGCB*), published by the National Society for the Preservation of Covered Bridges, lists its date of origin as 1896; *New Hampshire Covered Bridges* (*NHCB*), published by the New Hampshire Department of Transportation, indicates that the bridge was built in 1906 by the Bridge and Building Department of the Boston and Maine Railroad to replace an older wooden bridge built by the Sugar River Railroad in 1871 or 1872. Another variation exists in the identification of the truss—the *WGCB* identifies the truss structure as a double Town truss with arch, and *NHCB* identifies it as a double Town-Pratt truss. On our visit to the bridge in May 2003, our opinion of the truss agrees with that of the *WGCB*. A twenty-two ply laminated arch consisting of two one-by-nine-inch planks on the bottom, followed by one two-by-nine-inch plank next, and nineteen three-by-nine-inch planks on top, is sandwiched between single substantial Town lattice truss webs on each side of the bridge. For additional information on the Town-Pratt truss, we refer the reader to the page in this guide on the Fisher Railroad Bridge, Lamoille County, Vermont. The bridge was named for S. K. Wright, the former owner of the right-of-way that the railroad purchased.

NEW HAMPSHIRE /
VERMONT

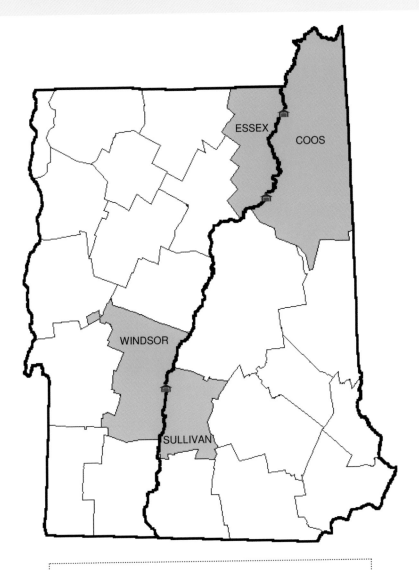

ESSEX

COOS

WINDSOR

SULLIVAN

Counties in green contain at least one interstate covered bridge

🏠 – location of a covered bridge

New Hampshire/Vermont and the Connecticut River

The Connecticut River is the only waterway in New England that required a bridge to connect neighboring states—New Hampshire and Vermont.

At one time a total of thirty-five covered bridges, both highway and railroad, spanned the mighty river from its northern extremities in the Town of Pittsburg, Coos County, New Hampshire, to the southern borders of the two states where the river enters Massachusetts. These ranged in size from the small farm bridges that stand in the northern lake country of New Hampshire to the massive 453-foot-long Cornish-Windsor Bridge that crosses from Cornish in Sullivan County, New Hampshire, to Windsor in Windsor County, Vermont. Not all of these bridges, however, were interstate bridges, for several of them crossed the Connecticut River where it originates entirely within the northern tip of New Hampshire, before it becomes the state border with Vermont.

Records indicate that the earliest bridge built across the Connecticut dates back to 1785, when Colonel Enoch Hale built a span from Walpole, New Hampshire, across the river to Bellows Falls, Vermont; however, it was not a covered bridge. Hale simply used a rock outcropping in the middle of the river as a central pier to support an open-deck bridge with timber bracing.

Federal law declared that the river, right up to the low watermark on the western shoreline, belonged to the state of New Hampshire. Consequently, the major responsibility for bridge maintenance, preservation, and repair fell on the shoulders of the eastern neighbor, making Vermont responsible for only the portion of each bridge that rested on the western banks of the river. Today, only three of the original covered spans are still standing. All are highway bridges, ranging in length from the northernmost, (the 146-foot, Howe truss, Columbia Bridge in Coos County) to the southernmost, longest covered span in New England (the aforementioned Cornish-Windsor Bridge, a Town lattice truss bridge in the central part of the two states). Also in Coos County, in between these two bridges, stands the 267-foot Mount Orne Bridge, also a Howe truss structure.

While not an interstate bridge, one other New Hampshire covered bridge spans the Connecticut, just south of Lake Francis in Coos County—the Pittsburg-Clarksville Bridge. It is no longer open to vehicular traffic but has been preserved in this northern part of the state. Nearby, just several miles east-northeast, situated between Lake Francis and the First Connecticut Lake, there are two other spans, the most northern covered bridges in New Hampshire—the Happy Corner Bridge and the River Road Bridge. Both of these bridges cross Perry Stream, one of the many small tributaries of the Connecticut River in this northern lake country.

Columbia Bridge

Location: Between the locality of Columbia, N.H., within the Columbia town line, and the locality of Lemington, Vt., within the Lemington town line.

Directions: In Colebrook, N.H., at the junction of US 3 and NH 26 East, go south on US 3 for 4.2 miles to Columbia Bridge Road on the right (west), turn right onto Columbia Bridge Road, and go 0.1 mile to the bridge.

GPS: 44° 51.179N 071° 33.082W (New Hampshire)

Year: 1912   **Truss:** Howe   **Waterway:** Connecticut River   **In Use:** Yes
Number of Spans: 1   **Owner:** Town of Columbia, N.H.
Builder: Charles Babbitt   **Length:** 145 ft. 7 in.   **Width:** 15 ft. 8 in.
Condition: Good   **Number:** NH-04-07/VT-05-02   **Register:** Dec. 12, 1976

This is the third covered bridge, from south to north, that spans the Connecticut River between New Hampshire and Vermont. Being the most northern, it crosses the river at a narrower point than the other two; consequently, it is also the shortest of the three structures. Columbia Bridge, like its southern neighbor, was built using the Howe truss. Because of its shorter length, however, the truss is a single span. The present span, built in 1912 by Charles Babbitt, rests on the abutments of an earlier span that have been reinforced with concrete. The earlier span was possibly an uncovered one. The photo, which was taken from the New Hampshire side of the bridge, quite clearly provides a view of the

Howe truss and also displays another unique feature of this span. Its two sides are treated differently—the upstream side of the bridge is covered only on the lower half, while the downstream side is completely covered. According to Herbert W. Congdon in *The Covered Bridge,* the downstream side was completely covered to protect it from the weather, and the upstream side was left more open to provide light. There is a record of the bridge having been rehabilitated only once during its less than one-hundred-year existence. That was in 1981, when the work was funded by the state of New Hampshire at a cost of $143,000. However, although there is no record of work having been done since then, there is a record of a grant of $4,920 having been awarded to the Town of Columbia from the Land and Community Heritage Investment Program made possible by Citizens for New Hampshire Land and Community Heritage. In its grant award statement this citizens' group said: "The bridge serves both NH and VT and is crucial in maintaining an active transportation corridor used by residents, farmers, and tourists. This bridge is essential to local and regional economies, and it is imminently threatened due to structural problems. . . . The project is of profound social and historic value." This is another example of people working together to preserve these fine examples of our historical heritage.

Mount Orne Bridge

Location: 5 miles southwest of the locality of Lancaster, within the town lines of Lancaster, N.H. and Lunenberg, Vt.

Directions: In Lancaster, N.H., at the junction of US 2 West/US 3 South and NH 135 South, go south on NH 135 for 5 miles. NH 135 turns 90° to the south; go straight to the bridge.

GPS: 44° 27.601N 071° 39.136W (New Hampshire)

Year: 1911   **Truss:** Howe   **Waterway:** Connecticut River   **In Use:** Yes
Number of Spans: 2   **Owner:** Towns of Lancaster, N.H. and Lunenberg, Vt.
Builder: Unknown   **Length:** 266 ft. 8½ in.   **Width:** 15 ft. 8½ in
Condition: Good   **Number:** NH-04-08/VT-05-03   **Register:** Dec. 12, 1976

This is the second covered bridge, from south to north, that spans the Connecticut River between New Hampshire and Vermont, and also the second longest. It is a two-span, Howe truss bridge, nearly 267 feet long. It was built in 1911 to replace another bridge, which had been operated as a toll bridge by the Union Bridge Company from the time it was built in the 1860s or 1870s until it was destroyed by a logjam in 1908. For three years transportation between the towns of Lancaster, New Hampshire, and Luneneburg, Vermont, was provided by ferry. In 1911 each town provided $2,500 toward the construction of a new covered span. The balance of $1,678 was raised by subscription. Timbers for

the bridge were precut and assembled at the bridge site. On July 5, 1983, it was necessary to close the bridge for a period of twelve weeks so that it could be rehabilitated. According to the New Hampshire Department of Transportation publication *New Hampshire Covered Bridges,* that rehabilitation cost $133,000. Funds were provided by the towns of Lancaster and Lunenburg, the states of New Hampshire and Vermont, and through a federal Historic Preservation Fund matching grant from the National Park Service of the U.S. Department of the Interior acquired by the New Hampshire Division of Historical Resources. The restored span was rededicated on November 23, 1983.

SULLIVAN / WINDSOR COUNTIES

Cornish-Windsor Bridge

Location: Between Cornish, N.H., and Windsor, Vt., within the town lines of Cornish and Windsor

Directions: In New Hampshire, approximately 1.5 miles northwest of the village of Cornish Mills, N.H., at the junction where NH 12A meets the road that crosses the river to I-91 in Vermont, go west to cross the bridge. In Vermont, in the village of Windsor, at the junction of US 5 and Bridge Street (which is VT 44 on the west side of US 5), go east on Bridge Street for 0.15 mile to the bridge.

GPS: 43° 28.402N 072° 22.982W (New Hampshire), 43° 28.445N 072° 23.087W (Vermont)

Year: 1866   **Truss:** Town   **Waterway:** Connecticut River
In Use: Yes   **Number of Spans:** 2   **Owner:** New Hampshire
Builder: James F. Tasker and Bela J. Fletcher   **Length:** 453 ft. 4 in.
Width: 19 ft. 4 in.   **Condition:** Very good   **Number:** NH-10-09/VT-14-14
Register: Nov. 21, 1976

This is the longest covered bridge in the United States and the longest two-span covered bridge in the world. In 1970, it was designated a National Historic Civil Engineering Landmark by the American Society of Civil Engineers. The present bridge is a restoration of the bridge built at this location in 1866 by Bela J. Fletcher of Claremont and James F. Tasker of Cornish. That structure was the fourth bridge built at the site since 1796. Others were built in 1824 and 1850. All the earlier spans were destroyed by floodwaters. The 1866 bridge was a Town lattice truss, built with squared timbers instead of planks. Repairs to the bridge were necessary many times during its existence. Within thirty years it lost all its positive camber and began to sag. Major repairs were made in 1887, 1892, 1925, 1938, 1954–55, and 1977. The New Hampshire Department of Transportation publication *New Hampshire Covered Bridges* states: "In 1935, the New Hampshire General Court authorized funds to purchase the bridge. The structure was purchased by the state in 1936 and operated . . . as a toll bridge until June 1, 1943." It was renovated by the state in 1954 but suffered again in 1977 when it was damaged by floodwater and ice. This led to repairs at a cost of $25,000. However, the span continued to deteriorate, and on July 2, 1987, it was closed to all traffic.

Before another rehabilitation of the bridge was undertaken, there was a great amount of dialogue and debate among covered bridge authorities, which included input from Arnold Graton, Jan Lewandoski, the New Hampshire De-

partment of Transportation, the New Hampshire Division of Historical Resources, the Town of Cornish, the Vermont Agency of Transportation, the Vermont Division of Preservation, and the Town of Windsor. In the spring of 1988 the actual rehabilitation project began.

The general contractor for the project was Chesterfield Associates; David Fischetti was the engineer, and Jan Lewandoski was the subcontractor for the wood framing, which primarily involved work on the trusses. In an article included in the *Society for Industrial Archeology,* Lewandoski highlighted some of the structural details—the old bed timbers were replaced, and eleven-by-thirty-five-inch glulam timbers that cantilever out thirteen feet were placed inside of them at both the abutments and the central pier; 60 percent of the chords were dismantled; positive camber was restored to eighteen inches; new lower chords of glue-laminated material consisting of southern yellow pine were installed (most of the new chord members were 100 or 116 feet long by eight inches by eleven inches); upper chords of similar material, 88 feet long, were replaced over the center pier; the overhead tie beams were doubled, and the lateral braces were mortised from the end of one into the middle of the next, allowing the original braces to be used; a new deck (possibly the fourth or fifth deck) of four-inch Douglas fir was installed on new six-by-eighteen-inch deck joists (at least the third set); and new pine siding, new spruce rafters, and a new galvanized metal roof (the fourth roof) were installed. Following this major reconstruction by the state of New Hampshire at a cost of $4,450,000, the bridge was rededicated and opened again to traffic on December 8, 1989.

In 2001, the Cornish-Windsor Bridge benefited from a $140,000 grant from the National Historic Covered Bridge Preservation Program, which was used to install upgraded fire protection in the form of a Protectowire fire detection system and a dry sprinkler system. Hopefully, these most recent improvements will allow this bridge to continue to serve as a Connecticut River crossing for many years into the twenty-first century and beyond.

RHODE ISLAND

PROVIDENCE

BRISTOL

KENT

WASHINGTON

NEWPORT

Counties in green contain at least
one covered bridge

 – location of a covered bridge

Rhode Island

"The Plantation State"

In his 1985 publication *Covered Bridges of the Northeast,* Richard Sanders Allen reports that few records could be found about covered bridges that once stood in the Plantation State. The topography of the small state is such that there never was much need for large, covered, trusswork bridges to span the relatively shallow tidal streams around Narragansett Bay or the small inland brooks and streams. What bridges were there were either pile structures near the bay or simple, uncovered truss structures farther inland. Allen, through careful research, could find records of only five covered bridges that were built in the state between 1820 and 1867. Rhode Island does, however, have the distinction of having had the first covered interstate railroad bridge in the United States. It was the India Point Bridge, built across the Seekonk River for the Boston and Providence Railroad.

Of the five bridges for which records could be found, two were highway bridges and three were railroad bridges. The last of the covered highway bridges to remain standing was the Narrow River Bridge, which crossed the Pettaquamscutt or Narrow River on the Boston Neck Road, now US 1, north of Narragansett. It was replaced by a wide, concrete, "modern" bridge in 1920.

The only covered bridge now standing in the state is one that was first discussed by the Town Council of Foster in Providence County. In 1986, the townspeople decided that in honor of the state's 350th birthday they were going to build a covered bridge that would cross Hemlock Brook on Central Pike. By May 23, 1993, after various delays, the Swamp Meadow Bridge was dedicated and placed into service just north of Foster Center. Unfortunately, vandals burned the lovely new structure on September 11 of the same year. However, with even greater determination, a replacement for the Swamp Meadow was rebuilt and dedicated at the same location just fourteen months after its destruction. Today, Rhode Island's only covered bridge, a beautiful Town lattice truss structure, stands proudly across Hemlock Brook in the Town of Foster—a true testament to the dreams, wishes, and aspirations of a proud rural community.

Swamp Meadow Bridge

Location: Just north of the locality of Foster Center, within the Foster town line.

Directions: North of Foster Center, at the junction of US 6 and RI 94, go south on RI 94 for 1.1 miles to Central Pike, turn right onto Central Pike, and go 0.1 mile to the bridge.

GPS: 41° 47.974N 071° 43.766W

Year: 1994   **Truss:** Town   **Waterway:** Hemlock Brook   **In Use:** Yes
Number of Spans: 1   **Owner:** Town of Foster   **Builder:** Foster townspeople
Length: 36 ft. 3¾ in.   **Width:** 15 ft. 10 in.   **Condition:** Very good
Number: RI-04-01 (2)   **Register:** Does not qualify

In 1986, the Town Council of Foster decided to build a covered bridge in their town in honor of Rhode Island's 350th birthday. The townspeople selected Central Pike, where it crosses Hemlock Brook, as the road on which the bridge should be built. By 1992, the town received approval from the State Department of Transportation to proceed with its project. On September 12, under the direction of Jed Dixon, designer of the bridge, a volunteer work party started construction on the two Town lattice trusses. By the end of that month the trusses were completed and ready to move to the bridge site. The first weekend of October 1992 marked the erection of the lattice trusses and the roof trusses, with all the structure's finishing touches being added by the end of November. The new bridge was dedicated on May 23, 1993.

Unfortunately, four months later, on September 11, the work of all those volunteers was destroyed by vandals who set the bridge on fire. By the time the Foster Fire Department could respond, the bridge was totally engulfed in flames. However, the outpouring of support from children, adults, businesses, and local organizations started an immediate campaign to replace their covered bridge. Just twelve days later, the Foster Town Council approved the rebuilding of the span. By November 5, 1994, the rebuilt Swamp Meadow Bridge was completed and rededicated.

The bridge is relatively short, only thirty-six feet three and three-quarters inches long, spans a very small waterway, Hemlock Brook, and is situated in a very picturesque setting. It is a lovely, natural wood structure substantially rebuilt in the traditional Town truss style complete with natural wood trunnels. The deck consists of crosswise planks laid on edge with lengthwise runners in the tire track area. The portion of the deck between the runners has been paved with macadam. Six I beam stringers support the entire deck structure. The roof is covered with cedar shakes, and the sides and portals with board and batten siding. The entire structure rests on concrete abutments that are extended to form road-level wingwalls. There is one diamond-shaped window located on each side. One other unusual feature is a heavy, curb-high timber that runs the entire length of the bridge, one on each side of the deck, which in turn supports six six-by-six-inch, vertical, square metal posts about two feet high. Each of these posts is welded to one-half inch metal plates, each of which is fastened to the curb-high timbers at equal intervals along the side. Our assumption was that these barriers have been erected to prevent vehicles from damaging the truss timbers. (A variety of techniques are being used in contemporary covered bridge restoration to deter extensive damage to these lovely structures.)

The enthusiasm and determination of the townspeople of Foster is clearly stated in the dedication program of November 5, 1994:

> Today we rededicate the resurrected "Swamp Meadow Bridge." This would not be possible without the unbelievable donation of services, of materials and of money by so many people. Not only has the bridge been rebuilt, but due to the generosity of so many, a fund can be established for its maintenance.
>
> Every day is a new beginning. We are proud of what the Swamp Meadow Bridge represents. We hope that future generations will be able to enjoy and respect the effort of so many.

VERMONT

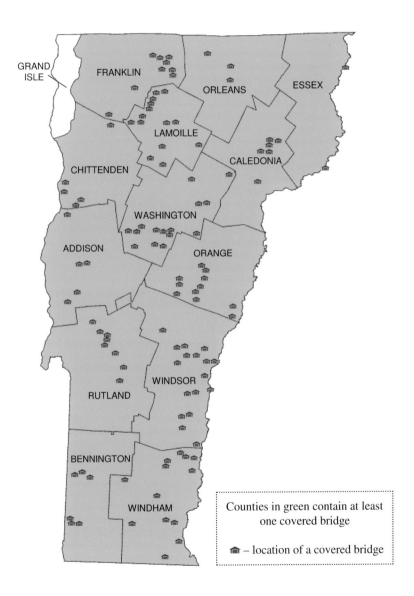

GRAND
ISLE

FRANKLIN

ORLEANS

ESSEX

LAMOILLE

CALEDONIA

CHITTENDEN

WASHINGTON

ADDISON

ORANGE

RUTLAND

WINDSOR

BENNINGTON

WINDHAM

Counties in green contain at least
one covered bridge

🏠 – location of a covered bridge

Vermont

"The Green Mountain State"

In October 1761, the Reverend Dr. Peters, one of the first clergymen to visit the thirty thousand settlers in the territory that is now Vermont, ceremoniously declared Verd Mont to be the "Green Mountain State" as he stood on top of a high mountain, then named Mount Pisgah, and looked out toward Lake Champlain on the west, the Connecticut River on the east, and the vast expanse of hills and trees to the north and the south. Today, covered bridge enthusiasts could travel through the numerous valleys, through which countless rivers, brooks, and streams flow, and call Vermont "The Covered Bridge State." This nickname would be justifiably applied because Vermont holds the distinct honor of having more covered bridges within its borders, per square mile, than any other state in the union.

There are records of well over five hundred covered spans that once stood in the state's 9,528 square miles. While that number has declined because of the usual causes of covered bridge loss—floods, ice, normal decay, and the destructive nature of man, it is quite remarkable that nearly one hundred historic spans can still be found in the Green Mountain State.

The earliest authenticated date for a covered bridge in the state is 1824. That was the year that the Keyes brothers built a long, single-span, arch truss bridge across the Mississquoi River at Highgate Falls. Lyman Burgess and Roderick Hill built similar crossings over the Lamoille River at Milton, and Sylvanus Baldwin spanned the Winooski River with another Burr-type arch truss bridge. For some time thereafter, this type of structure became the engineering style for bridges across the wider rivers in the northern region of the state.

At the age of twenty-one, Nicholas Montgomery Powers, a local young man raised on a farm just southwest of town, convinced the selectmen of Pittsford that he could erect a covered structure across Furnace Brook at Pittsford Mills. After some debate and the encouragement of his father, who put up bond and "agreed to make good any timbers the 'boy' might spoil," the selectmen agreed. The bridge that Powers erected was so substantial that it lasted ninety-six years, until it was replaced with a "modern," concrete bridge. That bridge assured Powers of numerous bridge-building jobs quite close to home. Today there are eight Town lattice truss covered bridges still standing in Powers's home county, Rutland, most of them attributed to Powers and his mentor, Abraham Owen, who favored the Town truss design. It was not long before Powers's reputation sent him as far away as Perryville, Maryland, for the erection of numerous covered bridges. Quoting Richard Sanders Allen again: "Writers have glibly credited him not only with 'all the lattice bridges in Vermont,' but with 'most of the covered bridges in New England and New York.' If Powers had built all the bridges attributed to him, he would have had to be working day and night for forty years. But the records of the ones he did build make him a man well worthy of the legends."

While Nick Powers was the most well known builder of bridges in Vermont and surrounding states, there were other builders whose names appear less frequently in the archives regarding the history of the state's covered bridges. Among them are Arthur Adams, John D. Colton, Sanford Granger, the Jewett brothers, Charles and Benjamin Sears, James F. Tasker, and, of course, the well-known twentieth-century covered bridge builder Milton Graton of New Hampshire. Several other builders will be documented in the following pages, but unfortunately there are no known builders on record for many of the Vermont bridges.

While the Town lattice truss appears to be the truss of choice throughout much of the state, several of the other truss styles are also well represented. In the northern part of the state, the Burr arch truss was the preferred type, and spread throughout the state are numerous examples of the multiple kingpost and the queenpost truss. In addition there is one adaptation of the extremely rare Haupt truss, one adaptation of the Pratt truss, and there are three examples of the Paddleford truss.

When we researched, documented, and photographed the Vermont bridges between August 2002 and May 2003, there were ninety-nine historic and/or authentic covered bridges still standing within the borders of the state and three spanning the Connecticut River connecting Vermont to New Hampshire. An additional twelve nonhistoric and in some cases nonauthentic bridges have also been included in this guide because mention of them has appeared on or in other state-related publications and we considered them worthy of being recorded herein. In any event, there are certainly a large number of covered spans that can be visited, photographed, and enjoyed throughout the Green Mountain State.

Halpin/High Bridge

Location: On Halpin Covered Bridge Road, 3.2 miles northeast of the center of the locality of Middlebury, near the town line of Middlebury and New Haven.

Directions: Entering Middlebury from the south on US 7/VT 125, where US 7/VT 125 turns left in the center of town, Washington St. bears right (northeast); go right on Washington St. 1.4 miles (Washington St. becomes Painter Road). Halpin Road goes straight ahead. Go straight on Halpin Road for 1.5 miles to Halpin Covered Bridge Road on the right (name is on the left), turn right onto Halpin Covered Bridge Road, and go 0.3 mile to the bridge. Entering Middlebury from the north, US 7 meets VT 125 near the middle of town; where US 7/VT 125 turns left, turn left again to Washington St. on the right (northeast). Follow directions on Washington St. as given above for approaching from the south.

GPS: 44° 03.001N 073° 08.452W

Year: 1850   **Truss:** Town   **Waterway:** Muddy Branch of the New Haven River
In Use: Yes   **Number of Spans:** 1   **Owner:** Town of Middlebury
Builder: Unknown   **Length:** 66 ft. $3\frac{3}{4}$ in.   **Width:** 11 ft. $11\frac{1}{2}$ in.
Condition: Good   **Number:** VT-01-03   **Register:** Sept. 10, 1974

This sixty-six-foot span is positioned higher above its waterway than any other covered bridge in Vermont. It rests forty-one feet above the Muddy Branch of

the New Haven River. It was originally built to bring loads of marble from the Halpin quarry at Marble Ledge to the marble-cutting mill powered by the waterfall at downtown Middlebury. Today its primary use is to provide access to the Halpin family farm property. There is some question about the date the bridge was constructed. The *World Guide to Covered Bridges* lists the date as 1850; most Vermont writings list it as 1824 (however, the historians of the Haverhill-Bath Bridge in New Hampshire, built in 1829, claim that the Haverhill-Bath is the oldest remaining covered bridge in New England). Minor repairs were made to the Halpin Bridge structure in the 1960s, and it received a complete restoration by Jan Lewandoski in 1994 after state bridge inspectors discovered that the abutments were in poor condition. The bridge was completely removed from the original abutments by crane, the original cut, white marble block abutments were replaced with cast concrete, and the bridge was repositioned on its new abutments. While the structure was removed from the abutments, some of the bottom chord and lattice truss members were replaced, as well as the siding and the roof. The bridge, especially when viewed from the riverbed below, is in a spectacular setting, with the waters of the river cascading over the rocky terrain of the Muddy Branch.

Pulp Mill/Paper Mill Bridge

Location: On Pulp Mill Bridge Road between the towns of Middlebury and Weybridge.

Directions: In Middlebury, at the junction of VT 30 and VT 125, go west on VT 125 for 0.1 mile to VT 23 on the right (northwest), turn right onto VT 23, and go 0.7 mile to Pulp Mill Bridge Road on the right; turn right onto Pulp Mill Bridge Road and go 0.4 mile. Pulp Mill Bridge Road bears to the right to cross the bridge.

GPS: 44° 01.489N 073° 10.673W

Year: 1820s   **Truss:** Burr–double barrel   **Waterway:** Otter Creek
In Use: Yes   **Num ber of Spans:** 1+
Owner: Towns of Middlebury and Weybridge   **Builder:** Unknown
Length: 199 ft.   **Width:** 22 ft. 8$\frac{1}{2}$ in.   **Condition:** Good
Number: VT-01-04   **Register:** Sept. 10, 1974

This is the only two-lane, twin portal bridge standing in the state of Vermont that still carries vehicular traffic, and quite a lot of it. We visited the bridge in the middle of a Monday afternoon in the month of April 2003, and there was an almost constant flow of traffic in both directions. Because several key factors were overlooked at the time the bridge was built, it has been under almost constant repair. The original segmented Burr arch trusses on each of the outside truss structures are no longer there. They have been replaced with arches

that reach to the eaves—laminated arches of nine three-by-six-inch planks bolted to the inside of the multiple kingpost trusses. These arches are seated in the abutments on each end. In addition to the side arches there are two center arches, which reach almost to the ridge pole of the span, that consist of ten laminated three-by-six-inch planks anchored to the center multiple kingpost truss. The original 199-foot Burr truss span crossed Otter Creek with no additional support. In 1979 two piers capped with timber cribs were built in the creek, providing additional support at equal thirds of the bridge. In 1991, Jan Lewandoski made additional improvements to the structure. In more recent years, through a grant provided to the Town of Weybridge, an uncovered pedestrian walkway has been added to the span. The bridge acquired its name because of a wood-pulp mill that was built nearby.

Salisbury Station/ Cedar Swamp/Station/ Cornwall-Salisbury/Creek Road Bridge

Location: On Swamp Road between the towns of Cornwall and Salisbury.

Directions: In Whiting, at the junction of Shoreham-Whiting Road and VT 30, go north on VT 30 for 3.5 miles to Swamp Road on the right (east), turn right onto Swamp Road, and go 1.7 miles to the bridge.

GPS: 43° 55.086N 073° 10.452W

Year: 1865   **Truss:** Town   **Waterway:** Otter Creek   **In Use:** Yes
Number of Spans: 1+   **Owner:** Towns of Cornwall and Salisbury
Builder: Unknown   **Length:** 153 ft. $6\frac{1}{4}$ in.   **Width:** 13 ft. $5\frac{1}{2}$ in.
Condition: Fairly good   **Number:** VT-01-01   **Register:** Sept. 10, 1974

This bridge, like many covered bridges, has been known by several names. Since no name is posted on the bridge, we have listed the name that seems to appear most frequently in various publications as the most common name. The edge of Great Cedar Swamp may seem to be a strange location for a covered bridge spanning Otter Creek, but in the 1860s the bridge provided a vital link between Cornwall and the railroad station at Salisbury. The fact that there is also a ford here indicates that this location has been a crossing even before a bridge was built here. One different feature of the Town truss in this bridge is the wide spacing of the lattice members of the truss. Whereas the usual spacing of the lattice members is three feet, the spacing on the Salisbury Station Bridge is four feet ten inches. In 1969, as part of a renovation project, a pier was erected in midstream to provide additional support to the long structure, and in the winter of 1992 Jan Lewandoski, a prominent restorer of covered bridges, did additional work to improve the span. On our visit to the bridge in 2003, we found it to be in fairly good condition.

Shoreham Railroad/East Shoreham Railroad/Rutland Railroad Bridge

Location: 3.4 miles east of the locality of Whiting, within the Whiting town line.

Directions: In Whiting, at the junction of VT 30 (Main St.) and Shoreham-Whiting Road, go west on Shoreham-Whiting Road for 2.8 miles to Shoreham Depot Road on the left (south), turn left onto Shoreham Depot Road, and go 0.6 mile to Dame Road on the left, where a driveway to a parking area is on the right; turn right into the parking area. The bridge is just ahead, down the old track bed.

GPS: 43° 51.611N 073° 15.209W (coordinates recorded at parking area near the bridge)

Year: 1897   **Truss:** Howe   **Waterway:** Lemon Fair River
In Use: Foot traffic only   **Number of Spans:** 1   **Owner:** State
Builder: Rutland Railroad Co.   **Length:** 108 ft. 9¾ in.   **Width:** 13 ft. 7¾ in.
Condition: Fair   **Number:** VT-01-05   **Register:** June 13, 1974

This bridge is one of only two covered railroad bridges still standing in Vermont. Both of them are now preserved by the Vermont Division for Historic Preservation. The other bridge is the Fisher Railroad Bridge, located in Lamoille County. (There had also been a third railroad bridge, but it was moved to Clark's Trading Post in Lincoln, New Hampshire, between 1960 and 1965.) The Shoreham Railroad Bridge was in constant use from the time it was built, 1897, until 1951. In 1983 is was carefully restored with a new roof, new siding, and a new eastern abutment. The railroad tracks were removed and replaced with a

wooden deck of lengthwise planks, laid across the original railroad ties, to provide pedestrian access along the railroad right-of-way trail. The bridge spans the Lemon Fair River, a rather strange name for a river in Vermont. Joseph Nelson, in *Spanning Time—Vermont's Covered Bridges,* explains that it might be "an English contraction of a French phrase describing a sometimes murky stream. The river flows over beds of limestone and through soils containing concentrations of hydrate of magnesium sulphate, or epsom salts."

Spade Farm/Old Hollow Bridge

Location: Just west of US 7, approximately 2 miles north of the locality of Ferrisburg, within the Ferrisburg town line.

Directions: Just north of Vergennes, at the junction of VT 22A and US 7 North, go north on US 7 for 3.9 miles to the bridge on the left (west) side of the highway. It is located just south of the Ferrisburg Artisans Group buildings and north of Starry Nite Café.

GPS: 44° 14.254N 073° 13.913W

Year: 1850   **Truss:** Town   **Waterway:** Entrance to pond
In Use: Foot traffic only   **Number of Spans:** 1
Owner: Ferrisburg Artisan Group   **Builder:** Justin Miller   **Length:** 85 ft. 6 in.
Width: 17 ft. 4½ in.   **Condition:** Fair   **Number:** VT-01-02
Register: Does not qualify

When the original Old Hollow Bridge was destined for dismantling and possible loss forever because of being replaced by a steel and concrete bridge, Sam

Spade, a local dairyman, had it moved to his farm to save it. Because it was then placed on private property and no longer eligible for state or federal aid, the bridge gradually fell into disrepair. However, because of the numerous advertising posters, metal signs, and stenciling on its interior, it was a valuable museum of advertising in a time when things moved much slower.

Ed Barna, in *Covered Bridges of Vermont,* tells the story of a relatively recent owner of the Spade Farm property who related an incident that occurred in 1988 shortly after her family came to the farm. Ed writes: "something started killing their ducks, but they couldn't figure out what it was. Then one day she came out of the house, looked into the bridge, and in the roof bracing saw the culprit: a big cat 'as big as a golden retriever, with a lot of hair on it. The first thing I could grab was a two-by-four, and I went after it. It never came back.'" Ed explains that this might have been a bobcat or lynx that had been sighted several times in a neighboring town. The new owner was advised by her neighbors to "never try that again."

As of 1997, the bridge was sadly in need of repair and was up for sale to anyone "who could afford to repair it." On our visit to the bridge in April 2003, we found that it is now part of the Ferrisburg Artisans Group, who have apparently made considerable repairs to the structure—roof boards, shakes, and rafters have been replaced on the east side of the bridge, and plywood with a variety of artistic designs has been placed on the deck, which was reported to have been in very poor shape previously. Spade Farm Bridge is certainly one that visitors to this part of Addison County should be sure to locate.

BENNINGTON COUNTY

Chiselville/High/Roaring Branch Bridge

Location: On East Arlington Road, northeast of the locality of Arlington–East Arlington, within the Sunderland town line.

Directions: In the Arlington–East Arlington Urban Compact, at the junction of US 7A and East Arlington Road, go east on East Arlington Road for 1.9 miles to the bridge (continue to bear left on the blacktop road).

GPS: 43° 04.317N 073° 08.001W

Year: 1870   **Truss:** Town   **Waterway:** Roaring Branch of the Batten Kill
In Use: Yes   **Number of Spans:** 1+   **Owner:** Town of Sunderland
Builder: Daniel Oatman   **Length:** 116 ft. 7$\frac{1}{2}$ in.   **Width:** 11 ft. 11$\frac{3}{4}$ in.
Condition: Good   **Number:** VT-02-05   **Register:** Does not qualify

Ed Barna, in *Covered Bridges of Vermont*, talks about a local doctor who nearly lost his life in 1779 crossing what was probably Sunderland's log stringer bridge during a spring torrent. In 1841, after a delegation traveled to Philadelphia to look at Timothy Palmer's Permanent Bridge built in 1805, the town decided to replace the stringer bridge with a Town lattice truss covered bridge. Barna tells that the aged doctor was the first to cross the new structure. Unfortunately, because of the location in a deep valley of the Roaring Branch of the Batten Kill, the amount of water carried through the gorge during the spring freshets and sudden downpours threatened any bridge crossing it. On October 4, 1869, a sudden storm sent wreckage-laden floodwater crashing into the bridge, completely destroying it. A local builder, Daniel Oatman, guaranteed the town that he could build a covered crossing over the chasm that would not be affected by floodwater. In 1870 he built a Town lattice truss bridge spanning 117 feet of the gorge that rested on cliffs forty feet above the Roaring Branch riverbed. That bridge, reported to be the second-highest bridge above the waterway of any bridge in Vermont, survived the floodwaters of 1927 that destroyed hundreds of Vermont covered bridges. In 1971 the bridge was severely damaged when two heavy trucks tried to cross at the same time. In 1973, the Agency of Transportation strengthened the bridge by placing concrete piers in the middle of the gorge, which support a huge concrete beam across the center of the bridge, which in turn supports three steel beams that span the entire independent slab roadway. The original, now rehabilitated truss structure built by Oatman supports only the bridge covering itself and any snow that might accumulate thereon. The bridge sides are also stabilized by cables to brace the structure against the strong winds that howl through the gorge. It's worth the descent into the gorge and the climb back up to view the bridge in its extremely high location.

Henry Bridge

Location: On the southern edge of the locality of North Bennington, within the Bennington town line.

Directions: In Bennington, at the junction of US 7A and VT 67A, go northwest on VT 67A for 2.1 miles to River Road on the left (67A turns 90 degrees to the right), turn left onto River Road (it become Harrington Road), and go 0.5 mile to the bridge on the left; turn left to cross the bridge.

GPS: 42° 54.761N 073° 15.276W

Year: ca. 1840, rebuilt ca. 1990   **Truss:** Town   **Waterway:** Walloomsac River
In Use: Yes   **Number of Spans:** 1   **Owner:** Town of Bennington
Builder: Blow and Cote, Inc. (restoration)   **Length:** 120 ft. 8 in.
Width: 14 ft. 9½ in.   **Condition:** Good   **Number:** VT-02-02 (2)
Register: Aug. 28, 1973

There are three covered bridges very close to the Bennington urban area that span the Walloomsac River, and they lie within two miles of each other. The most distant from the urban center is the Henry Bridge. The closest to the center is the Silk Bridge, and the one in between is the Paper Mill Bridge. The original bridge built at this crossing of the Walloomsac River around 1840 was named for the Henry family, who owned fifty acres nearby. Elnathan Henry, an Irish immigrant, purchased the land from the original owner, James Breckenridge. Elnathan built the Henry House, which was operated as a store and tavern by a later Irish immigrant, William Henry. Other members of the Henry family operated a gristmill just southeast of the bridge. In the 1860s iron ore was discovered nearby. The Burden Iron Company of Troy, New York, which

began operations in this area, added additional lattice planks to the Town truss structure as well as additional decking to support the ore-laden wagons that crossed the bridge. When repairs were necessitated in 1952, it was discovered that the extra lattice timbers and additional decking really were not necessary. All they did was add extra dead load to the bridge. Consequently, most of the extra material was removed. By 1989, extensive repairs were needed. A contract for $223,617 was awarded to Blow and Cote, Inc., Morrisville, Vermont, to make the needed repairs. In the process, it was discovered that many of the timbers were bent, and the contractor asked if they could go a step further. Somehow the Division for Historic Preservation was bypassed, and the bridge was replaced with all new material using southern pine with ash trunnels whereas the original bridge was Vermont spruce and oak. According to Barna, "the old timbers were saved, but at last report they were sitting uncovered in a town pile, still awaiting creative reuse."

Kreffer's Crossing Bridge

Location: On Sandgate Road, in the locality of Sandgate, within the Sandgate town line.

Directions: In West Arlington, at the junction of VT 313 and Sandgate Road, go north on Sandgate Road for 2.5 miles to the covered bridge on the right (east) side of the road.

GPS: 43° 08.350N 073° 12.230W

Year: 1977   **Truss:** Stringer with Town   **Waterway:** Green River
In Use: Yes, private   **Number of Spans:** 1   **Owner:** Private, Kreffer family
Builder: Unknown   **Length:** 39 ft. 2$\frac{1}{2}$ in.   **Width:** 13 ft. 4$\frac{1}{2}$ in.
Condition: Fairly good   **Number:** VT-02-A   **Register:** Does not qualify

This is one of the bridges documented in this guide that is not an authentic covered bridge. We have included it because it is documented in some of the Vermont tourist information about covered bridges and in the DeLorme *Vermont Atlas & Gazetteer*. Travelers in the vicinity of the West Arlington Bridge will find the Kreffer's Crossing Bridge just a few miles away. The first crossing in this location was built for Mr. Kreffer as an uncovered stringer in 1975. However, in conversation with some of his neighbors along the Green River, Mr. Kreffer was advised to cover his crossing in order to preserve its longevity. In 1977, with the addition of a Town lattice truss covering, Kreffer's Crossing became a covered bridge. Mr. Kreffer relates that the rough edges along the bottom of the upstream side of the bridge were created during a recent winter freeze when the entire river froze up to the level of the bottom stringers of the bridge. Fearing that the spring thaw might possibly carry his bridge away with the ice pack, Mr. Kreffer kept his fingers crossed. Early one Sunday morning

when he approached the bridge he discovered that in the overnight hours the entire ice pack had broken free, leaving his bridge completely unharmed except for the bottom edges of the upstream side boards. He had survived another hard winter freeze. The bridge is very easy to locate if you are traveling along Sandgate Road between West Arlington and Sandgate.

Paper Mill Bridge

Location: Just southeast of the locality of North Bennington, within the Bennington town line.

Directions: In Bennington, at the junction of US 7A and VT 67A, go northwest on VT 67A for 1.4 miles to an unnamed road on the left; turn left to cross the bridge.

GPS: 42° 54.772N 073° 13.998W

Year: 1889, rebuilt 2000   **Truss:** Town   **Waterway:** Walloomsac River
In Use: Yes   **Number of Spans:** 1   **Owner:** Town of Bennington
Builder: Charles F. Sears   **Length:** 125 ft. 9 in.   **Width:** 14 ft. $5\frac{1}{2}$ in.
Condition: Excellent, new   **Number:** VT-02-03 (2)
Register: Does not qualify

The original Paper Mill Bridge, built in 1889 on this site, very closely resembled the Silk Bridge located just a short distance away. According to the Vermont Division of Historic Sites, the Paper Mill Bridge was built by Charles F. Sears, son of Benjamin Sears, who built the Silk Bridge. The Paper Mill Bridge was named for a paper mill adjacent to the bridge that dates back to the 1790s. The

location of the dam adjacent to the mill used to be called Bennington Falls, hence one of the former names of this area. Paper Mill, like the other two Bennington area bridges, had extensive repairs made in 1952. By 1994 an inspection by the state discovered that the bridge was once again in need of extensive repairs. Much of the damage had occurred because of a leaky roof. (Youngsters had removed a number of the roof boards to achieve easy access to the roof area, from which they dove into the deep waters of the Walloomsac River.) In 1998 the bridge was scheduled for a $300,000 reconstruction. The work was done by Blow and Cote, Inc., the same construction company that reconstructed the Henry Bridge. By July 13, 2000, the work was completed and the bridge was rededicated.

Silk/Silk Road/Locust Grove/ Robinson Bridge

Location: Just southeast of the locality of North Bennington, within the Bennington town line.

Directions: In Bennington, at the junction of US 7A and VT 67A, go northwest on VT 67A for 1.1 miles to Silk Road on the left (south), turn left onto Silk Road, and go 0.2 mile to the bridge.

GPS: 42° 54.571N 073° 13.517W

Year: ca. 1840, rebuilt 1991   **Truss:** Town   **Waterway:** Walloomsac River
In Use: Yes   **Number of Spans:** 1   **Owner:** Town of Bennington

Builder: Benjamin Sears   **Length:** 88 ft. $3\frac{1}{2}$ in.   **Width:** 15 ft.
Condition: Good   **Number:** VT-02-04 (2)   **Register:** Aug. 28, 1973

According to all records that we have been able to find, the Silk Bridge was built around 1840 by Benjamin Sears, the father of Charles Sears, builder of the Paper Mill Bridge. The original name of the bridge, according to the Bennington Museum director, was Robinson Bridge. The present name of the bridge and the road on which it is located has nothing to do with a silk mill or silk manufacturing; it is simply connected to residents by the name of Silk who lived nearby. This bridge, like the other two bridges close by, Paper Mill and Henry, had extensive repairs made to it in 1952. Additional work was done on the bridge in 1991. The contractor was Wright Construction, Inc., with designer and resident engineer Gilbert Newbury overseeing the rehabilitation project. The major focus was on the repair and replacement of decayed and damaged material. Roof boards were replaced as needed, the old wood shingles were replaced with new cedar shakes, missing collar ties were added to the roof rafters, and members of the Town lattice truce and upper and lower chord members were replaced with similar material where possible. New structural material was mostly southern yellow pine with some Douglas fir. The new trunnels were all white oak. The approximate cost of the project was $115,000.

West Arlington/Arlington/ Bridge-at-the-Green Bridge

Location: In the locality of West Arlington, within the Arlington town line.

Directions: In Arlington, at the junction of US 7A North and VT 313 West, go west on VT 313 for 4.2 miles; the bridge is just to the left (south).

GPS: 43° 06.253N 073° 13.220W

Year: 1852 **Truss:** Town **Waterway:** Batten Kill **In Use:** Yes
Number of Spans: 1 **Owner:** Town of Arlington **Builder:** Unknown
Length: 84 ft. $\frac{1}{2}$ in. **Width:** 14 ft. 1 in. **Condition:** Very good
Number: VT-02-01 **Register:** Aug. 28, 1973

According to several references, the West Arlington Bridge is one of the most photographed covered bridges in Vermont. Several factors may have something to do with this claim. First, the bridge is easily accessed. It is located just south of a fairly heavily traveled highway between the Arlington area of Vermont and the Cambridge/Greenwich area of New York—Vermont 313. It is also quite easy to photograph from almost any angle because of the open space around it. It spans a world-renowned trout stream, the Batten Kill, and it is located near one of Vermont's listed "favorite swimming holes," also in the Batten Kill. Our photo shows cables that have been attached to the upper side of the bridge close to the end. There is one on each upper corner. The main purpose of these cables is to stabilize the bridge and prevent it from being toppled into the river. It is reported that very strong winds whip through the Batten Kill Valley. There's a story of the bridge having been blown off its abut-

ments shortly after it was built and lying on its side in the river until it could be replaced. Persons needing to cross the stream continued to do so by walking or driving on the upturned side—a testimony to the strength of the truss structure.

Chamberlin/Chamberlin Mill/Sawmill/ Witcomb Bridge

Location: In the locality of Lyndon, within the Lyndon town line.

Directions: In Lyndon, at the junction of US 5 and the I-91 North exit 23 ramp, go south on US 5 for 0.3 mile to York St. on the right (west), turn right onto York St., and go 0.3 mile to the road on the right (unmarked at this end, Chamberlin Bridge Road at the junction with South Wheelock Road at the north end of the bridge); the bridge is just to the right (north).

GPS: 44° 30.978N 072° 00.996W

Year: 1881   **Truss:** Queenpost
Waterway: South Wheelock Branch of Passumpsic River   **In Use:** Yes
Number of Spans: 1   **Owner:** Town of Lyndon
Builder: Covered by W. W. Heath   **Length:** 69 ft.   **Width:** 16 ft. 6 in.
Condition: Good   **Number:** VT-03-04   **Register:** July 30, 1974

The date of 1881, given as the date of origin for this bridge, is based on a news item that was printed in the *Vermont Union* in August 1881: "The Chamberlin Bridge at the west of this village is having a new abutment and is to be built as a covered bridge." Until that time, there had been several bridges at this location, but presumably none of them covered. A map dating back to 1795 shows a bridge over the South Wheelock Branch of the Passumpsic River at this location.

It is always interesting to try to determine how some of the covered bridges have acquired so many names, some of them quite different. In the case of the Chamberlin Bridge, the names are relatively easy to trace. In 1817, Ephraim Chamberlin built a gristmill nearby, hence the name Chamberlin and/or Chamberlin Mill. A little later, he added a sawmill, which accounts for the third name—Sawmill. In 1818, Anson Miller built a wagon and sleigh works at the north end of the existing crossing. In 1840, Ephraim's son, Myron, built a new gristmill in the same area. By this time, in addition to the businesses operated by the Chamberlins and the Millers, there were a carding mill, a fulling mill, a bark mill, a saddler's shop, and an oil mill, all sharing the waterpower provided by the Wheelock Branch. The mill started by the Chamberlins changed hands a number of times through the years, but each time it retained the name of the first owners until it was purchased in 1905 by Harold Witcomb. This name change led to the last name of the bridge, Witcomb. However, when Whitcomb sold out in 1937, both the mill name and the bridge name changed back to Chamberlin.

Greenbanks Hollow/Greenbank Hollow Bridge

Location: 2.7 miles south of the locality of Danville, within the Danville town line.

Directions: In Danville, at the junction of US 2 with an unmarked road to the north, Peacham Road, and Brainerd St. to the south, go south on Brainerd St. for 0.8 mile to a junction with Joes Brook Road and Greenbank Hollow Rd 2; go straight on Greenbank Hollow Rd 2 for 1.9 miles to the bridge.

GPS: 44° 22.662N 072° 07.315W

Year: 1886, rebuilt 2000s   **Truss:** Queenpost   **Waterway:** Joe's Brook
In Use: Yes   **Number of Spans:** 1   **Owner:** Town of Danville
Builder: Unknown   **Length:** 74 ft. 9$\frac{1}{2}$ in.   **Width:** 14 ft. 6$\frac{1}{2}$ in.
Condition: Excellent   **Number:** VT-03-01 (2)   **Register:** June 13, 1974

Records show that the first bridge built at this site dates back to the early 1800s, but like many other bridges built during those early years of our country's development, it was left uncovered. Historians tell us that a Benjamin Green-

banks came to this area from England in 1840. At that time England was one of the leading producers of woolen cloth. Greenbanks established a large, five-story woolen mill near the bridge that crossed Joe's Brook. At its height of operation, the mill employed forty-five men, women, and children. Unfortunately, a fire in 1885 destroyed the mill, a store, several farms, and the nearby bridge, which by this time was covered. The mill was never rebuilt, but the bridge that stood in this location was the successor to the one destroyed in the fire.

By the 1970s the bridge needed improvements in order to accommodate the vehicular use of the time. In renovations that took place, a pier was built in the middle of Joe's Brook, and two steel beams were tie-bolted to the bottom chords. In 1994, as part of a statewide study of town-owned covered bridges, the inspectors recommended that Danville build a bypass bridge or replace the covered bridge entirely and move it to a nearby preservation site. A bridge replacement was estimated to cost $315,000. Instead, the town applied for funds through the National Historic Covered Bridge Preservation Program and in 2000 received a $300,000 grant. Grants from this source provide 80 percent of the funding necessary for historic bridge restoration.

When we visited the bridge in January 2003, we found it beautifully restored. The pier in the middle of the brook and the steel beams supporting the deck had been removed. The abutments had been refurbished, the truss structure was completely rebuilt, and the bridge had a new deck, roof, and siding. Another historic covered bridge had been saved through the diligent efforts of townspeople and funding made available through the Transportation Equity Act for the Twenty-first Century.

Miller's Run/Bradley Bridge

Location: 0.5 mile west of the locality of Lyndon Center, within the Lyndon town line.

Directions: In Lyndon Center, at the junction of US 5 and VT 122 (Stevens Loop TH3), go west on VT 122 for 0.5 mile to Center St. on the left (south), turn left onto Center St., and go 0.05 mile to the bridge.

GPS: 44° 32.516N 072° 00.597W

Year: 1878   **Truss:** Queenpost   **Waterway:** Passumpsic River   **In Use:** Yes
Number of Spans: 1   **Owner:** Town of Lyndon   **Builder:** E. H. Stone
Length: 59 ft. 5 in.   **Width:** 15 ft. 9 in.   **Condition:** Very good
Number: VT-03-06   **Register:** June 13, 1977

A brief news article in the *Vermont Union* announced the first covered bridge to appear on this site in an August 1878 issue: "The Selectmen have completed a new covered bridge over Miller's Run." Town records indicate that there was at least one other, uncovered span in this location as early as 1800, when a special tax was levied to build a bridge. The present bridge is the result of a restoration project in 1995. At that time it was completely disassembled and rebuilt with a modern steel structure to support the live load. The roadway of the restored span is a little wider than the original, and a pedestrian walkway has been added. The original queenpost truss has been refurbished, but at this point it supports only the siding and the roof. It no longer serves the major function of a truss—that of carrying both the live load and the dead load of the bridge. The bridge now has a covering of white, vertical boards on both the

sides and the portals, has a deck of lengthwise planks laid over the modern steel substructure, and has a roof of green, standing-rib sheet metal.

The bridge has always carried a considerable amount of traffic. On our visit to the site in January 2003, we made a notation that "traffic on the bridge was *very* heavy, not just moderate." However, the bridge is a modern reconstruction that remains as true to the original as possible in appearance while still being able to accommodate contemporary travel.

Randall/Sawmill/Burrington/ Old Burrington Bridge

Location: 1.8 miles east-northeast of the locality of Lyndon Center, within the Lyndon town line.

Directions: In Lyndon Center, at the junction of US 5 and VT 114, go north on VT 114 for 1.7 miles to Burrington Bridge Road on the right (south); turn right to the bypassed bridge.

GPS: 44° 33.203N 071° 58.161W

Year: 1865   **Truss:** Queenpost   **Waterway:** East Branch of Passumpsic River
In Use: Foot and snowmobile   **Number of Spans:** 1   **Owner:** Town of Lyndon
Builder: Unknown   **Length:** 71 ft.   **Width:** 13 ft. 1 in.   **Condition:** Fair
Number: VT-03-07   **Register:** June 13, 1974

In 1965, the Randall Covered Bridge, built in 1865, was bypassed when Burrington Bridge Road was rerouted over a new concrete and steel bridge. The only reference available regarding restoration work on the old bridge is a news item published in the spring 2001 issue of *The Bridger,* the newsletter of the Vermont Covered Bridge Society, which announced that the Lyndon Historical Society had mounted a $50,000 drive for the restoration of four historic landmarks, among them the Randall Covered Bridge. The article went on to say: "The bridge is critically in need of abutment work as well as roof alignment and roof restoration. The amount needed for the restoration is $15,000."

On our visit to the bridge in January 2003, it appeared to be in fairly good condition, indicating that some of the restoration work may have been accomplished. The structure looked a bit better than earlier photos we had seen of it. The portal gables, which earlier documentation described as "stained brown," looked like new vertical boards that were now stained barn red. Since the roof area was completely snow covered, it was not possible to determine if any of the roof alignment work had been accomplished. An active snowmobile trail was using the bridge as a regular crossing and, of course, it is open to foot traffic.

Sanborn/Centre Bridge

Location: Just north of the locality of Lyndonville, within the Lyndon town line.

Directions: In Lyndon Center, just south of the junction of US 5 and VT 114, on the west side of US 5, the bridge is on the property of the Lynburke Motel, south of the motel buildings.

GPS: 44° 32.633N 072° 00.047W (coordinates recorded on parking lot close to the bridge)

Year: ca. 1867   **Truss:** Paddleford   **Waterway:** Passumpsic River
In Use: Storage and foot traffic   **Number of Spans:** 1   **Owner:** Private
Builder: Unknown   **Length:** 118 ft. 9 in.   **Width:** 18 ft. $4\frac{3}{4}$ in.
Condition: Fair   **Number:** VT-03-05   **Register:** June 20, 1974

This bridge has a feature that is common to all the Lyndon area bridges. The roof has quite wide, overhanging eaves that help to protect the sides, which are generally open for at least one-half of the upper portion, and it has gable ends that are extended on corbels. The exact date the original bridge was built is not certain. However, all the documented dates are around the late 1860s or early 1870s. A sign posted on a gable end at one time indicated 1867, the pamphlet *Vermont's Covered Bridges* lists the year as 1869, and noted bridge builder and restorer Milton Graton dates the origin as 1873.

The location of the bridge, when it was first built, was in a meadow area on the farm of Benjamin Sanborn, where a road was built to connect Lyndon

Center with the farms on the west side of the Passumpsic River. According to Arthur and Jeanne Elliott, present owners of Lyneburke Motel, in 1960, when the bridge was to be torn down, Armand Morin, then owner of the motel, and Herbert Gallagher had the bridge moved to the motel grounds, where it now spans the East Branch of the Passumpsic River. In his book *Spanning Time— Vermont's Covered Bridges,* Joseph Nelson credits Milton Graton with the actual moving of the bridge. There are accounts of various businesses occupying a small officelike structure that has been built inside the bridge in its present location.

The owners welcome visitors who come to see and photograph the bridge. Always be careful when visiting any covered bridge, especially those on private property. Treat the property as if it were your own highly prized possession.

School House/Schoolhouse/ Chase Bridge

Location: In the locality of Lyndon, within the Lyndon town line.

Directions: In Lyndon, at the junction of US 5 and the I-91 North exit 23 ramp, go south on US 5 for 0.1 mile to South Wheelock Road, turn right (west) onto South Wheelock Road, and go 0.1 mile to the bridge parking area on the left (south) side of the road.

GPS: 44° 30.966N 072° 00.598W (coordinates recorded on parking lot close to the bridge)

Year: 1879 **Truss:** Queenpost
Waterway: South Wheelock Branch of Passumpsic River
In Use: Foot traffic only **Number of Spans:** 1 **Owner:** Town of Lyndon
Builder: J. C. Jones, Lee Goodall, and John Clement **Length:** 45 ft. 2 in.
Width: 16 ft. 5 in. **Condition:** Good **Number:** VT-03-03
Register: Mar. 31, 1971

A profile of the School House Bridge that is prominently displayed inside the bridge by the Lyndon Area Chamber of Commerce indicates that the plans for the bridge were drawn by J. C. Jones, the framing was done by Lee Goodall, and the abutments were made by John Clement. Other documentation credits John Clement for having laid the foundations of twenty-nine other Lyndon bridges. The Chamber's profile continues by saying:

> The School House bridge was designed to be light and graceful, suggesting a bird poised to take wing. The builder wanted to protect the structure from the effect of weather, and so spread the eaves much wider than usual and also carried the gable out on tall sloping brackets.
>
> It is perhaps the only bridge remaining in the state to have the trusses boarded on both sides (possibly to keep the school children from climbing the rafters).
>
> The first bridge at this crossing was built to service the new brick Lyndon Academy and Graded School in 1871–72 and was uncovered.

By 1879 the present bridge had been designed and built. Originally, it was built with walkways on both sides of the bridge, possibly to accommodate the children on the way to and from the school. Today only the north walkway remains. In 1971, when Interstate 91 was built, the road that passed over the bridge was relocated, bypassing the covered bridge. An acre of land was donated by a local business, creating a green around the bridge where it is being maintained. The profile posted by the Chamber of Commerce also credits the doctors and staff of the medical clinic presently using the old schoolhouse with maintaining the bridge as a service to the community.

CHITTENDON COUNTY

Lake Shore/Holmes Creek/ Holmes Bridge

Location: 3.1 miles northwest of the locality of Charlotte, within the Charlotte town line.

Directions: Just east of Charlotte, at the junction of US 7and Church Hill Road on the east and VT F5 on the west, go west on VT F5 for 1.3 miles to the junction with Lake Road, turn right (north) onto Lake Road, and go 1.8 miles to the bridge.

GPS: 44° 19.979N 073° 16.942W

Year: 1898   **Truss:** Tied arch with kingpost   **Waterway:** Holmes Creek
In Use: Yes   **Number of Spans:** 1   **Owner:** Town of Charlotte
Builder: Leonard Sherman   **Length:** 40 ft. 1 in.   **Width:** 12 ft. 1 in.
Condition: Good   **Number:** VT-04-01   **Register:** Sept. 6, 1974

This covered bridge is located at the lowest elevation of any covered bridge in Vermont. It is just a few feet from the banks of Lake Champlain, where it spans the Holmes Creek. It is also one of only three tied arch truss bridges that are still standing in the state. The other two are the Best Bridge and the Bowers Bridge, both located in Windsor County. The Lake Shore Bridge, however, differs from the other two tied arch bridges because of the use of the arch in conjunction with a kingpost truss, almost in the same way that the Burr arch has been used in conjunction with the multiple kingpost truss. However, in this bridge there is only one arch anchored to the kingpost truss members on each side of the bridge. In 1993, an inspection done by the Vermont Agency of Transportation found that the superstructure of the bridge was in trouble under normal traffic loading. Also in 1993, the entire structure was rehabilitated by Milton Graton Associates with additional work done in 1994 by Paul Ide and Jan Lewandoski. Because of repeated damage caused by overweight vehicles, the Agency of Transportation has recommended the construction of a permanent bypass bridge next to the covered bridge. On our visit to the bridge in April 2003, we found that it is still in use and from outward appearances seems to be in good shape. It is obviously being maintained—some of the vertical boards on the portals are new, and it has a relatively new, black, standing-seam metal roof, which might have been installed in conjunction with the repairs of 1993–94 or as part of the reroofing of thirty-eight Vermont bridges as the result of $461,600 granted to the state in 2001 by the National Historic Covered Bridge Preservation Program.

Quinlan/Lower/Sherman Bridge

Location: Approximately 3 miles east of US 7 within the extreme southern part of the Charlotte town line.

Directions: From the Spade Farm Covered Bridge, north of Ferrisburg, go north on US 7 for 1.4 miles to Old Hollow Road on the right (east), turn right onto Old Hollow Road, go 0.4 mile to Philo Road on the left (north), turn left onto Philo Road, go 0.5 mile to Spear St. on the right (northeast), turn right onto Spear St., go 1.9 mile to Mountain Road on the right, and turn right to go through the bridge.

GPS: 44° 16.584N 073° 11.039W

Year: 1849   **Truss:** Burr   **Waterway:** Lewis Creek   **In Use:** Yes
Number of Spans: 1   **Owner:** Town of Charlotte   **Builder:** Unknown
Length: 88 ft. 1 in.   **Width:** 13 ft. $10\frac{1}{4}$ in.   **Condition:** Fair
Number: VT-04-03   **Register:** Sept. 10, 1974

Although the builders of this bridge and a neighboring bridge, Sequin, located over the same waterway and within the Charlotte town line, are unknown, it is

likely that both bridges were built by the same person or persons. The website "Vermontbridges Dot Com Covered Bridge Directory," prepared by Joseph Nelson, states that "Gilbert Newbury, a structural engineer trained in timber bridges, points out that very sophisticated and intricate construction details make these two the best built wooden bridges in the state. Intricate 'keys,' especially visible in the Seguin Bridge, are used in the tension connections in the bottom chords. The elaborate roof framing systems include 'birds-mouth' notches in the rafters and beams." The common name of this bridge is derived

The Burr truss system of the Quinlan Bridge.

from the Quinlans, a family that at one time had extensive farm property in this area. The second name, Lower, is derived from the bridge's position over Lewis Creek in relation to its neighboring bridge. And the third name is acquired from Sherman's sawmill, which was located next to the bridge at the time the bridge was constructed. The live load capacity of the bridge was increased in 1949 or 1950 with the addition of two steel beams under the deck. The original stone abutments may have been capped and faced with concrete at the same time. Even though the bridge was missing a few siding boards on our visit in April 2003, we found that otherwise it appeared to be in fair condition. The interior photo depicts the Burr truss as it was used in the Quinlan Bridge.

Sequin/Seguin/Upper/Brown's Bridge

Location: Approximately 2.8 miles east-northeast of Quinlan Bridge, at the southeast boundary of Charlotte-Hinesburg town line, within the Charlotte town line.

Directions: From the Quinlan Covered Bridge (see previous bridge), go through the bridge from Spear St. to the junction on the south side with Mountain Road and Lewis Creek Road, turn left (east) onto Lewis Creek Road, go 1.6 miles to a T with Roscoe Road, turn left onto Roscoe Road, and go 1.2 miles to the bridge.

GPS: 44° 17.333N 073° 09.010W

Year: 1849 **Truss:** Burr **Waterway:** Lewis Creek **In Use:** Yes
Number of Spans: 1 **Owner:** Town of Charlotte **Builder:** Unknown
Length: 70 ft. 5 in. **Width:** 13 ft. $3\frac{1}{2}$ in. **Condition:** Good
Number: VT-04-02 **Register:** Sept. 6, 1974

This bridge is the "upper" neighbor of the Quinlan Bridge discussed earlier in the Chittenden County section. Extensive repairs made to the span in 1949 did nothing to change it from the original builder's plan. Additional authentic repairs were made in the fall of 1994 by Paul Ide and Jan Lewandoski. At that time portions of the bottom chords and some of the vertical timbers of the multiple kingpost portion of the Burr truss system required replacements. The photo provides a good view through the bridge of the Burr truss system. The bridge presently rests on one abutment of stone and mortar capped with concrete and one of poured concrete. The sides and portals are covered with random-width, vertical board siding. Much of the siding on the downstream side of the bridge appears to be new. The bridge also has a new standing seam black metal roof, possibly as a result of the overall reroofing program of thirty-eight Vermont bridges in 2001. This was made possible by a grant of $461,600 through the National Historic Covered Bridge Preservation Program. The bridge appeared to be in good condition when we saw it in April 2003.

Shelburne Museum/Museum/ Cambridge Bridge

Location: In the locality of Shelburne on the Shelburne Museum property, within the Shelburne town line.

Directions: In Shelburne, at the junction of US 7 and Harbor Road on the west and Falls Road on the east, go south on US 7 for 0.2 mile to the bridge on the west side of the highway. To see the bridge from the inside of the museum grounds, the entrance to the parking area for the museum is 0.25 mile to the south along US 7.

GPS: 44° 22.610N 073° 13.749W

Year: 1845 **Truss:** Burr–double barrel **Waterway:** Burr Pond
In Use: For museum visitors **Number of Spans:** 1
Owner: Shelburne Museum **Builder:** Fairwell Weatherby
Length: 164 ft. $6\frac{1}{2}$ in. **Width:** 12 ft. $9\frac{1}{2}$ in. each side **Condition:** Fairly good
Number: VT-04-06 **Register:** Does not qualify

The original location of this bridge was in the town of Cambridge, forty-five miles north of its present location. In 1949, when the state replaced the two-lane or "double barrel" bridge with a modern span, Mrs. J. Watson Webb re-

quested that the state donate the structure to the Shelburne Museum. Since the museum had been successful in moving a number of historical structures to its grounds, the state was quite willing to donate the bridge if the museum took care of the moving. The moving project was under the careful eye of R. V. Milbank, professor of civil engineering at the University of Vermont, and W. B. Hill and Company of Tilton, New Hampshire, who helped the museum staff disassemble the bridge, move it by truck, and reassemble it on the museum grounds. Now only one thing was missing. The bridge was on dry land. Consequently, the museum dug a pond over which the bridge now stands to make the restoration complete. The pond was named Burr Pond, possibly in honor of Theodore Burr, the creator of the Burr arch truss. For a number of years the bridge provided the main entrance to the museum grounds. However, when the continual usage of the bridge for vehicular traffic proved to be too taxing for the span, the museum's main entrance was moved approximately one-quarter of a mile south along US 7, and the bridge was retired from "active duty."

Westford / Brown's River / Brown's Bridge

Location: In the locality of Westford, just north of Cambridge Road, within the Westford town line.

Directions: In Essex Center, at the junction of VT 15 and VT 128, go north on VT 128 for 8.2 miles to Cambridge Road in Westford; turn right (northeast) onto Cambridge Road to the bypassed bridge on the north side of the road.

GPS: 44° 36.748N 073° 00.500W

Year: 1838, rebuilt 2001   **Truss:** Burr   **Waterway:** Browns River
In Use: Foot traffic only   **Number of Spans:** 1   **Owner:** Town of Westford
Builder: Unknown   Length: 96 ft. 6 in.   **Width:** 13 ft. 6½ in.
Condition: Excellent   **Number:** VT-04-05   **Register:** Does not qualify

In 1836, voters in the Town of Westford resolved to build a single bridge over Browns River not to exceed a cost of $600. By 1838 the Burr truss bridge was completed. It served the Westford area well for 127 years until it was bypassed by a modern bridge, part of which can be seen in the photo. The covered bridge stood, nearly abandoned, until 1976, when a group of local townspeople and a reserve Seabee battalion from Burlington repaired it for the national bicentennial celebration. The repairs, however, did not take care of the wooden arches, which were sagging noticeably, and the bridge was closed even to foot traffic in 1987. At that time the Westford Historical Society was formed and a campaign was started to raise funds to restore the bridge. Graton Associates of Ashland, New Hampshire, was the firm contracted to take care of the restoration. In Graton's usual, outstanding fashion the work began. The bridge was raised on timber cribbing, false work was built beneath it, and a team of oxen pulled the bridge off the river on log rollers. The event was of such importance that the National Geographic Society filmed the entire operation as part of a documentary on the life of Milton Graton, legendary covered bridge restorer. The bridge was moved to the town garage property, where Graton's team set out to restore the span. Finally, by September 21, 2001, the town, through its own efforts—community fairs, ham suppers, and grants—had raised $50,000; the Vermont Agency of Transportation had provided $35,000 through the Federal

Intermodal Surface Transportation Enhancement Act; and the Westford Bridge had been placed back on its abutments across Browns River and rededicated. A plaque to be placed on the bridge reads: "In grateful recognition to Caroline Brown for her determination and tireless efforts from 1987 to 2001 in the rehabilitation of the Brown's River Covered Bridge. From her friends in the Covered Bridge Community."

Comstock Bridge

Location: On the western edge of the locality of Montgomery, within the Montgomery town line.

Directions: In Montgomery Center, at the junction of VT 118 and VT 242, go north on VT 118 through Montgomery for 2.7 miles to Comstock Bridge Road on the left (south), turn left onto Comstock Bridge Road, and go 0.1 mile to the bridge.

GPS: 44° 53.979N 072° 38.687W

Year: 1883   **Truss:** Town   **Waterway:** Trout River   **In Use:** Yes
Number of Spans: 1   **Owner:** Town of Montgomery
Builder: Sheldon and Savannah Jewett   **Length:** 68 ft. $10\frac{1}{2}$ in.
Width: 16 ft. $1\frac{1}{4}$ in.   **Condition:** Appears good, scheduled for restoration
Number: VT-06-04   **Register:** Nov. 19, 1974

The Town lattice truss system of the Comstock Bridge.

When we visited the Comstock Bridge in April 2003, we felt that it was in good condition. However, while we were measuring and documenting the bridge, a local Montgomery resident happened to walk by and informed us that "it's good that we visited the bridge now, because later this year it's to be disassembled and restored." The bridge is a lovely Town lattice plank bridge built by the Jewett brothers in 1883 (see the interior photo). It is one of the seven bridges constructed by Sheldon and Savannah Jewett between 1863 and 1890. When erected, it was near the mill of John Comstock, a millwright, grain dealer, and manufacturer of carriages and sleighs. As we saw it in 2003, the bridge had natural, unpainted, vertical board siding, some of it recently replaced; white, random-width, vertical board portals; a standing-seam sheet metal roof; and a deck of lengthwise planks installed on edge. There is a long, narrow, window-like opening on the downstream side of the bridge, primarily to provide a view of the approaching traffic along the bend in the streamside road. This opening is quite noticeable in the photo. The entire structure rests on abutments of stone and concrete on the north end and concrete on the south end. The abutments are extended to road-level wingwalls of similar material on each end. It will be interesting to return to this bridge after it is rebuilt. A grant of $576,000 has been awarded through the National Historic Covered Bridge Preservation Program to help fund the rebuilding project.

Creamery/West Hill/Crystal Springs Bridge

Location: Approximately 2.7 miles south-southwest of the locality of Montgomery, within the Montgomery town line.

Directions: In Montgomery Center, at the junction of VT 118 and VT 242, go north on VT 118 through Montgomery for 2.8 miles to Hill West Road on the southwest (left); go left on Hill West Road for 2.5 miles to an unmarked, very rough road on the right (west). It is suggested that one walk to the right (west) for the remaining approximately 0.2 mile to the bridge.

GPS: 44° 52.084N 072° 38.693W (coordinates recorded at beginning of the rough road to the bridge)

Year: 1883   **Truss:** Town   **Waterway:** West Hill Brook
In Use: Foot traffic only, with extreme caution   **Number of Spans:** 1
Owner: Town of Montgomery   **Builder:** Sheldon and Savannah Jewett
Length: 58 ft. 9 in.   **Width:** 16 ft. 6 in.
Condition: Closed, for structural defects   **Number:** VT-06-09
Register: Dec. 31, 1974

At the time this bridge was built, again by the Jewett brothers, this area was quite prosperous. In addition to the Jewett family farm and lumber mill along the West Hill Brook, there were forty-nine active farms. There was a creamery just east of the bridge, hence the bridge's name, and a furniture factory in the lower part of the West Hill Brook gorge. Today, the bridge, as well as the access

road to it, stands nearly abandoned. We say "nearly" because, although the majority of the bridge structure is in very poor condition, it sports a brand-new, shiny, green, standing-seam sheet metal roof. Today, this is probably the one thing that will preserve the otherwise decaying structure. Mother Nature is reclaiming the access road, which, even for a four-wheel drive vehicle, is rather rough; trees and wild growth are rapidly closing in on the once busy, narrow road. The bridge itself is missing many siding boards and has a deck that had gradually deteriorated before the new roof was installed. Hopefully, there will be an effort to save this bridge, but we are not aware of any movements at the time of this writing.

East Fairfield Bridge

Location: In the locality of East Fairfield, within the Fairfield town line.

Directions: In Bakersfield, at the junction of VT 108 and VT 36, go west on VT 36 for 3.15 miles to Bridge St. in East Fairfield; turn left (south) to the bridge.

GPS: 44° 47.183N 072° 51.721W

Year: 1865   **Truss:** Queenpost   **Waterway:** Black Creek
In Use: Foot traffic only   **Number of Spans:** 1   **Owner:** Town of Fairfield
Builder: Unknown   **Length:** 66 ft. $9\frac{1}{2}$ in.   **Width:** 12 ft. $8\frac{1}{4}$ in.
Condition: Very poor   **Number:** VT-06-03   **Register:** Nov. 19, 1974

The East Fairfield Bridge is located in an area that at one time was the center of considerable small-town industrial activity. The bridge spans a millpond created along the Black Creek that provided power to a gristmill. Some of the mill foundation can still be seen south of the bridge. Remnants of a sawmill are visible on the upstream side of the span. Closer to Bakersfield there was a factory that made tubs—butter, sugar, and watering troughs—and a fulling mill, a tannery, and a brickyard. Today, the bridge stands isolated without a trace of these enterprises. The Town of East Fairfield has tried to maintain the bridge. Repairs were made early in the 1940s, it was reconstructed in 1967, and in the winter of 1973–74, while the millpond was frozen, several of the town selectmen made additional repairs. Finally, in 1987, it was necessary to close the bridge to all traffic. Its condition declined quickly. Repair to the deck early in the 1990s made the bridge usable for pedestrian traffic only. After a study by the Vermont Agency of Transportation in 1995, the inspection team advised that the bridge should remain closed to any vehicular traffic and that it should be extensively stabilized to allow foot traffic. On our visit to the bridge in April 2003, we found that it had been stabilized with large I beams anchored to the truss structure and the deck on the interior of the bridge. Only because these provide stability is the bridge usable for pedestrian traffic.

Fuller/Black Falls Bridge

Location: On Fuller Bridge Road, in the locality of Montgomery, within the Montgomery town line.

Directions: In Montgomery, where VT 118 North bears west, Fuller Bridge Road continues north to the bridge approximately 0.1 mile ahead.

GPS: 44° 54.188N 072° 38.375W

Year: 1890, rebuilt 2000s   **Truss:** Town   **Waterway:** Black Falls Brook
In Use: Yes   **Number of Spans:** 1   **Owner:** Town of Montgomery
Builder: Sheldon and Savannah Jewett   **Length:** 49 ft. 6 in.   **Width:** 16 ft. 4$\frac{3}{4}$ in.
Condition: Very good   **Number:** VT-06-05 (2)   **Register:** Dec. 23, 1974

Various accounts trace the troubled history of this bridge. It was built originally in 1890, one of the last ones built by the Jewett brothers, to replace an open bridge that had collapsed under the weight of a four-horse team and a load of bobbins from the Black Falls Bobbin Mill located at the north end of town. After being restored in 1981, it was hit by a logging truck's loading beam, late in 1982, which severly damaged the roof and even removed many of the Christmas decorations that had just been strung that day. After the sides of the remaining structure were braced, it served the town through the winter. Further weakness was found in the trunnels, which were made of beech. It seems that powder beetles, which prefer hardwood to softwood, had damaged

many of them. Then arrived the flood of 1997, which came to within inches of a complete washout of the northeast corner of the span.

Since 2000, the history of the bridge looks much brighter. The bridge has seen a complete transformation. The firm of Blow and Cote, Inc., general contractors of Morrisville, Vermont, submitted the winning bid for a complete restoration of the bridge. When we visited it in April 2003, we found a complete, authentic reproduction of the original span, a very substantial structure that is sure to serve the Town of Montgomery for many years to come.

Hectorville/Gibou Road/Gibou Bridge

Location: Stored in the locality of Montgomery, within the Montgomery town line on the property of A. L. St. Onge Contractor, Inc.

GPS: Unknown at time of writing

Year: 1883   **Truss:** Town and kingpost
Waterway: South Branch of Trout River   **In Use:** No, in storage
Number of Spans: 1   **Owner:** Town of Montgomery
Builder: Sheldon and Savannah Jewett   **Length:** 54 ft.
Width: Unable to measure
Condition: Dismantled, to be rebuilt in new location
Number: VT-06-06   **Register:** Nov. 20, 1974

The Hectorville Bridge, which at one time spanned the South Branch of the Trout River along Gibou Road just north of Hectorville, is no longer standing. It had been the target of vandals for some time since it was bypassed around

1950 with a modern steel and concrete structure. About three years ago the town selectmen hired a consultant to advise them on the condition of the bridge and what might be done with it. Last fall, a representative of the Vermont Historical Division advised the selectmen that the bridge might not survive another severe winter of heavy snows. In October 2002, the A. L. St. Onge Contractor, Inc., of Montgomery was hired to dismantle the bridge and salvage whatever might be usable. On our visit to Montgomery in April 2003, we found the trusses stored under cover of the bridge's roof on the property of the St. Onge company. In a conversation with a staff member of the company and other members of the Montgomery Historical Society, we learned that the society hopes to raise sufficient funds to rebuild the bridge as a footbridge, possibly on property owned by the Jewett family, descendants of the original builders of seven other Montgomery covered bridges. This bridge was originally built in Montgomery village in 1883 and moved to the Gibou Road location in 1899 to serve a thriving tub factory located in that area.

Hopkins Bridge

Location: Approximately 2.4 miles west-northwest of the locality of Montgomery, just inside the Enosburg town line.

Directions: In Montgomery Center, at the junction of VT 118 and VT 242, go north on VT 118 through Montgomery for 4.8 miles to Hopkins Bridge Road on the left (south); turn left to the bridge.

GPS: 44° 55.236N 072° 40.364W

Year: 1875, rebuilt 1999   **Truss:** Town   **Waterway:** Trout River
In Use: Yes   **Number of Spans:** 1   **Owner:** Town of Enosburg
Builder: Sheldon and Savannah Jewett   **Length:** 90 ft. 5 in.   **Width:** 15 ft. 8¾ in.
Condition: Excellent   **Number:** VT-06-01 (2)   **Register:** Nov. 20, 1974

This bridge is located just west of the Montgomery town line in the Town of Enosburg. It is another one of the seven area bridges built by the Jewett brothers. This one was completed in 1875. There is nothing to identify the bridge other than its location. Two signs are posted on the bridge portal facing Vermont Route 118. One reads: "Lattice Type Bridge . . . Built by . . . The Jewett Bros. 1875"; the other: "SLOW . . . AUTOS TO 10 MILES AN HOUR . . . HORSES TO A WALK . . . PER ORDER . . . SELECTMEN." A humorous story is related, regarding the latter sign, from Montgomery's town history by Ed Barna in *Covered Bridges of Vermont:* "A man who owned a fine team of horses, and who freely disregarded such posted admonitions, was brought into court to pay the $5 fine. He handed the judge a $10 bill and told him to keep the change, as he was going back through the bridge again in about 15 minutes."

In 1993, the Agency of Transportation inspection team reported that the bridge was "severely overstressed." Consequently it was closed, and a temporary span provided for the local farm that the bridge served late in the twentieth century. In 1999, at a cost of $320,649, the bridge was completely renovated by Renaud Bros. of Vernon, Vermont, under the supervision of the Vermont Agency of Transportation. An interesting feature of the restored bridge is that it has two thicknesses of vertical board siding, possibly to make it more difficult for vandals to remove them.

Hutchins Bridge

Location: 1.3 miles south of the locality of Montgomery Center, within the Montgomery town line.

Directions: In Montgomery Center, at the junction of VT 58 and VT 118, go south on VT 118 for 1.2 miles to South Brook Road on the right (west) side of the highway; go right on South Brook Road, cross the intersection with Hutchins Bridge Road #40, and continue for 0.15 mile to the bridge.

GPS: 44° 51.513N 072° 36.737W

Year: 1883 **Truss:** Town **Waterway:** South Branch of Trout River
In Use: Yes **Number of Spans:** 1 **Owner:** Town of Montgomery
Builder: Sheldon and Savannah Jewett **Length:** 76 ft. $11\frac{1}{2}$ in. **Width:** 16 ft.
Condition: Very poor **Number:** VT-06-07 **Register:** Dec. 30, 1974

This is another Town of Montgomery covered bridge constructed by the Jewett brothers. Today it serves a dead-end road with no other access. Consequently, when the Agency of Transportation inspected it in 1994, it recommended "prompt attention to restore its capacity to safely support traffic."

According to a note posted in September 1999 on "The Changing Scene" website maintained by Joseph Nelson, president of the Vermont Covered Bridge Society, the bridge "has been secured with 3-foot I-beams on each side of the deck, the stringers below supported by loops of steel cable." On our visit to the bridge in April 2003, we found that these I beams are still in place and the bridge is open to traffic. However, other than those beams, there is little else supporting the structure. Many siding boards are missing, but the bridge has been covered with a new, green, standing-seam sheet metal roof. We have no reports of any intended repairs or rehabilitation.

Longley/Harnois/Head Bridge

Location: Approximately 1 mile west-northwest of the locality of Montgomery, within the Montgomery town line.

Directions: In Montgomery Center, at the junction of VT 118 and VT 242, go north on VT 118 for 3.4 miles to Longley Road on the left (south); go left to the bridge.

GPS: 44° 54.432N 072° 39.321W

Year: 1863   **Truss:** Town   **Waterway:** Trout River   **In Use:** Yes
Number of Spans: 1   **Owner:** Town of Montgomery
Builder: Sheldon and Savannah Jewett   **Length:** 84 ft. 7 in.
Width: 16 ft. 1¼ in.   **Condition:** Very good   **Number:** VT-06-08
Register: Dec. 30, 1974

This is one of the earliest covered bridges in the Montgomery area built by the Jewett brothers. It was erected in 1863. It provides access across the Trout River by way of Longley Road to the Enosburg Forest area and East Enosburg. The span has had some repair work done during its 140-year existence. In 1979, the original abutments were capped and faced with concrete, and three steel beams were installed from the base of the north abutment to three of the lengthwise deck timbers. This is a support technique that we have not often seen. A complete restoration was made during the winter of 1992 by Jan Lewandoski. This is another Montgomery area bridge that is sided with two layers of vertical board material. It has a deck of lengthwise planks with runners in the traffic area and has a ribbed sheet metal roof. The vertical-board portal siding is painted white. The Lewandoski restoration has made this a very substantial bridge that should continue to serve the Montgomery and Enosburg area for some time.

Maple Street/Village/Fairfax/ Lower Bridge

Location: In the locality of Fairfax, within the Fairfax town line.

Directions: In the center of Fairfax, at the junction of VT 104 North and the road to Fletcher and Binghamville to the east, Maple St. goes southwest down the hill (it is not identified); turn onto Maple St. and follow it to the bridge.

GPS: 44° 39.821N 073° 00.617W

Year: 1865   **Truss:** Town   **Waterway:** Mill Brook   **In Use:** Yes
Number of Spans: 1   **Owner:** Town of Fairfax   **Builder:** Kingsbury and Stone
Length: 56 ft. 4½ in.   **Width:** 17 ft.   **Condition:** Very good   **Number:** VT-06-02
Register: Not listed

With an inside clearance of seventeen feet, this is one of the widest single-portal bridges in Vermont. When the span was washed from its abutments in the 1927 flood, some say it was replaced on its abutments in a different orientation—that is, the east portal faced west and the west portal faced east. This may account for a slight lean that seemed to exist after its return. In 1975, major work was done on the span—the original stone abutments were faced with concrete, and a ribbed metal roof was installed over the old wooden shakes. Further improvements were made to the bridge again in 1990 when Jan Lewandoski made repairs to some of the timbers. Early in 2002, after the structure was damaged by a truck driven by a local resident, Lewandoski was again contracted to correct the damage. It was necessary to remove the roof and siding in order to replace some of the main truss members. When replacing the

roof, it was necessary to use quite a bit of new material. Consequently, the new material is quite noticeable against the original, time-worn roof stringers, rafters, and kingposts. This most recent Lewandoski restoration has also corrected the slight lean that was apparent after the 1927 replacement. When we visited the bridge in April 2003, we found a very sturdy, well-restored bridge that should serve the community for many years to come. However, it is unfortunate that it has already been attacked by some of the local graffiti vandals, especially on the red portal and on several of the interior lattice truss members.

LAMOILLE COUNTY

Brook Road/White Caps Bridge

Location: 4.4 miles northwest of the locality of Stowe, within the Stowe town line.

Directions: In Stowe, at the junction of VT 100 and VT 108, go northwest on VT 108 for 4.3 miles to Brook Road on the left (southwest), turn left onto Brook Road, and go 0.1 mile to the bridge.

GPS: 44° 29.829N 072° 44.708W

Year: 1970   **Truss:** Stringer with simulated Howe
Waterway: West Branch of Waterbury River   **In Use:** Yes
Number of Spans: 1   **Owner:** Private   **Builder:** Unknown
Length: 54 ft. 1½ in.   **Width:** 22 ft. 8½ in.   **Condition:** Good
Number: VT-08-D   **Register:** Does not qualify

This bridge is not an authentic covered bridge but one that is classified as a "romantic" or "modern shelter." It has been included in this guide because it is a "covered bridge" that might be encountered as one travels along the Smugglers Notch Scenic Highway, Vermont Route 108, just a few miles northwest of Stowe. Its location is charted on the "Vermont Covered Bridges" map prepared by the State of Vermont Agency of Transportation in 1988 and is documented in *Romantic Shelters* by Arthur F. Hammer, published by the National Society for the Preservation of Covered Bridges in 1989. It is also included here because, even though it is built on a stringer deck, the truss structures that support the dead weight of the bridge are excellent examples of a Howe truss, of which there are only a few scattered throughout New England. The bridge provides a crossing for Brook Road where it enters an attractive residential area over the West Branch of the Waterbury River. It is worth making a stop there, if only to examine the truss structure.

Cambridge Junction/Poland/Junction/Station/Kissing Bridge

Location: 0.7 mile east of the locality of Jeffersonville, within the Cambridge town line.

Directions: At the junction of VT 15 and VT 108 North/to VT 109, at the east end of Jeffersonville, go east on VT 15 for 0.6 mile to the road sign on the north (left) that says "Jct Rd Th 23," turn left onto Jct Rd Th 23, and go 0.1 mile to the bridge site across the railroad tracks.

GPS: 44° 39.044N 072° 48.877W

Year: 1887 **Truss:** Burr **Waterway:** Lamoille River
In Use: Closed, foot traffic only **Number of Spans:** 1
Owner: Town of Cambridge
Builder: George W. Holmes, abutments by Luther A. Wheelock
Length: 152 ft. 10¾ in. **Width:** 16 ft. ½ in. **Condition:** Very poor
Number: VT-08-02 **Register:** Oct. 9, 1974

At the time this bridge was built, it was surrounded by controversy. In the 1880s, Cambridge Junction was an important railroad station. Residents of the villages of Belvidere and Waterville to the north, looking for ready access to the station, requested that a bridge be built across the Lamoille River. The residents of Cambridge saw no need for an additional tax burden and blocked the request. Finally, after the debate had continued for some time, Luke P. Poland, a prominent lawyer and political figure in both state and national circles, returned to his hometown after retiring in 1884 and led the two towns in a legal

battle against the town of Cambridge. In 1887, after some additional stalling on the part of Cambridge, the bridge was built. Consequently, the name Poland is still attached to the bridge. When the bridge was inspected in the 1990s, as part of a statewide inspection program, the Agency of Transportation found that the original twelve-inch positive camber of the bridge had fallen to a negative eighteen-inch camber and closed the bridge to all traffic. Almost immediately, concerned citizens applied for funds to rehabilitate the span. At the time of our visit to the bridge in April 2003, we found that the structure had been stabilized with many heavy timbers reinforcing the trusses and three large A-frame supports erected, one at each end and one at the center kingposts of the multiple kingpost portion of the trusses. We understand that the final stage of rehabilitation will take place during the spring, summer, and fall of 2003.

Church Street/Village/Meat Market/ Lower Bridge

Location: On Church Street in the locality of Waterville, within the Waterville town line.

Directions: Just northeast of Jeffersonville, at the junction of VT 108 and VT 109, go north on VT 109 for 4.3 miles to Church St. in Waterville; go left (west) on Church St. for 0.1 mile to the bridge.

GPS: 44° 41.410N 072° 46.250W

Year: ca. 1877   **Truss:** Queenpost   **Waterway:** North Branch of Lamoille River
In Use: Yes   **Number of Spans:** 1   **Owner:** Town of Waterville
Builder: Unknown   **Length:** 61 ft. 3$\frac{1}{4}$ in.   **Width:** 12 ft. 11 in.
Condition: Good   **Number:** VT-08-13   **Register:** Dec. 16, 1974

Most of the accounts of this bridge list its date of construction as "around 1877," although the Vermont Agency of Transportation lists it as 1895. The bridge served the Waterville area quite well until December of 1979, when the rear wheels of a truck driven by a local resident broke through the bridge deck. The next year the deck was reinforced with four lengthwise steel beams. The bridge was also threatened by a fire at a neighboring house in 1970, but the fire department avoided damage to the bridge by hosing the bridge down at the same time that it fought the house fire. In October of 1999, it was necessary to close the bridge again because of damage done to some of the internal overhead knee braces and roof stringers by an oversize truck. By March 2000, the bridge was reopened with the west portal resheathed with board and batten siding to match the rest of the bridge. Of course, it will take a number of years before the new siding matches the weathered appearance of the original sides and east portal. When we visited the bridge in April 2003, we found that it has also received a new, green, standing-seam sheet metal roof. The name Lower has been given to the bridge because it is the lowest bridge within the Waterville town line spanning the North Branch of the Lamoille River. It's a lovely, queenpost span in a quiet village setting.

Fisher Railroad/Chubb/Chub Bridge

Location: South of VT 15 between Wolcott and Hardwick, within the Wolcott town line.

Directions: In Wolcott, at the junction of VT 15 and School Road (south side of VT 15), go east on VT 15 for 2 miles to the roadside park on the right (south) side of the highway. Or, in Hardwick, at the junction of VT 14 South and VT 15, go west on VT 15 for 4 miles to the roadside park on the left (south). The bridge is a state historic site within the park.

GPS: 44° 31.967N 072° 25.654W (coordinates recorded in roadside park for the bridge)

Year: 1908   **Truss:** Town-Pratt   **Waterway:** Lamoille River
In Use: For railroad tours only   **Number of Spans:** 1   **Owner:** State
Builder: Pratt Construction Co.   **Length:** 103 ft.   **Width:** 15 ft.
Condition: Good   **Number:** VT-08-16   **Register:** Oct. 1, 1974

A historic marker placed at the site of this bridge by the Vermont Board of Historic Sites states:

> FISHER BRIDGE . . . WOLCOTT, VERMONT . . . This bridge, spanning the Lamoille River on the St. Johnsbury & Lamoille County R. R., is the last railroad covered bridge still in regular use in Vermont and one of a very few left in the U.S. Built in 1908, it is the only one remaining with full-length cupola, which provided a smoke escape. In 1968 the bridge was scheduled for destruction to make way for a new steel span. It was saved by placing heavy steel beams underneath. This preservation was achieved with State funds and with generous private donations raised by the Lamoille County Development Council.

The three names of the bridge listed above are derived from the families that lived nearby when it was built. The name by which the bridge is known today is associated with farmer Christopher "Crit" Fisher, the more recent owner (during the early 1900s) of the land that borders the tracks and the bridge crossing. When the bridge was built, the railroad line was owned by the Boston & Maine Railroad; in more recent years, the St. Johnsbury and Lamoille Railroad. The contractor for the bridge construction was the Pratt Construction Company, which adapted the Town lattice truss. For this bridge Pratt increased the size of the lattice truss members and doubled the lattice web on each side. With these changes the truss structure was called a Town-Pratt. We understand from various accounts that although there is no regular service along the railroad line, the bridge is used occasionally during railroad tours for railroad buffs and "leaf peepers."

Gates Farm Bridge

Location: In the locality of Cambridge, within the Cambridge town line.

Directions: Just west of Cambridge, at the junction of VT 104 and VT 15, go east on VT 15 for 0.8 mile and look to the south; the bridge is in the field, over Seymour River.

GPS: 44° 38.738N 072° 52.424W (coordinates recorded along VT 15 close to the bridge)

Year: 1897, rebuilt 1994   **Truss:** Burr   **Waterway:** Seymour River
In Use: Yes   **Number of Spans:** 1   **Owner:** Town of Cambridge
Builder: George W. Holmes   **Length:** 81 ft. 10 in.   **Width:** 15 ft. 9½ in.
Condition: Very good   **Number:** VT-08-04 (2)   **Register:** Nov. 19, 1974

At one time there were two covered bridges in the Cambridge area. One of these was a two-lane bridge crossing the Lamoille River referred to as the Big

Bridge; the other, a single-lane bridge spanning the Seymour River referred to as the Little Bridge. In 1950, when the state bypassed the Big Bridge with a modern span, it also diverted the Seymour River so that it emptied into the Lamoille River farther upstream. This left the Little Bridge high and dry without a waterway to span, and the Big Bridge was moved to the Shelburne Museum through an arrangement between the state and the museum. However, the diverting of the Seymour River left the Earl Gates family without access to sixty acres of their farmland. Since the Little Bridge was no longer needed in its original location, the state moved it to the Seymour crossing on Gates Farm. Hence the bridge's present name—Gates Farm. Through the next forty-plus years, the bridge gradually deteriorated. In the 1990s the state informed Rex Gates, Earl's son, that the bridge was his to maintain. However, an agreement signed by the elder Gates and his wife, but never signed by the state, indicated that the state would maintain the Gates Farm Bridge until other access could be provided. Consequently, the younger Gates informed the state that it had created the problem that diverted Seymour River, so it was responsible for repairing the bridge. After some discussion, the state agreed. When Blow and Cote, Inc., of Morrisville started to dismantle the ninety-seven-year-old span, it discovered that many of the timbers were in bad shape and had to be replaced. On a visit to the bridge in 2003, we saw what appears to be a lovely new bridge, in the middle of a farm field, going nowhere.

Gold Brook/Emily's/ Stowe Hollow Bridge

Location: 3 miles south-southeast of the locality of Stowe, within the Stowe town line.

Directions: In Stowe, at the junction of VT 100 and VT 108, go south on VT 108 for 1.8 miles to Gold Brook Road on the left (east), turn left onto Gold Brook Road, and go 0.3 mile to crossroads. Gold Brook Road goes left (north); turn left to stay on Gold Brook Road and go 0.9 mile to Covered Bridge Road. The bridge is just to the left.

GPS: 44° 26.416N 072° 40.797W

Year: 1844   **Truss:** Howe   **Waterway:** Gold Brook   **In Use:** Yes
Number of Spans: 1   **Owner:** Town of Stowe   **Builder:** John W. Smith
Length: 48 ft. 5 in.   **Width:** 13 ft. 7$\frac{3}{4}$ in.   **Condition:** Good
Number: VT-08-12   **Register:** Oct. 1, 1974

This is another bridge that has acquired some interesting names. "Stowe Hollow" is rather easy to understand because the bridge is located in an area called Stowe Hollow in the southern part of Stowe. "Gold Brook" is understandable because the bridge crosses Gold Brook, aptly named for the so-called placer gold that can be found in tiny nuggets panned or sluiced in the stream. But the second name has a more interesting background. Emily was a young girl who, according to various tales told by the local residents, suffered a rather untimely death. The most interesting legend might be that poor Emily, daughter of a mid-1800s local farmer, found herself in "a family way," was deserted by her lover,

and hanged herself in the bridge. Occasionally, on moonlit nights her ghost may be seen wandering through the bridge still looking for her lover.

While the bridge has this "dark" story, it also has a dark appearance because of the vertical board siding, which may have been stained walnut brown at one time. It is one of the few Howe truss bridges to be found in Vermont, being especially unusual for such a short span. On our visit in January, 2003, we found that even though the original covered bridge at this site dates back to 1844, the current structure was in good condition. This may be due to the fact that the town made a resolution for perpetual care of the bridge in 1969. According to Nelson's documentation, this resolution is displayed on a bronze plaque in a grassy area near the east portal. That plaque was not visible in the deep snow of our 2003 visit.

Grist Mill/Scott/Bryant/Brewster River/ Grand Canyon/Canyon Bridge

Location: In the locality of Jeffersonville, within the Cambridge town line.

Directions: In Jeffersonville, at the junction of VT 15 and VT 108, go south on VT 108 for 0.45 mile to Canyon Road on the left (east); turn left onto Canyon Road to the bridge.

GPS: 44° 38.199N 072° 49.531W

Year: 1872   **Truss:** Burr   **Waterway:** Brewster River   **In Use:** Yes
Number of Spans: 1   **Owner:** Town of Cambridge   **Builder:** Unknown
Length: 84 ft. 7½ in.   **Width:** 14 ft. 8¾ in.   **Condition:** Good
Number: VT-08-01   **Register:** June 13, 1974

There is little information available about the Grist Mill Bridge. Even the exact date of its construction is questionable. Most sources list the date of origin as unknown. One source, however, the *World Guide to Covered Bridges,* published by the National Society for the Preservation of Covered Bridges, lists the date of origin as 1872. One story related by Ed Barna, in *Covered Bridges of Vermont,* describes a near disaster following the 1952 freshet: "Selectman Clark Dodge Sr. was about to drive onto it (the bridge) when he noticed that the end had settled considerably. Stopping his car, he found a 4-foot washout between the road and the bridge abutment. The town built a cribbing (crisscross stack) of railroad ties and jacked up the bridge, only to have another rainfall wash the cribbing out. Finally, a new concrete abutment was poured." With this solid foundation, the town was able to return the bridge to regular use. As recently as 2001, there have been discussions between the town selectmen and Vtrans and the Historic Covered Bridge Committee regarding the present-day condition of the structure. Specific needs have been outlined, bids were sought, and

the work was scheduled for 2003. In 2002, a request for $336,000 was made of the National Historic Covered Bridge Preservation Program, and that exact amount was granted for work needed on the Grist Mill (Canyon) Bridge. We felt that the outward appearance of the bridge was quite good when we saw it in April 2003. It will be interesting to see how much improvement is made through the planned restoration.

Jaynes/Codding Hollow/Upper/ Kissing Bridge

Location: 1.7 miles north of the locality of Waterville, within the Waterville town line.

Directions: Just north of Jeffersonville, at the junction of VT 108 and VT 109, go north on VT 109 for 6 miles to Codding Hollow Road; turn right (east) onto Codding Hollow Road and go 0.1 mile to the bridge.

GPS: 44° 42.730N 072° 45.374W

Year: ca. 1877   **Truss:** Queenpost   **Waterway:** North Branch of Lamoille River
In Use: Yes   **Number of Spans:** 1   **Owner:** Town of Waterville
Builder: Unknown   **Length:** 60 ft. 9 in.   **Width:** 11 ft. 11 in.
Condition: Fairly good   **Number:** VT-08-15   **Register:** Oct. 1, 1974

This is another bridge that is known by multiple names, but it is easy to account for the four names given to it. When it was built, the Jaynes family lived and worked nearby; it is along Codding Hollow Road; it is the uppermost cov-

ered bridge crossing the North Branch of the Lamoille River within the Waterville town line; and a weathered sign on the west portal gable end identifies it as the Kissing Bridge. According to a longtime resident, that sign was placed there by a visitor in the 1950s. The name Kissing, however, is not unusual because most covered bridges have been given that nickname at some time or other. This bridge is located in a lovely rural setting where it provides access to the farmland and homes that lie on the eastern side of a rapidly moving stream in the foothills of the Green Mountains. Codding Hollow is about two miles to the east. The bridge is a moderate-length, queenpost truss structure with random-width, vertical board siding on both the sides and the portals, has a deck of crosswise planks set on edge with runners in the traffic area, and has a relatively new, green, standing-seam sheet metal roof. The latter may have been installed as a part of the reroofing program of thirty-eight Vermont bridges in 2001. One account tells of the rear end of a local contractor's gravel truck crashing through the floor in the fall of 1960, after which the deck was reinforced with four lengthwise steel girders.

Lumber Mill/Mill/Lower Bridge

Location: 3.8 miles north of the locality of Waterville, within the Belvidere town line.

Directions: Just northeast of Jeffersonville, at the junction of VT 108 and VT 109, go north on VT 109 for 8.1 miles to Back Road on the left (west), turn left onto Back Road, and go 0.45 mile to the bridge. Or, in Belvidere Corners, at the junction of VT 118 and VT 109, go south on VT 109 through

Belvidere Center for 6.4 miles to Back Road on the right (west) (the road sign is blank on the north side), turn right onto Back Road, and go 0.45 mile to the bridge.

GPS: 44° 44.614N 072° 44.496W

Year: ca. 1895   **Truss:** Queenpost   **Waterway:** North Branch of Lamoille River
In Use: Yes   **Number of Spans:** 1   **Owner:** Town of Belvidere
Builder: Lewis Robinson   **Length:** 70 ft. 4¾ in.   **Width:** 11 ft. 11½ in.
Condition: Good   **Number:** VT-08-06   **Register:** Nov. 19, 1974

Some accounts refer to this bridge simply as Mill Bridge because there was a tub factory or mill upstream from the bridge and a lumber mill downstream. Other accounts refer to it specifically as the Lumber Mill Bridge. It has also been called the Lower Bridge because, within the Belvidere town line, it is the lower of the two bridges that span the North Branch of the Lamoille River. It, too, was repaired because of a failure in the floor system, which occurred in November 1971 when a local contractor's snowplow broke through the deck. Within six weeks the deck was reinforced with four lengthwise steel girders, at which time the abutments were also reinforced with concrete. After this renovation, the live load of the bridge was no longer supported by the truss structure. The queenpost truss structure now supports only the dead load of the sides and roof of the span. The original truss portion of the span was repaired in 1995 by Jan Lewandoski, a Vermont restorer of covered bridges, and Paul Ide, a post and beam carpenter. The bridge also has a relatively new, green, standing-seam metal roof, which may have been installed in conjunction with the reroofing program in 2001 as a result of a $461,600 grant awarded to Vermont through the National Historic Covered Bridge Preservation Program.

Montgomery/Middle/Dallas/ Potter Bridge

Location: 1.3 miles north of the locality of Waterville, within the Waterville town line.

Directions: Just northeast of Jeffersonville, at the junction of VT 108 and VT 109, go north on VT 109 for 5.6 miles to Montgomery Road on the right (east); turn right to the bridge.

GPS: 44° 42.349N 072° 45.625W

Year: 1887 **Truss:** Queenpost **Waterway:** North Branch of Lamoille River
In Use: Yes **Number of Spans:** 1 **Owner:** Town of Waterville
Builder: Unknown **Length:** 70 ft. 3¾ in. **Width:** 12 ft. 5¼ in.
Condition: Very good **Number:** VT-08-14 **Register:** Oct. 18, 1974

Originally this bridge was named for a nearby resident, Luke Potter. However, it later took the name Montgomery or Dallas, being named after the Dallas Montgomery Farm east of the North Branch of the Lamoille River. It has also been referred to as the Middle Bridge because it is located between the Jaynes or Upper Bridge, upstream, and the Church Street or Lower Bridge, downstream. All three of these bridges span the North Branch within the Waterville town line. This bridge, like several others in this area, required restoration work between 1969 and 1971. In 1969, an early January snowstorm deposited five feet of snow on one side of the roof, causing it to groan and lean a little to one side. According to Ed Barna in *Covered Bridges of Vermont*, Dallas Mont-

gomery, owner of the farm for whom the bridge is named, climbed up on the roof to clear some of the snow, and local resident Wilmer Locke winched the structure back into shape and reinforced it with additional bracing and iron rods. A second incident in August 1971 caused further damage when an asphalt truck headed for the Montgomery Farm crashed through the floor, ending in the stream on its back. Fortunately, the driver escaped through a window with only minor cuts and bruises. In 1971, following these occurrences, this bridge, too, had its deck reinforced with steel girders. Later accounts indicate that the bridge had major repairs made in 1997. On our visit to the bridge in April 2003, we found it to be in good condition with new, unpainted, vertical board siding.

Morgan/Upper Bridge

Location: 4.5 miles north of the locality of Waterville, within the Belvidere town line.

Directions: Just northeast of Jeffersonvile, at the junction of VT 108 and VT 109, go north on VT 109 for 8.8 miles to Morgan Bridge Road on the left (west), turn left onto Morgan Bridge Road, and go 0.15 mile to the bridge. Or, in Belvidere Corners, at the junction of VT 118 and VT 109, go south on VT 109 through Belvidere Center for 5.7 miles to Morgan Bridge Road on the right (west), turn right onto Morgan Bridge Road, and go 0.15 mile to the bridge.

GPS: 44° 44.600N 072° 43.682W

Year: 1887   **Truss:** Queenpost   **Waterway:** North Branch of Lamoille River
In Use: Yes   **Number of Spans:** 1   **Owner:** Town of Belvidere
Builder: Lewis Robinson, Charles Leonard, and Fred Tracy
Length: 70 ft. 11 in.   **Width:** 12 ft. $2\frac{3}{4}$ in.   **Condition:** Good
Number: VT-08-07   **Register:** Nov. 19, 1974

This bridge was named for the Morgan family that owned the property at the north portal. The name Upper Bridge is derived, like Lower Bridge, from the span's upstream position along the North Branch of the Lamoille River within the Belvidere town line. A recent inspection of the Morgan Bridge in the 1990s by the Vermont Agency of Transportation indicated that the bridge has unique features that could enable it to carry at least nine tons, more than the stated load limit of eight tons for a bridge with wooden decks. According to Joseph Nelson in *Spanning Time—Vermont's Covered Bridges,* the report of the inspectors stated: "The queenpost truss incorporates three small king-post trusses within the queenpost truss to help support floor loads. Also, queen-rods are positioned next to the queenposts. Two other rods drop from near the bottom of the queenpost main-braces as well. Another design feature includes double

six-by-eight tie beams at each queenpost allowing for two tenons and two pairs of knee braces." Another unique feature of this bridge in comparison with the other queenpost bridges of the area is its overhanging gables, which extend five feet beyond the bridge deck at each end. This bridge, too, may have been reroofed in recent years. It sports a green, standing-seam sheet metal roof.

Power House/Johnson/School Street Bridge

Location: On the northeast edge of the locality of Johnson, within the Johnson town line.

Directions: In Johnson, at the junction of VT 15 and VT 100C, go northeast on VT 100C for 0.3 mile. Turn left to the bridge.

GPS: 44° 38.168N 072° 40.212W

Year: 1870, rebuilt 2002   **Truss:** Queenpost   **Waterway:** Gihon River
In Use: Yes   **Number of Spans:** 1   **Owner:** Town of Johnson
Builder: Unknown   **Length:** 66 ft. 5 in.   **Width:** 16 ft. $4\frac{1}{2}$ in.
Condition: Excellent   **Number:** VT-08-08 (2)   **Register:** Oct. 9, 1974

Originally known as the School Street Bridge, this bridge was built in 1870 to extend School Street across the Gihon River. It was also known as Johnson Bridge because it is in the Town of Johnson. However, after the town constructed a power plant upstream from the village in the 1890s, the bridge has

been known as the Power House Bridge. The queenpost truss structure was built with massive timbers—the main members of the truss are ten inches by twelve inches, and the additional supporting diagonals measure ten inches by ten inches (see the internal photo). Records indicate that the span has seen several repairs or restorations during its 133-year history. It was reconstructed in 1960 and again in 1993 because the deck had developed quite a sag. In 1995 it was closed again because the bridge continued to sag. As the result of a comprehensive covered bridge survey that was conducted in the 1990s, the deck had metal girders placed under it to bring the bridge up to contemporary load-limit requirements, and the truss members were refurbished. On Mach 8, 2001, need for another major change occurred when the roof of the bridge collapsed onto the deck under the weight of winter snows. The sides of the bridge collapsed outward and fell into the river below. Fortunately, no one was crossing the bridge at the time. The practice of removing snow from covered bridges had been discontinued after many of the structures had their roofs replaced with standing-rib sheet metal, which readily allows the snow to melt and slide from the roof. However, the Power House Bridge still had wooden shakes.

After much discussion and deliberation over a period of five or six months, the town selectmen decided to completely restore the old structure. In November 2001, a bid of $139,855 was accepted from Blow and Cote, Inc., Morrisville, Vermont, for the project. The restoration was begun with a "snowbreaking" ceremony on February 19, 2002, and completed with a "ribbon-cutting" re-dedication ceremony on June 29, 2002. Obviously, when we visited the bridge in January 2003, we found a beautifully restored structure. Many thanks are due to the enthusiastic supporters of covered bridges in the Johnson area.

The massive timbers of the queenpost truss system of the Power House Bridge.

Red/Sterling/Sterling Brook/ Chaffee Bridge

Location: 5.1 miles north of the locality of Stowe, within the Morristown town line.

Directions: In Stowe, at the junction of VT 100 and VT 108, go north on VT 100 for 1.6 miles to Stagecoach Road (Stagecoach Road continues straight from VT 100), go north on Stagecoach Road for 1.8 miles to Sterling Valley Road on the left (west), turn left onto Sterling Valley Road, and go 1.7 miles to Cole Hill Road. The bridge is just to the right on Cole Hill Road.

GPS: 44° 31.105N 072° 40.663W

Year: 1896　**Truss:** Kingpost within queenpost　**Waterway:** Sterling Brook
In Use: Yes　**Number of Spans:** 1　**Owner:** Town of Morristown
Builder: Unknown　**Length:** 64 ft. 1 in.　**Width:** 15 ft. 1$\frac{1}{4}$ in.
Condition: Good　**Number:** VT-08-11　**Register:** Oct. 16, 1974

The oldest name of this bridge, Chaffee, was given to it by the local residents because a Chaffee family lived nearby. Other residents have referred to it as Sterling or Sterling Brook because of the waterway it spans. In recent years, since its been painted barn red, it is simply known as the Red Bridge. The bridge was originally built in 1896 by an unknown builder who chose the king-

post truss surrounded by a queenpost truss as the superstructure for the crossing (see the interior photo). After the truss was damaged by a storm in 1897, additional iron rods were added for rigidity.

In order to bring the bridge up to contemporary live load standards, the Vermont Department of Highways rebuilt the span in 1971 with an independent, reinforced concrete deck supported on two steel girders. The original stone abutments were reinforced with concrete. The only thing the trusses support at this time is the dead weight of the sides and roof. The vertical board sides are open along the eaves approximately one-fourth of their height. In keeping with the overall bridge coloration, the roof is covered with red standing-rib sheet metal.

The combination of a kingpost truss surrounded by a queenpost truss of the Red Bridge.

Scribner/East Johnson/DeGoosh/ Mudget Bridge

Location: 1.7 miles east of the locality of Johnson, within the Johnson town line.

Directions: In Johnson, at the junction of VT 15 and VT 100C, go north on VT 100C for 0.9 mile to Sinclair Road on the right (southeast), turn right onto Sinclair Road, go 0.7 mile to a T (no road name is evident), turn left, and go 0.1 mile to the bridge.

GPS: 44° 38.286N 072° 38.915W

Year: 1919 **Truss:** Queenpost **Waterway:** Gihon River **In Use:** Yes
Number of Spans: 1 **Owner:** Town of Johnson **Builder:** Unknown
Length: 47 ft. 8½ in. **Width:** 13 ft. 6 in. **Condition:** Very good
Number: VT-08-09 **Register:** Oct. 1, 1974

The name used originally for this bridge, and the one that appears to have remained the most common name, is Scribner. It is the name of two local residents who lived in the vicinity of the bridge at the time it was built—Leroy Scribner and Sam Scribner. Since the bridge is located just east of the locality of East Johnson, that accounts for the second name. A later resident of one of the Scribner farms was Ellsworth DeGoosh, hence the third name. The fourth name, Mudget, is recorded by Joseph Nelson in *Spanning Time—Vermont's Covered Bridges*. It is also listed on the "Vermont Covered Bridges" website, of Virtual Vermont. However, no explanation is given in either of these references.

The queenpost trusses are built of very substantial members—ten-by-eleven-inch timbers for the horizontal members with ten-by-ten-inch timbers for the diagonal members. The date of the first span crossing the Gihon River at

this point is not known, but it is assumed that it was originally uncovered. How-ever, the Agency of Transportation lists 1919 as the year of construction for the covered structure. Like many bridges, the Scribner Bridge was brought up to contemporary load limits. In 1960, the original stone abutments were replaced with concrete, and the deck was supported with four steel girders independent of the queenpost trusses, which now support only the sides and the roof.

ORANGE COUNTY

Braley/Johnson/Blaisdell/ Upper Blaisdell Bridge

Location: 0.8 mile south of the locality of East Randolph, within the Randolph town line.

Directions: In East Randolph, at the junction of VT 66 and VT 14, go south on VT 14 for 0.8 mile to Braley Covered Bridge Road on the right (west), turn right onto Braley Covered Bridge Road, and go 0.1 mile to the bridge. Or, from the junction of VT 107 and VT 14, south of East Bethel, go north on VT 14 for 8 miles to Braley Covered Bridge Road on the left (west), turn left, and go 0.1 mile to the bridge.

GPS: 43° 55.711N 072° 33.302W

Year: 1904   **Truss:** Multiple kingpost
Waterway: Second Branch of White River   **In Use:** Yes
Number of Spans: 1   **Owner:** Town of Randolph   **Builder:** Unknown
Length: 40 ft. 4 in.   **Width:** 14 ft. 2 in.   **Condition:** Good
Number: VT-09-04   **Register:** June 13, 1974

Ed Barna in *Covered Bridges of Vermont,* Joseph Nelson in *Spanning Time—Vermont's Covered Bridges,* and the *World Guide to Covered Bridges* document the origin of this bridge as 1904. It is one of only two "half-high" multiple kingpost truss bridges in Vermont (see the interior photo). Since the truss, which supported both the live load and the dead load of the bridge, reaches only halfway up the interior of the bridge, it is assumed that the first bridge on this site was an open span with its truss covered on the outside to the top of the actual multiple kingpost portion. This left the deck of the bridge open to the elements. Decks, even in covered bridges, had to be replaced on a fairly regular basis because of deterioration caused by dirt and moisture that were carried in. At least, with an open deck, it was not necessary to hire someone to "snow" the bridge in the winter to accommodate the numerous sleighs. According to Herbert W. Congdon in *The Covered Bridge,* the date of 1909 appeared on the

portal of this bridge when he documented it in the mid-1900s. The earlier documented dates of origin, the "half-high" multiple kingpost truss, and the date of 1909 on the portal lead one to the conclusion that the first covered bridge on this site did not appear until 1909. At that time additional vertical timbers and upper chords were placed above the original truss to provide sufficient overhead clearance for a roof. Records indicate that the deck of the bridge was reinforced with four metal girders when it was restored in 1977.

The other "half-high" multiple kingpost truss is the Gifford Bridge, also in this county, just a mile south of the Braley Bridge.

The "half high" multiple kingpost truss system of the Braley Bridge.

Cilley/Lower Bridge

Location: Between the localities of South Tunbridge and Tunbridge, within the Tunbridge town line.

Directions: In South Royalton, at the junction of VT 14 and VT 110, go north on VT 110 for 4.5 miles to Howe Lane on the left (west), turn left onto Howe Lane, and go 0.1 mile to the bridge.

GPS: 43° 52.975N 072° 30.221W

Year: 1883   **Truss:** Multiple kingpost   **Waterway:** First Branch of White River
In Use: Yes   **Number of Spans:** 1   **Owner:** Town of Tunbridge
Builder: Arthur C. Adams   **Length:** 67 ft. 4 in.   **Width:** 15 ft. $7\frac{1}{2}$ in.
Condition: Fair   **Number:** VT-09-08   **Register:** Sept. 10, 1974

Arthur C. Adams is credited with the construction of this full-height, multiple kingpost truss span in 1883. It is a lovely rustic structure nestled in the low hills of the Tunbridge area with East Hill to the east, the Pinnacle to the southwest, and Goodwin Hill to the northwest. At sixty-seven feet four inches, it is a relatively short multiple kingpost bridge. It is covered with random-width, vertical board siding on both the sides and the portals and has an opening near the southwest end where Howe Lane makes a hard turn after leaving the bridge. The roof is covered with standing-rib sheet metal, and the deck consists of random-width, lengthwise planks. There is no record of recent work having been done on the bridge, but on our two visits in August 2002 and February 2003 we found the bridge in fairly good condition.

Flint Bridge

Location: 3.2 miles north of the locality of North Tunbridge, within the Tunbridge town line.

Directions: Starting in Tunbridge along VT 110, at the "Mill Bridge" sign, go north on VT 110 for 4.7 miles through North Tunbridge to Bicknell Hill Road on the right (east), turn right onto Bicknell Hill Road, and go 0.1 mile to the bridge.

GPS: 43° 56.962N 072° 27.530W

Year: 1845   **Truss:** Queenpost   **Waterway:** First Branch of White River
In Use: Yes   **Number of Spans:** 1   **Owner:** Town of Tunbridge
Builder: Unknown   **Length:** 87 ft. 8 in.   **Width:** 15 ft. 8 in.
Condition: Good   **Number:** VT-09-11   **Register:** Sept. 10, 1974

This bridge is the oldest of six bridges located along a seven-mile stretch of Vermont Route 110 between South Royalton in the south and Chelsea in the north. According to Joseph Nelson in *Spanning Time—Vermont's Covered Bridges* and Ed Barna in *Covered Bridges of Vermont,* the bridge was built in 1845. However, the *World Guide to Covered Bridges* and the sign on one gable end show the date as 1874. The builder is unknown, but he used a queenpost truss structure to span a fairly long distance. The overall length of the bridge was measured at eighty seven feet eight inches. The bridge was restored in 1969 by well-known covered bridge builder and restorer Milton Graton of New Hampshire. The original stone abutments were capped with concrete, which

raised the bridge for better drainage, the ends were rebuilt, camber was restored to the deck, the deck system was replaced, and new siding was installed. After completion of the project, the state bridge inspector commented that Graton's restoration was "an outstanding example of functional preservation of an historic structure."

In his 1997 publication, Nelson indicated that the Vermont Agency of Transportation recommended closing the bridge and constructing a bypass as the "best long-term action to preserve the bridge for the future." However, when we visited the bridge in February 2003, it was still open to traffic, and there was no evidence that a bypass was being constructed.

Gifford/C. K. Smith Bridge

Location: 1.6 miles south of the locality of East Randolph, within the Randolph town line.

Directions: In East Randolph, at the junction of VT 66 and VT 14, go south on VT 14 for 1.6 miles to Hyde Road on the left (east), turn left, and go 0.1 mile to the bridge. Or, from the junction of VT 107 and VT 14, south of East Bethel, go north on VT 14 for 7.2 miles to Hyde Road on the right (east), turn right, and go 0.1 mile to the bridge.

GPS: 43° 54.973N 072° 33.310W

Year: 1904   **Truss:** Multiple kingpost
Waterway: Second Branch of White River   **In Use:** Yes
Number of Spans: 1   **Owner:** Town of Randolph   **Builder:** Unknown
Length: 54 ft. 9 in.   **Width:** 14 ft. $10\frac{1}{2}$ in.   **Condition:** Good
Number: VT-09-03   **Register:** July 30, 1974

This is one of only two "half-high," multiple kingpost truss bridges in Vermont. Its northern neighbor, the Braley Bridge, is the other one. Therefore, it is assumed that the Gifford Bridge, like its neighbor, was uncovered in the earlier years of its existence. The upward extension of the sides in the Gifford Bridge, however, was done quite differently than in the Braley Bridge. In the Gifford Bridge, the truss structure above the "half-high" multiple kingpost is a single kingpost within a queenpost (see the interior photo). The deck of the bridge has been reinforced with large, full-length, steel I beams or girders which are located against the trusses on either side of the roadway. They, in turn, are connected with tie rods to shorter I beams or girders located directly below them under the deck. Nevertheless, when the statewide covered bridge assessment was conducted in the 1990s, it was recommended that the bridge be closed and bypassed by a contemporary bridge.

When we visited the bridge in August 2002 and February 2003, we found a beautifully refurbished bridge at this location. In 2001, the Town of Randolph did an extensive amount of work on the span. The bridge was raised by pouring concrete caps on top of the original stone abutments, rotted truss timbers were replaced, and it received new, random-width, barn-red siding on both the sides and the portals and a new standing-rib sheet metal roof. The steel girders, however, are still there, lending support to the live load that the bridge carries. The load limit is still three tons.

The Gifford Bridge is an excellent example of why the people of Vermont are justifiably proud of their covered bridges. It might be interesting to note, at this point, that at one time this was called the Blue Bridge because it was painted that strange color—something we have never seen on our "bridging" ventures.

The different-truss combination of the Gifford Bridge.

Howe Bridge

Location: Just north of the locality of South Tunbridge, within the Tunbridge town line.

Directions: In South Royalton, at the junction of VT 14 and VT 110, go north on VT 110 for 3.3 miles to Belknap Brook Road on the right (east), turn right onto Belknap Brook Road, and go 0.05 mile to the bridge.

GPS: 43° 51.894N 072° 29.948W

Year: 1879   **Truss:** Multiple kingpost   **Waterway:** First Branch of White River
In Use: Yes   **Number of Spans:** 1   **Owner:** Town of Tunbridge
Builder: Ira Mudget, Edward Wells, Chauncey Tenney   **Length:** 75 ft. 11 in.
Width: 12 ft. 9½ in.   **Condition:** Good   **Number:** VT-09-07
Register: Sept. 10, 1974

Members of the Howe family live on both sides of Vermont Route 110. The bridge, through which Belknap Road passes, provides an attractive entrance to the well-structured and maintained Howe farm just to the east of the bridge. Built in 1879, the bridge appears to have been well preserved. The Howes themselves place pots of flowers or other appropriate decorations at the western portal. In 1994, it was necessary to replace the deck, floor beams, and the bottom chords of the truss structure. In 2001, funds received through the National Historic Covered Bridge Preservation Program provided new sheet metal roofs for this and some other covered bridges across the state. The towns had a choice of green, silver, black, or red. Tunbridge selected silver as the color that would be used on the bridges receiving new roofs in its area.

A long ladder, approximately eighteen feet in length, hangs inside the bridge along the multiple kingpost truss. When asked by a writer why the ladder was there, members of the Howe family replied: "I don't know, it's always been there." We certainly hope that the same will be true of both the Howe Bridge and the Howe Farm—they'll always be there. This is another bridge that the Agency of Transportation recommended closing and bypassing. We were delighted to see that it was still there and in use on our visit of February 2003.

Hyde/Kingsbury Bridge

Location: On the north edge of the locality of East Bethel, within the Randolph town line.

Directions: In East Randolph, at the junction of VT 66 and VT 14, go south on VT 14 for 4.4 miles to Kingsbury Road on the right (west); turn right onto Kingsbury Road to the bridge. Or, from the junction of VT 107 and VT 14, south of East Bethel, go north on VT 14 for 4.4 miles to Kingsbury Road on the left (west); turn left onto Kingsbury Road to the bridge.

GPS: 43° 52.848N 072° 34.906W

Year: 1904   **Truss:** Multiple kingpost
Waterway: Second Branch of White River   **In Use:** Yes
Number of Spans: 1   **Owner:** Town of Randolph   **Builder:** Unknown
Length: 51 ft. 9 in.   **Width:** 15 ft. 8$\frac{1}{4}$ in.   **Condition:** Fairly good
Number: VT-09-02   **Register:** July 30, 1974

All the covered bridges that are located within the Randolph town line can be considered the younger generation of the old historic bridges of Vermont. The Hyde, like the Gifford and Braley Bridges was built in 1904. Unfortunately, the builders of all three are unknown. The Hyde, however, has a full-size multiple kingpost truss, while its two northern neighbors have "half-high," multiple kingpost trusses. In 1980 it was restored. Between that restoration and 1994, it was closed for a number of years because of ice damage. In 1994, after another restoration, it was reopened and continues to be in use. The work done in 1994 consisted of replacing portions of the top and bottom chords and replacing some of the bracing, vertical truss members, bolster beams, and miscellaneous structural members. This span, like eight other Orange County bridges, had its roof replaced in 2001 with standing-rib sheet metal.

Larkin Bridge

Location: 1.3 miles north of the locality of North Tunbridge, within the Tunbridge town line.

Directions: Starting in the village of Tunbridge along VT 110, at the "Mill Bridge" sign, go north on VT 110 for 2.8 miles through the village of North Tunbridge to a dirt road on the right (east) (no markings). Turn right onto the dirt road, and go 0.1 mile to the bridge.

GPS: 43° 55.385N 072° 27.936W

Year: 1902   **Truss:** Multiple kingpost   **Waterway:** First Branch of White River
In Use: Yes   **Number of Spans:** 1   **Owner:** Town of Tunbridge
Builder: Arthur C. Adams   **Length:** 68 ft. 5 in.   **Width:** 12 ft. 11 in.
Condition: Fairly good   **Number:** VT-09-10   **Register:** July 30, 1974

This bridge, like the three Randolph bridges—Braley, Gifford, and Hyde, is one of the few historic bridges that were built in the early years of the twentieth century. Being built in 1902, the Larkin is just two years older than the Randolph spans. An interesting feature of this bridge is that because Larkin Road, which runs through the bridge, does not cross perpendicular to the First Branch of the White River, the abutments supporting the bridge could not be built perpendicular to the bridge deck. Consequently, the two multiple kingpost trusses supporting the deck, the side walls, and the roof of the bridge, while being parallel to each other, are noticeably skewed to the abutments.

This is another of the Orange County bridges that, during the covered bridge surveys of the 1990s, the state recommended either closing and bypassing or rehabilitating to accommodate contemporary traffic. However, on our visits to the bridge in August 2002 and February 2003, we found that it was still in use and had received a new standing-rib metal roof during the 2001 reroofing program of the bridges in this area. We do not have any record of other work having been done on the bridge, but it appears to be regularly maintained by the Town of Tunbridge.

Mill/Spring Road/Hayward/ Noble Bridge

Location: In the locality of Tunbridge, within the Tunbridge town line.

Directions: In South Royalton, at the junction of VT 14 and VT 110, go north on VT 110 for 5.3 miles to the center of the village of Tunbridge. Look for a sign on the left (west) side of the road: Mill Bridge 1883–2000. Turn left to the bridge.

GPS: 43° 53.495N 072° 29.485W

Year: 1883, rebuilt 2000   **Truss:** Multiple kingpost
Waterway: First Branch of White River   **In Use:** Yes   **Number of Spans:** 1
Owner: Town of Tunbridge   **Builder:** Arthur C. Adams   **Length:** 74 ft. 5 in.
Width: 16 ft. 1 in.   **Condition:** Excellent   **Number:** VT-09-09 (2)
Register: July 30, 1974

The present bridge in Tunbridge, the Mill Bridge, is a beautiful reconstruction of the original bridge built in 1883. It was designed by James Tasker of Cornish, New Hampshire, and constructed by Arthur Adams. Adams was not a highly educated man. Records indicate that he could not read or write, but he was a highly skilled, master builder. The historic structure had been raised once, in the 1970s, because of frequent flooding in this area. When it was nominated for inclusion in the National Register of Historic Places, the Vermont Division of Historic Sites indicated that it was located in the heart of the nineteenth-century Tunbridge Mill District. The bridge was 116 years old when it was de-

stroyed by an ice jam on March 4, 1999. An exceptionally warm spring accompanied by heavy rains sent hundreds of tons of ice and water down the First Branch of the White River until the ice jammed under and around the old bridge, which was normally ten feet above the river. Despite valiant efforts of the townspeople, nothing could save the bridge. Eventually the huge ice jam, with the "roar of a freight train," tore the bridge from its abutments and sent it tumbling into the river. Fearful that the damaged bridge would float on downriver and destroy other historic covered bridges, one of them just about one mile south, the town selectmen decided to set the fallen structure on fire. The smoke from the fire had hardly settled before plans were under way to rebuild the historic span. Funds were provided by the Vermont Agency of Transportation. While the original bridge was built at a cost of $532.32, the new bridge required an expenditure of $230,000. Daniels Construction, Ascutney, Vermont, was contracted for the reconstruction. On July 3, 2000, just sixteen months after the 1883 structure was lost, the seventy-four-foot five-inch, re-creation was pulled into place the "old-fashioned way" by four teams of oxen. The dedication ceremony officially opening the new span was held on July 22, 2000.

Moxley/Guy Bridge

Location: 3.9 miles north of the locality of North Tunbridge, within the Chelsea town line.

Directions: Starting in Tunbridge along VT 110 at the "Mill Bridge" sign, go north on VT 110 for 5.3 miles to Moxley Road on the right (east), turn right onto Moxley Road, and go 0.15 mile to the bridge.

GPS: 43° 57.425N 072° 27.808W

Year: 1883   **Truss:** Queenpost   **Waterway:** First Branch of White River
In Use: Yes   **Number of Spans:** 1   **Owner:** Town of Chelsea
Builder: Arthur C. Adams   **Length:** 58 ft. 8 in.   **Width:** 14 ft. 7 in.
Condition: Fairly good   **Number:** VT-09-01   **Register:** Sept. 10, 1974

An attractive, scrolled sign on the gable end of this bridge indicates 1883 as the date of its completion; however, the National Register of Historic Places lists the date as 1886–87. It is one of four bridges, all along Vermont Route 110, attributed to Arthur C. Adams as the builder. This bridge, like one of its downstream neighbors, the Larkin Bridge, is also built on a skew because of the angle at which the road crosses the First Branch of the White River. According to available records, the Moxley Bridge has been maintained in true nineteenth-century fashion. The only modification that has been recorded is the addition of distribution beams under the random-width, lengthwise plank deck. The queenpost trusses are reinforced with additional kingpost-like diagonals in the center of each truss. Like eight other bridges in this area of Orange County,

the Moxley received a new standing-rib, sheet metal roof in 2001. Its roof was silver. The unpainted, vertical-board-sided structure is resting on cut stone abutments that have been reinforced with concrete. It is the northernmost bridge of six that are located in this quiet river valley along Route 110.

Sayers/Thetford Center Bridge

Location: 0.2 mile west of the locality of Thetford Center, within the Thetford town line.

Directions: From I-91 exit 14, to VT 113, go northwest on VT 113 through Thetford Center for 2.3 miles to Tucker Hill Road on the left (west), turn left onto Tucker Hill Road, and go 0.2 mile to the bridge.

GPS: 43° 49.940N 072° 15.149W

Year: Unknown   **Truss:** Haupt with arch
Waterway: Ompompanoosuc River   **In Use:** Yes   **Number of Spans:** 1 +
Owner: Town of Thetford   **Builder:** Unknown   **Length:** 128 ft. 11 in
Width: 18 ft. 7½ in.   **Condition:** Fairly good   **Number:** VT-09-06
Register: Sept. 17, 1974

There is some question about the type of truss used in the Sayers Bridge. It is listed as a Haupt truss variant with arch in the *World Guide to Covered Bridges;* Nelson lists it as a Haupt with arch in *Spanning Time—Vermont's Covered Bridges;* and Barna lists it as Haupt in *Covered Bridges of Vermont.* A quote that appears in Nelson's book expresses Jan Lewandoski's opinion about the truss:

The Haupt truss system with arch of the Sayers Bridge.

"Some people think that the Sayers Bridge is a Haupt Truss, mostly because some of the diagonals cross more than one bridge panel, but there is no evidence that the builder knew he was building a Haupt Truss." In any event, there is certainly no other bridge in Vermont or any of the other New England states with a truss that begins to resemble this one (see the interior photo). The Bunker Hill Bridge in North Carolina is one of the few other bridges in the country that has a similar truss (see the introduction, section III). In 1963 the span was strengthened with a nail-laminated deck resting on four lengthwise girders, which in turn are supported by a concrete pier in the middle of the Ompompanoosuc River. On our visit to the bridge in February 2003, we noticed that all the roof stringers, the rafters, and some knee braces appeared to be new. These improvements may have been the result of a $24,000 grant awarded to Vermont by the National Historic Covered Bridge Preservation Program.

Union Village Bridge

Location: 2.4 miles northwest of the locality of Pompanoosuc, within the Thetford town line.

Directions: In Pompanoosuc, at the junction of US 5 and VT 132, go northwest on VT 132 for 2.4 miles to a fork in the road with Acadamy Road to the right, bear right onto Acadamy Road, and go 0.6 mile to the bridge on the right (east).

GPS: 43° 47.319N 072° 15.270W

Year: 1867   **Truss:** Multiple kingpost   **Waterway:** Ompompanoosuc River
In Use: Yes   **Number of Spans:** 1   **Owner:** Town of Thetford
Builder: Unknown   **Length:** 117 ft. 9 in.   **Width:** 15 ft. 1 in.
Condition: Excellent   **Number:** VT-09-05   **Register:** Sept. 17, 1974

We made two visits to this bridge—the first in September 2002 and the second in February 2003. On the first visit a complete restoration was in progress. Work had begun in April 2002 with a completion target date of November 2002. The successful bid of $609,213 was awarded to Alpine Construction, L.L.C., of Stillwater, New York. One hundred percent of the funding was provided through the efforts of U.S. Senator James Jeffords. The description of the project called for improvement of the original abutments with concrete; return the original camber of the bridge to a positive camber by installing six heavy, Douglas fir, glue-laminated beams measuring ten inches thick by five feet high extending the entire length of the bridge; replacement of the original deck with glulam stringers and five-inch-thick glulam floor panels; replacement of a portion of both the north and south bottom chords as well as a few vertical truss members; replacement of the roof rafters; installation of a new, standing-seam, copper roof; replacement of the siding with new vertical boards on both the sides and the portals; and installation of interior lighting. On our return in February 2003, we found a beautifully rebuilt covered bridge. It will take some time until the natural board siding acquires the original siding's weathered patina, but in all other respects the wood retains the appearance of the lumber in an original nineteenth-century covered bridge, even though some contemporary building materials were used in this reconstruction.

Irasburg/Orne/Black River/Coventry/Lower Bridge

Location: 0.5 mile southwest of the locality of Coventry on Covered Bridge Road, within the town line of Irasburg, almost on the town line with Coventry.

Directions: Just south of Coventry, at the junction of US 5 and VT 14, go north on US 5 for 0.2 mile to Main St. on the left (west) side of the highway, turn left onto Main St., and go 0.2 mile to Heermanville Road on the left (west); turn left, then left immediately onto Covered Bridge Road; continue on Covered Bridge Road for 0.5 mile to the bridge.

GPS: 44° 51.661N 072° 16.390W

Year: 1881, rebuilt 1999   **Truss:** Paddleford   **Waterway:** Black River
In Use: Yes   **Number of Spans:** 1   **Owner:** Town of Irasburg
Builder: John D. Colton   **Length:** 88 ft.   **Width:** 14 ft. 9½ in.
Condition: Excellent   **Number:** VT-10-02 (2)   **Register:** Nov. 20, 1974

This bridge is an extremely substantial replica of the original 1881 structure that was destroyed by arsonists on Hallowe'en night, November 1, 1997. The new bridge was designed by the Vermont Agency of Transportation (Vtrans) and built by Blow and Cote, Inc., of Morrisville, Vermont. The original bridge was one of two bridges credited to John D. Colton as the builder and was listed

The extremely substantial Paddleford truss system of the Irasburg Bridge.

on the National Register as the Orne Covered Bridge. The most recent documented name of the bridge appears to be Irasburg, as found in various news reports about the structure. The name Black River is understandable because the bridge crosses the Black River. The name Coventry is understandable because the bridge is located on Coventry Road if one is traveling from Irasburg to Coventry, and it is located just over the Coventry town line in the Town of Irasburg. The only explanation we have for the name Lower is that the bridge is located in the southern part of the county. An interesting fact pointed out by the designer of the new bridge is that the original span was built with a fourteen-panel Paddleford truss representing the fourteen counties in the state of Vermont and the fact that Vermont was the fourteenth state to enter the union. The new bridge, likewise, is a fourteen-panel Paddleford truss structure (see the interior photo). Neither bridge required any additional support such as a laminated arch, so familiar in many Paddleford truss bridges. The new bridge, while a replica of the historic one, is built with timbers generally of a larger dimension than the original, and some of these are contemporary glulam materials—the top and bottom chords are eight and one-half by eleven inches, and the floor is five inches thick, all of glulam southern yellow pine. The posted limit on the original bridge was four and one-half tons. The posted limit on the new bridge is sixteen thousand pounds, but the Vtrans assistant engineer of the bridge has indicated that it is designed for twenty-ton, two-axle trucks.

With the use of sturdy timbers and fireproofing chemicals, the new bridge should stand up well against traffic and the threat of arson. There is no question that this bridge will be around for many years into the twenty-first century and possibly well beyond.

Lords Creek Bridge

Location: 1.3 miles east-northeast of the locality of Irasburg, within the Irasburg town line.

Directions: In Irasburg, at the junction of VT 14 South and VT 58, go east on VT 58 for 0.5 mile to an unnamed road on the left (north), turn left, and go 0.8 mile to the bridge on the left (west).

GPS: 44° 48.997N 072° 15.980W

Year: 1881   **Truss:** Paddleford   **Waterway:** Black River
In Use: Yes, private   **Number of Spans:** 1   **Owner:** Private
Builder: John D. Colton   **Length:** 50 ft. 4 in.   **Width:** 15 ft. $2\frac{1}{4}$ in.
Condition: Very poor   **Number:** VT-10-01   **Register:** Does not qualify

Seeing this bridge immediately after the Irasburg Bridge, we were certainly struck by their extremely contrasting structures. In its days as a serviceable crossing over Lords Creek, this was a fine bridge, but the ravages of time and neglect have left it in rather sad condition. It, too, is a short Paddleford truss structure that at one time spanned Lords Creek in the southern part of Irasburg. In the 1950s the abutment of the covered bridge was washed out, and the bridge was replaced with a steel and concrete span. Joseph LaBond, a local farmer, acquired the wooden structure and moved it to a farm lane crossing over the Black River where it flows through his farm property. On our visit to the bridge in January 2003, we found that all the siding has been stripped from both the sides and the portals, which will eventually lead to total deterioration of the bridge. However, a visit to it, as long as the bridge is still standing, is an excellent opportunity to see the skeletal structure of a Paddleford truss.

River Road/School House/School/ Upper Bridge

Location: Approximately 4.5 miles north-northeast of the locality of Troy or approximately 3 miles south-southeast of the locality of North Troy, within the Troy town line.

Directions: Approximately 3 miles north of Troy, at the junction of VT 101 and VT 242, go north on VT 101 for 1.1 miles to an unmarked road on the right (east), turn right onto the unmarked road, and go 1.2 miles to the bridge.

GPS: 44° 57.384N 072° 23.623W

Year: 1910   **Truss:** Town   **Waterway:** Missisquoi River   **In Use:** Yes
Number of Spans: 1   **Owner:** Town of Troy   **Builder:** Unknown
Length: 92 ft. 3½ in.   **Width:** 11 ft. 10½ in.   **Condition:** Fair
Number: VT-10-03   **Register:** Nov. 19, 1974

This is the most northern location of any covered bridge in Vermont. That may be the reason for the last name listed above, or Upper may simply refer to the fact that it is in the upper part of Orleans County in comparison with the Irasburg Bridge, which is in the lower part of the county. There are several unique facts about this bridge that require mentioning. The Town truss timber material is probably the lightest of any Town truss we have seen in the entire New England area. Where most lattice members are at least three inches by ten or eleven inches, the lattice timbers of this bridge are only two by nine; and where most Town trusses have four sets of chords—a primary bottom chord, a sec-

The exceptionally light Town truss system of the River Road Bridge.

ondary bottom chord, a secondary top chord, and a primary top chord—the trusses of this bridge have only three. There is no secondary top chord. Also, where two planks are usually used in the primary chords on each side of the lattice webbing, the River Road Bridge has only one on each side. However, although there is only one chord on each side of the lattice webbing, the dimensions of the chords are twice as thick, six inches rather than the usual three. Another positive fact is that the lattice timbers are placed on twenty-nine-inch centers rather than the usual thirty-six, but instead of the timbers being anchored with two trunnels at each lattice intersection, there is only one. (This is evident in the interior photo.) The height of the lattice trusses is also about two feet shorter than in the average Town truss; consequently, the conventional method of bracing the roof rafter framing with knee braces as well as lateral stringers would not have allowed the usual-height hay wagon to pass through. Therefore, knee braces were not used, but in order to prevent too much vertical shift in the trusses, the builder used external buttresses to provide resistance against strong winds. Notice, too, in the external photo, the exceptionally low roofline that extends quite far over the sides of the bridge, which, although faded now, were painted barn red. This is quite a contrast to most Vermont bridges, the sides of which are unpainted and left to darken naturally from exposure to the weather. Even with all these differences, River Road Bridge has served the Troy area quite well during the past century. Notice how straight and proud it stands with its new, silver, standing-seam sheet metal roof, possibly another beneficiary of the 2001 grant from the National Historic Covered Bridge Preservation Program.

Brown Bridge

Location: Approximately 2.5 miles east of the locality of North Clarendon, within the Shrewsbury town line.

Directions: South of Rutland, at the junction of US 7 South and US 4 West, go south on US 7 for 0.9 mile to North Shrewsbury Road, turn left (east) onto North Shrewsbury Road, go 0.6 mile to the crossroad with East Clarendon Road, cross East Clarendon Road, go 0.2 mile to Cold River Road, turn right onto Cold River Road, go 1.7 miles to a dirt road on the left (if a sign is still there the road name is Upper Cold River Road), turn left onto Upper Cold River Road, and go 0.1 mile to the bridge. Upper Cold River Road is not maintained during the winter months.

GPS: 43° 34.078N 072° 55.275W (coordinates recorded at beginning of Upper Cold River Road)

Year: 1880   **Truss:** Town   **Waterway:** Cold River   **In Use:** Yes
Number of Spans: 1   **Owner:** Town of Shrewsbury
Builder: Nicholas Powers   **Length:** 115 ft. 4¾ in.   **Width:** 15 ft.
Condition: Very good   **Number:** VT-11-09   **Register:** Jan. 21, 1974

This is reported to be the last covered bridge built by master covered bridge builder Nicholas Powers, at the age of sixty-three. According to contemporary restorers of covered bridges, it is one of his finest Town lattice truss bridges. We

have no record of recent work having been performed on the bridge, but when we visited it in September 2002, we found new, unpainted vertical boards on the sides. According to the Vermont Covered Bridge Society newsletter, the siding and a few members of the Town truss had been replaced during the month of June 2002. The sides are completely closed with the exception of narrow openings that run the entire length of the bridge directly under the eaves. The abutment on one end of the bridge consists primarily of a huge streamside boulder, a testament to Powers's Yankee ingenuity, and the other abutment consists of stone laid dry on the bottom and stone with mortar toward the top, all of which is capped with concrete. The deck of the bridge consists of lengthwise planks set on edge and covered with runners in the tire track area. The bridge still has a slate roof, true to the original. This is one of the few Vermont covered bridges that may not be easily accessible after the snows begin to fall. The last tenth of a mile to the bridge traverses Upper Cold River Road, which is not maintained in the winter. The GPS coordinates printed above were taken at the beginning of that last tenth of a mile.

Cooley Bridge

Location: 1.1 miles south of the locality of Pittsford, within the Pittsford town line.

Directions: In Pittsford Mills, at the junction of US 7 and VT 3, go north on US 7 for 0.9 mile to Elm St. on the left (west), turn left onto Elm St., and go 1.1 mile to the bridge.

GPS: 43° 41.430N 073° 01.708W

Year: 1849   **Truss:** Town   **Waterway:** Furnace Brook   **In Use:** Yes
Number of Spans: 1   **Owner:** Town of Pittsford   **Builder:** Nicholas Powers
Length: 50 ft. 3 in.   **Width:** 15 ft. $1\frac{1}{4}$ in.   **Condition:** Fair   **Number:** VT-11-07
Register: Jan. 24, 1974

In several accounts of this bridge, the authors have indicated that on first approach it has the appearance of a "misplaced Conestoga wagon." But, on close observation, it is in reality a very substantial Ithiel Town lattice truss covered bridge. On our visits to the bridge in September 2002 and again in February 2003, we felt that although the bridge is still in use, it is beginning to show the need for some refurbishing. In 2001, a grant of $200,000 was requested from the National Historic Covered Bridge Preservation Program, and that exact amount was awarded. Minutes of the Vermont Agency of Transportation Historic Bridge Committee, which are available through the Vermont Covered Bridge Society website, indicate that reconditioning of this bridge has been discussed at both the February 2002 and the May 2002 meetings. Presently the faded red, vertical, tongue-and-groove siding is in need of work. Discussions

indicate that it may be replaced. Discussions also indicate that a fire-retardant material may be used to paint whatever siding is installed. Because of heavy truck traffic, there is also a need to upgrade the bridge's load limit. All these items and several others are under consideration. It appears to be quite certain that there will be some positive changes made to the bridge in the near future, possibly even before this guide is off the press. This is one of four covered bridges in relatively close proximity to the town center of Pittsford. The other three are the Depot, the Gorham, and the Hammond Bridges.

Depot/Florence Station Bridge

Location: 0.7 mile west of the locality of Pittsford, within the Pittsford town line.

Directions: In Pittsford Mills, at the junction of US 7 and VT 3, go north on US 7 for 1.1 miles to Depot Hill Road on the left (west), turn left onto Depot Hill Road, and go 0.7 mile to the bridge.

GPS: 43° 42.583N 073° 02.544W

Year: 1840   **Truss:** Town   **Waterway:** Otter Creek   **In Use:** Yes
Number of Spans: 1   **Owner:** Town of Pittsford   **Builder:** Abraham Owen
Length: 122 ft. $5\frac{1}{2}$ in.   **Width:** 18 ft. 1 in.   **Condition:** Fairly good
Number: VT-11-06   **Register:** Jan. 21, 1974

According to Joseph Nelson in *Spanning Time—Vermont's Covered Bridges* and Ed Barna in *Covered Bridges of Vermont,* this bridge was built in 1840. However, the *World Guide to Covered Bridges* places its origin at 1853. In either case,

the bridge has been in this location for at least a century and a half. Sometime after the bridge was built, a railroad station was built nearby. Consequently the bridge soon acquired the name Depot and/or Florence Station. In its history, there are records of its having been repaired three times. One of the early repairs required that the southeast side of the bridge be given additional support because it had always been subjected to damage from the prevailing winds, and especially because some of the internal knee braces had been damaged by tall vehicles. This additional support consisted of two steel beams, which are braced against the outside of the upper chord of the Town truss. They are still there today and are quite noticeable in the bridge photo. During the 1974 reconstruction, four steel beams were placed under the deck to bring the live load limit up to contemporary road standards. At this time the truss structure simply supports the dead load of the bridge—its sides and its very heavy slate roof, one of the few remaining slate roofs still in existence on a covered bridge. We have found no record of recent work having been performed, but the bridge does appear to be in fairly good condition. This is another of the four bridges near the town center of Pittsford.

Gorham/Goodnough Bridge

Location: 2 miles south of the locality of Pittsford, within the Pittsford town line.

Directions: In Pittsford Mills, at the junction of US 7 and VT 3, go north on US 7 for 0.9 mile to Elm St. on the left (west), turn left onto Elm St., and go 2 miles through Cooley Covered Bridge to Gorham Bridge Road. The bridge is immediately to the right.

GPS: 43° 40.797N 073° 02.229W

Year: 1842 **Truss:** Town **Waterway:** Otter Creek
In Use: Foot and snowmobile **Number of Spans:** 1
Owner: Town of Pittsford **Builder:** Abraham Owen and Nicholas Powers
Length: 114 ft. 2 in. **Width:** 17 ft. 10¼ in **Condition:** Poor
Number: VT-11-04 **Register:** Feb. 12, 1974

Nicholas Powers was only twenty-four years old when he worked with Abraham Owen on this bridge. Up until this time he had been Owen's apprentice, but on this project they were equal partners. The truss they used for this bridge was the one Owen preferred—the Town lattice truss. Records indicate that the original bridge has been rehabilitated at least two times in its history, once in 1956 and again in 1979. However, when we visited the bridge in September 2002 and February 2003, it was closed to traffic other than pedestrian or snowmobile, and vehicular traffic was carried by a temporary bridge. To the untrained eye, the 1842 span appeared to be in poor condition. Since vehicular traffic was being carried by a temporary bridge, we assumed that the bridge might be rehabilitated again in the near future. Further research indicated that an amount of $576,000 was requested from the National Historic Covered Bridge Preservation Program and in 2001 that exact amount was awarded to Vermont for the rehabilitation of the Gorham Bridge. Minutes of the Vermont Agency of Transportation Historic Bridge Committee of both January and May 2002 indicate that a considerable amount of work is anticipated with this extensive grant. It will probably include work on the abutments, deck, trusses, siding, knee braces, and roof. Hopefully, this work will begin sometime in 2003, and the century-and-one-half-plus span will again be carrying vehicular traffic. This is another of the four spans located near the town center of Pittsford.

Hammond Bridge

Location: 1.6 miles northwest of the locality of Pittsford, within the Pittsford town line.

Directions: In Pittsford Mills, at the junction of US 7 and VT 3, go north on US 7 for 2.1 miles to Kendall Hill Road on the left (west), turn left onto Kendall Hill Road, and go 0.7 mile to the bypassed bridge.

GPS: 43° 43.238N 073° 03.236W

Year: 1842   **Truss:** Town   **Waterway:** Otter Creek
In Use: Foot and snowmobile   **Number of Spans:** 1
Owner: Town of Pittsford   **Builder:** Asa Norse   **Length:** 138 ft. 11$\frac{1}{4}$ in.
Width: 17 ft. 10$\frac{1}{2}$ in.   **Condition:** Fair   **Number:** VT-11-05
Register: Jan. 21, 1974

According to a news item that appeared in the *Boston Phoenix* during the summer of 2001, "the Hammond is known as 'the bridge that went on a voyage,' as it went on a mile-and-a-half-long journey during the flood of 1927. Undamaged, it was mounted on barrels and towed back to its original location, a few miles north of Rutland." The bridge is still resting where it was replaced in 1927, but it was bypassed by a new steel and concrete bridge sometime during the twentieth-century improvement of Kendall Hill Road. The photo was taken from that new bridge.

The Hammond Bridge is listed as a Vermont Historic Site. A news item in the *Rutland Herald* on August 2, 2000, reported that a state official indicated that $250,000 would be required just to preserve this historic structure. On our visits to the bridge in September 2002 and February 2003, it did appear that

some efforts are being made to preserve the bridge. The standing-seam, green, sheet metal roof had the appearance of a relatively recent improvement. However, we can find no records of other specific work having been done. This is a lovely, long specimen of a Town lattice truss bridge and certainly should be preserved.

Kingsley/Mill River Bridge

Location: In the locality of East Clarendon, within the Clarendon town line.

Directions: South of Rutland at the junction of VT 7B and VT 103, go east on VT 103 for 0.1 mile to the road toward the airport on the right, turn right, go 1.3 miles to Gorge Road on the right, turn right onto Gorge Road, go 0.1 mile to East St., turn left onto East St., and go 0.1 mile to the bridge

GPS: 43° 31.445N 072° 56.468W (coordinates recorded in parking area north of the bridge)

Year: 1836   **Truss:** Town   **Waterway:** Mill River   **In Use:** Yes
Number of Spans: 1   **Owner:** Town of Clarendon
Builder: Timothy K. Horton   **Length:** 120 ft. 5 in.   **Width:** 13 ft. 11 in.
Condition: Good   **Number:** VT-11-03   **Register:** Feb. 12, 1974

This covered span, like many others, was named for a family that lived nearby. As early as 1825, Mr. and Mrs. John H. Kingsley operated several mills near the site of the bridge—a carding mill, a sawmill, and a gristmill. Consequently,

the bridge built eleven years later acquired the Kingsley name. The gristmill is still standing a short distance from the bridge and appears to have been converted into a private residence. The bridge was built by a local carpenter, Timothy K. Horton, from the Town of Clarendon. Records indicate that the bridge was closed in 1950 for repairs and again in 1983 for restoration. There are cables attached to each of the four corners in order to provide additional lateral reinforcement against the winds that sweep through the Mill River Valley. In 2001, the state of Vermont was awarded $461,600 to replace roofs on thirty-eight covered bridges statewide by the National Historic Covered Bridge Preservation Program. The Clarendon town selectmen, while they felt that the monies could be used for other, more essential bridge repairs, accepted the funds to install a new green, standing-seam, sheet metal roof. On our visits to the bridge in 2002 and 2003, we felt that it was being well maintained by Clarendon.

Sanderson Bridge

Location: 1.3 miles southwest of the locality of Brandon, within the Brandon town line.

Directions: In Brandon, just south of the junction of US 7 and VT 73 West, Pearl St. goes west (a post office is on the corner of US 7 and Pearl St.). Go west on Pearl St. for 0.3 mile to Maple St., bear right to stay on Pearl St., and go 1 mile to the bridge.

GPS: 43° 47.374N 073° 06.683W

Year: 1838   **Truss:** Town   **Waterway:** Otter Creek
In Use: Closed for restoration   **Number of Spans:** 1
Owner: Town of Brandon   **Builder:** Unknown   **Length:** 131 ft. 3 in.
Width: 17 ft. 5 in.   **Condition:** Disassembled prior to restoration
Number: VT-11-02   **Register:** June 13, 1974

On our visit to this bridge in September 2002, all that we found standing was the deck and the skeleton of the Town lattice trusses. Restoration of the 164-year-old bridge had started just a month earlier. The bridge was closed in 1987 when state inspectors found serious deficiencies in its timber framing. In 2000, upon a request for $500,000 from the National Historic Covered Bridge Preservation Program, the state received an award of $450,000. Because of a series of delays brought on by other considerations nearby, such as discovery of a wealth of Native American remains of significant archaeological importance, work on the bridge project slowed, and the monies allocated to it were used for other covered bridge projects by the Vermont Agency of Transportation. According to the winter 2002 issue of *The Bridger* newsletter of the Vermont Covered Bridge Society, work had resumed in August 2002, when the contract for the

project was awarded to the Blow and Cote construction company of Morrisville, Vermont. On a more recent visit to the bridge site in February 2003, we found that the trusses had been removed, stacked, and covered along the side of the bridge site and work was continuing on the abutments. The target date for completion of the restoration is June 2003 at an anticipated cost of $1,200,000.

Twin Bridge

Location: Approximately 2.6 miles north of the locality of Rutland, within the Rutland town line.

Directions: In Rutland, at the junction of US 7 and US 4 East, go north on US 7 for 1.8 miles. US 7 curves to the left where a secondary road goes straight ahead. Follow the secondary road for 0.8 mile to a dirt road on the right. The large storage building on the right is the Twin Bridge.

GPS: 43° 38.922N 072° 50.359W

Year: 1850   **Truss:** Town   **Waterway:** Dry land   **In Use:** Storage only
Number of Spans: 1   **Owner:** Town of Rutland   **Builder:** Nicholas Powers
Length: 64 ft. 3½ in.   **Width:** 15 ft. 3½ in.   **Condition:** Poor   **Number:** VT-11-10
Register: Does not qualify

In 1849, Nicholas Powers was contracted by the Town of Rutland to build a covered bridge to replace a span over the East Creek lost to floodwaters. The bridge had been in use only for a short time when another flood diverted the

waters of the East Creek about twenty feet from the end of the bridge. Again, Powers was contracted by the town selectmen to build a second bridge over the new waterway. Both bridges remained in service until June of 1947, when 3.7 inches of rain fell on the area and the dam on the East Creek, located in East Pittsford, burst, sending a fifteen-foot wall of water down the creek valley. One of the two bridges was destroyed outright. The other one survived, and after the floodwaters receded it was hauled up onto dry land where it is still resting on temporary abutments to preserve the trusses. There it has served primarily as a storage shed for the Town of Rutland.

A news item that appeared in *The Bridger* newsletter of the Vermont Covered Bridge Society indicates that the Twin is slated for "new life." The 153-year-old structure is to be restored and enjoyed again as part of a recreational bicycle path. The location mentioned is Northwood Park in the Town of Rutland. A $10,000 grant has been secured, and there is another $8,000 of local money available. The total anticipated cost of the project is not known, but it is hoped that it will be completed sometime in 2003.

A. M. Foster Bridge

Location: On Cabot Plains Farm, approximately 5 miles west of the locality of West Danville, within the Cabot town line.

Directions: In West Danville, at the junction of US 2 and VT 15, go west on US 2 for 1.3 miles to West Shore Road on the right (north), go north on West Shore Road for 2.1 miles to the junction with Bricketts Crossing Road and Cabot Plains Road, turn left (southwest) onto Cabot Plains Road, go 0.6 mile to the junction with Bolton Road (Cabot Plains Road bears right), go right to stay on Cabot Plains Road for 0.8 mile to a T, bear right to stay on Cabot Plains Road, and go 0.1 mile to an open field with the bridge in sight over a pond outlet to the left (west).

GPS: 44° 25.423N 072° 16.041W (coordinates recorded on Cabot Plains Road close to the bridge)

Year: 1988   **Truss:** Queenpost   **Waterway:** Pond on farm property
In Use: Yes, private   **Number of Spans:** 1   **Owner:** Richard W. Spaulding
Builder: Richard W. Spaulding   **Length:** 47 ft. $6\frac{1}{2}$ in.   **Width:** 10 ft. $7\frac{3}{4}$ in.
Condition: Excellent   **Number:** VT-12-75   **Register:** Does not qualify

As a young boy, Richard Spaulding, the great-grandson of A. M. Foster, would watch with awe as the sun set over the Green Mountains as he looked out across Cabot Plains from the local cemetery, one of the spots that he and his

The substantial queenpost truss system of the A. M. Foster Bridge.

family would frequent when they returned to Cabot to visit. The family would often go to the Orton Bridge, too, in Marshfield, which fascinated Richard as a boy. His boyhood dream was to someday build a covered bridge that would be just like the Orton Farm Bridge. After Spaulding purchased the farm next to the land once owned by his mother, he decided to build his dream bridge to join the two properties. In 1988, using lumber harvested from the surrounding property, Richard and two relatives, Doug Blondin, a Cabot builder familiar with the old ways of timber joinery, and Frank Foster, who Richard says "has more skill and native knowledge than most anyone I know," set out to erect Richard's own queenpost truss covered bridge. (The substantial truss is shown in the internal photo.) The bridge now spans a man-made pond created where a gully between the properties once existed. The forty-seven-and-one-half-foot structure is covered with unpainted, random-width, vertical board and batten siding on both the sides and the portals, has a deck of lengthwise planks, and has a roof covered with wooden shakes. Upon completion, the covered span was dedicated to Richard's great-grandfather, Alonso Merrill Foster. A. M. Foster was the inventor and patent holder of the well-known Foster Maple Spout and Bucket Cover, which his great-grandson uses now, in the twenty-first century, to harvest maple sap from the sugar maple trees on his Cabot Plains farm property.

Battleground Bridge

Location: 3.4 miles west of the locality of Irasville along VT 17, within the Fayston town line.

Directions: In Irasville, at the junction of VT 100 and VT 17, go west on VT 17 for 3.4 miles to the entrance to the Battleground condominiums on the right. The bridge is at the entrance.

GPS: 44° 12.047N 072° 53.689W

Year: 1975   **Truss:** Stringer with Town   **Waterway:** Mill Brook
In Use: Yes   **Number of Spans:** 1   **Owner:** Private   **Builder:** Unknown
Length: 50 ft. 8 in.   **Width:** 20 ft. $\frac{1}{2}$ in.   **Condition:** Very good
Number: VT-12-D   **Register:** Does not qualify

This is one of the "romantic/modern" shelters that have been mentioned elsewhere in this guide. Battleground Bridge will be readily noticed as one travels along the McCullough Highway, Vermont Route 17, about three and one-half miles west of Irasville. It is located at the entrance to the Battleground Condominium Development. To the untrained eye, it appears to be an authentic covered bridge. However, it is a simulated Town truss built on a concrete, stringer deck. Close examination readily indicates that the truss structure is considerably lighter than an authentic Town truss and the concrete deck is certainly not true to the deck of an authentic covered bridge. The inside portal width is twenty feet, which will comfortably accommodate two-lane traffic, and the structure has a pedestrian walkway on the east side. It appears to have been stained a dark walnut color at some time since it was built in 1975. Although not an authentic or historic bridge, it does lend a typical Vermont atmosphere to the entrance of the housing complex.

Chamberlin Bridge

Location: Approximately 5 miles west-southwest of the locality of Northfield, within the Northfield town line.

Directions: Just south of Northfield, at the junction of VT 125 and VT 12A, go southwest on VT 12A for 1.5 miles to Stony Brook Road on the right (north), turn right onto Stony Brook Road, and go 0.2 mile to a fork in the road. Bear left to stay on Stony Brook Road. After another 0.6 mile, pass through Stony Brook Covered Bridge and continue for 1.9 miles to Chamberlin Road on the right (north), turn right onto Chamberlin Road, and go 0.8 mile to the bridge on the right.

GPS: 44° 08.926N 072° 43.095W

Year: 1956   **Truss:** Stringer with kingpost   **Waterway:** Stony Brook
In Use: Yes, private   **Number of Spans:** 1   **Owner:** Private
Builder: Mahlon Chamberlin   **Length:** 20 ft. 7 in.   **Width:** 11 ft. 11 in.
Condition: Good   **Number:** VT-12-A   **Register:** Does not qualify

This is another "romantic/modern" shelter that has been documented in other covered bridge publications. It is located on private property in the Town of Northfield, where there are also five authentic and historic covered bridges. The Chamberlin Bridge was built in the middle of the twentieth century by the owner of the property on which it is located—Mahlon Chamberlin. On our visit in January 2003, there was too much snow around the bridge to examine it carefully, but we have been told that it has a stringer deck with a kingpost truss to support the sides and the roof. It rests on irregular stone and brick abutments that are extended to short road-level wingwalls. It is covered with random-width, vertical boards on the sides and regular-width, vertical boards on

the gable ends of the portals, all of which are painted pale yellow. The portals have white trim. The deck consists of crosswise planks, and the roof appeared to be covered with standard roofing shingles. According to the DeLorme *Vermont Atlas & Gazeteer,* the bridge spans the same Stony Brook crossed by the bridge of the same name about three miles downstream. If you're an avid bridger in the vicinity of the Stony Brook Bridge, it is certainly worth traveling a few miles farther to see what a twentieth-century craftsman has built.

Coburn/Cemetery Bridge

Location: 2.5 miles northeast of the locality of East Montpelier, within the East Montpelier town line.

Directions: In East Montpelier, at the junction of VT 14 North and US 2 East, go east on US 2 for 2 miles to Coburn Road on the left (north), turn left onto Coburn Road, and go 0.5 mile to the bridge.

GPS: 44° 16.854N 072° 27.275W

Year: 1851   **Truss:** Queenpost   **Waterway:** Winooski River
In Use: Yes   **Number of Spans:** 1   **Owner:** Town of East Montpelier
Builder: Larned Coburn   **Length:** 69 ft. 5 in.   **Width:** 13 ft. 5 in.
Condition: Good   **Number:** VT-12-02   **Register:** Oct. 9, 1974

In *Spanning Time—Vermont's Covered Bridges,* Joseph Nelson has this to say about this bridge:

The Coburn Bridge is not just a covered bridge, it is a fine representation of the bridge-builder's art. The eaves are wide, shedding rain and snow far away from the structure. The gable ends are deep for the same purpose. The sheathing on the sides is three-quarter height, letting in light and air. These are the features that craftsmen employed to ensure a long life for their bridges. But the pilasters and trim at the portals serve no practical purpose—these finishing touches are marks of the builder's pride.

Larned Coburn offered to build this bridge for the town in 1851, if the road would run closer to his home. The town agreed, and Coburn built the bridge. Today, it is on a less used back road that also runs past a local cemetery, hence the second name for the bridge. In 1972 the bridge was reconstructed by the Agency of Transportation, at which time the deck was replaced with a concrete deck supported on three steel beams. Because of its proximity to a gravel quarry, the bridge has had to support heavy loads. The truss structure now supports only the sides, roof, and gable ends of the portal. Further restoration to the bridge was made during the winter of 1996–97.

Kent's Corner Bridge

Location: 4.2 miles west of the locality of East Calais, within the Calais town line.

Directions: In North Montpelier, at the junction of VT 214 and VT 14, go north on VT 14 for 4.9 miles to East Calais; at the junction with Moscow Woods Road on the left(west), turn left onto Moscow Woods Road (be sure to stay onto Moscow Woods Road) and go 2.0 miles to a T with North Calais Road (there is a stop sign). Turn left onto North Calais Road, and go 1.3 miles to Kents Hill Road on the right, turn right, and go 0.9 mile to private property on the right (north), on which the bridge is located in a meadow behind the house.

GPS: 44° 22.101N 072° 29.006W (coordinates recorded on Kents Hill Road across the meadow from the bridge)

Year: 1963, rebuilt 1994   **Truss:** Kingpost   **Waterway:** Curtis Brook
In Use: Yes, private   **Number of Spans:** 1   **Owner:** Private
Builder: Ralph Weeks, reconstructed by Jan Lewandoski   **Length:** 23 ft.
Width: 10 ft. 7$\frac{1}{4}$ in.   **Condition:** Good   **Number:** VT-12-19 (2)
Register: Does not qualify

For a little background on this bridge, we must go back in history to 1798, when the Kent family settled in the area west of East Calais. In that area, Abdiel Kent together with one of six brothers built a tavern and a general store, operated a post office, sold shoes, ran a brickyard and sawmill, and farmed. The tavern served as a stagecoach stopover on the main road between Boston and Montreal. The Kent family holdings became known as Kent's Corner. In 1912,

Louise Andrews from Brookline, Massachusetts, married Ira Rich Kent from Calais, Vermont. Thereafter, they lived in Brookline, where they raised three children and Louise had a successful career as a newspaper columnist. However, the family spent their summers in Vermont in the Kent's Corner area. In the early 1960s, while Louise was writing children's books and cookbooks under the pen name Mrs. Appleyard, she wanted to have a little covered bridge behind the summer residence. So Ralph Weeks, according to Ed Barna in *Covered Bridges of Vermont*, "toggled one up for her" because "he was a great toggler." (For those unfamiliar with the term, a toggler is one who fixes things, perhaps a Vermont term.) By the time Kurt Janson and Eileen Murray bought the summer Kent residence in 1990, Weeks's small kingpost covered bridge was in rather poor condition. Consequently, Kurt and Eileen hired Jan Lewandoski to rebuild the structure. In its restored condition, they now claim, it is probably the smallest covered bridge in Vermont that is a real covered bridge. Look carefully after you find the Janson-Murray home or you'll miss the bridge hidden attractively in their backyard.

Lincoln Gap/Warren Bridge

Location: On Covered Bridge Road in the locality of Warren, within the Warren town line.

Directions: In Irasville, at the junction of VT 17 and VT 100, go south on VT 100 for 4.8 miles to Main St. in Warren on the left (east), turn left onto Main St., and go 0.5 mile to Covered Bridge Road on the right, and turn right to cross the bridge. Or, in Roxbury, at the junction of VT 12A and Warren Road, go west on Warren Road for 5.8 miles (portions are unimproved through Roxbury Gap) to a crossroad, turn left (southwest) toward Warren, go 2.4 miles to Main St. in Warren, turn left, go 0.3 mile to Covered Bridge Road, and turn right to cross the bridge.

GPS: 44° 06.665N 072° 51.410W

Year: 1880, rebuilt 2000   **Truss:** Queenpost   **Waterway:** Mad River
In Use: Yes   **Number of Spans:** 1   **Owner:** Town of Warren
Builder: Walter Bagley   **Length:** 57 ft. 6 in.   **Width:** 13 ft. 10¾ in.
Condition: Very good   **Number:** VT-12-15 (2)   **Register:** Aug. 7, 1974

This bridge is a "good model for a partnership between the State and the Federal Government, and local folks," Governor Howard Dean commented when he spoke at the dedication of the restored Lincoln Gap Bridge in Warren on October 2, 2000. The queenpost truss sturcture was built originally in 1880 by Walter Bagley. Records indicate that in 1995 the deck was strengthened with timber cross braces and stringers and the roof was reshingled. In 1998, when the Agency of Transportation examined all the bridges along the Mad River, it felt that this bridge was in fairly good condition. However, a flood that occurred after that examination removed some of the boards on the upstream side, exposing the truss system, and the town engineers realized they had a problem. Consequently, the bridge was closed in the fall of 1998. After discussions with state officials and research on what funds would be available to assist with the project, it was decided that a complete restoration was the most practical way to proceed. The contract for the restoration was awarded to Jan Lewandoski and his company, Restoration and Traditional Building, which has specialized in historic preservation and the restoration of timber structures

since the 1980s. Repairs were made to the truss system and the deck—which included three-inch transverse planking covered with two-and-one-half-inch runners—and some new siding was added. The total cost of the restoration was $122,500.

Martin/Orton/Orton Farm Bridge

Location: Just east of the locality of Plainfield, within the Marshfield town line.

Directions: In Plainfield, at the junction of US 2 and VT 214 North, go east on US 2 for 1.5 miles. The bridge is visible approximately 100 feet south of the highway in an open field.

GPS: 44° 17.265N 072° 24.517W (coordinates recorded along US 2, across the field, north of the bridge)

Year: 1890   **Truss:** Queenpost   **Waterway:** Winooski River
In Use: No   **Number of Spans:** 1   **Owner:** Private
Builder: Harry Martin or Herman Townsend   **Length:** 44 ft. 8¾ in.
Width: 11 ft. 2¼ in.   **Condition:** Poor   **Number:** VT-12-06
Register: Oct. 9, 1974

According to Joseph Nelson in *Spanning Time—Vermont's Covered Bridges,* this bridge might be one of the last covered bridges built by Herman F. Townsend. On the other hand, Ed Barna in *Covered Bridges of Vermont* attributes the bridge to Harry Martin. Other accounts indicate that a William Martin bought

a farm in the Plainfield locality that was reputed to be one of the finest in the area. From the information available to us, we can only surmise that Harry Martin was a descendant of William Martin and that he might have had the covered bridge built by Townsend. In any event, the bridge has always been located on this farm property, which was eventually purchased by the Orton family, hence its second name. In recent years, however, the land was purchased by Charles Thorndike of Meredith, New Hampshire, who has graciously given us permission to include information about his covered bridge in our book. With this new ownership, the name has reverted to the original name of Martin Bridge. At some time during its use, the structure may have been used to prevent livestock from crossing the Winooski River, because there is still a gate that is hinged to the queenpost truss closest to the highway. Otherwise it appears that the bridge remains basically the way it was built over one hundred years ago, except that, according to a local neighbor, the shake roof was replaced about twenty years ago. There is no road or lane leading to the bridge, but it is accessible to visitors and is an interesting subject to photograph with its weathered, one-hundred-year-old, siding.

Moseley/Stony Brook Bridge

Location: Approximately 2.3 miles west-southwest of the locality of Northfield, within the Northfield town line.

Directions: Just south of Northfield, at the junction of VT 12 South and VT 12A, go southwest on VT 12A for 1.5 miles to Stony Brook Road on the right (north), turn right onto Stony Brook Road, go 0.2 mile to a fork in the road, bear left to stay on Stony Brook Road, and go 0.6 mile to the bridge.

GPS: 44° 07.221N 072° 41.342W

Year: 1899   **Truss:** Kingpost   **Waterway:** Stony Brook   **In Use:** Yes
Number of Spans: 1   **Owner:** Town of Northfield   **Builder:** John Moseley
Length: 36 ft. 8 in.   **Width:** 15 ft. 10 in.   **Condition:** Fairly good
Number: VT-12-07   **Register:** Nov. 20, 1974

This bridge derives one of its names from its builder, John Moseley, and the other from the stream it crosses. It is a relatively short kingpost span and has an unusual truss. Where the center post and diagonals on most kingpost truss bridges go from the bottom chord to the top chord, on this bridge they originate on a second chord placed above the bottom chord and do not extend to the upper chord, which in turn supports the roof truss members. In a restoration of 1971, five steel beams were installed under the deck, and in 1990 the original abutments of large granite blocks were faced with concrete. The abutments extend to short road-level wingwalls. The sides are covered with random-

width, vertical boards and the portals with vertical boards and battens, all of which are painted barn red. The present deck consists of crosswise planks set on edge, and the roof is covered with gray, standing-seam sheet metal. It is a lovely, short covered span located on a peaceful, rural road that winds west from the village of Northfield into the Northfield Mountains.

Newell/Middle/Lower Cox Brook/ Second Bridge

Location: On Cox Brook Road, just northwest of the locality of Northfield Falls, within the Northfield town line.

Directions: In Northfield Falls, at the junction of VT 12 and Cox Brook Road, go northwest on Cox Brook Road for 0.2 mile to the bridge.

GPS: 44° 10.364N 072° 39.170W

Year: 1872   **Truss:** Queenpost   **Waterway:** Cox Brook   **In Use:** Yes
Number of Spans: 1   **Owner:** Town of Northfield   **Builder:** Unknown
Length: 56 ft. 9 in.   **Width:** 15 ft. $6\frac{1}{2}$ in.   **Condition:** Good   **Number:** VT-12-10
Register: Oct. 15, 1974

There is a cluster of four covered bridges in the village of Northfield Falls that are all within one mile of each other. Three of them are on the same road—Cox Brook Road. Ed Barna, in *Covered Bridges of Vermont*, refers to these as "three red jewels strung on the same necklace, all within 0.4 mile of each

other." This is the only place in the Northeast where it is possible to view and even photograph one covered bridge from its nearest neighbor on the same road. These three bridges all have an assortment of names. All the names are easy to explain except the first one listed for this bridge, and all seem to be used interchangeably in any account written about the bridges. No record has been found to explain the name Newell, although, as has frequently happened, the name may originate from a family that lived near the bridge at the time it was built. The Newell Bridge is the middle bridge of the three; it is built over the lower part of Cox Brook, and it is the second bridge in the red jewel "necklace." Records indicate that it was built in 1872, and the only reference to changes indicates that Newell, like the other two bridges on Cox Brook Road, had its deck reinforced with steel beams in the 1960s. However, its present condition indicates that it has definitely been well maintained by the Town of Northfield.

Pine Brook/Wilder Bridge

Location: Approximately 2.5 miles northeast of the locality of Waitsfield, within the Waitsfield town line.

Directions: Approximately 1 mile north of Waitsfield village center, at the junction of VT 100 and Tremblay Road on the east, go east on Tremblay Road for 0.8 mile to a T at North Road, turn left (north), and go 0.3 mile to the bridge. At North Road, a sign also points to the covered bridge.

GPS: 44° 12.339N 072° 47.527W

Year: 1872 **Truss:** Kingpost **Waterway:** Pine Brook **In Use:** Yes
Number of Spans: 1 **Owner:** Town of Waitsfield **Builder:** Unknown
Length: 48 ft. $6\frac{1}{2}$ in. **Width:** 14 ft. 2 in. **Condition:** Good **Number:** VT-12-12
Register: June 13, 1974

All references to this bridge indicate that it was built in 1872; however, a sign posted directly below the name of the bridge on its portal indicates 1870. The bridge contains a classic kingpost truss. When Milton Graton was called on to restore the bridge in 1976, he found it in very poor condition. Both chords of the kingpost truss were rotted, one of the corners had sagged almost a foot, and the deck was being supported by posts placed in the middle of Pine Brook. Realizing that the bridge required a greater load limit for the twentieth century but still wanting to retain the authenticity of the historic structure, he proposed placing steel beams one-half inch below the deck system so that only an overload would cause the deck to bend enough to require the additional support. Consequently, concrete caps were poured on top of the original cut stone abutments, steel beams were installed, the chords of the trusses were repaired, and the sides and roof were replaced. In a more recent rehabilitation of 1989, the lengthwise deck planks were also replaced. The structure also has a new standing-seam metal roof, which, we assume, may have been installed during the 2001 reroofing project of the Vermont Agency of Transportation. On our visit in January 2003, we found the bridge in good condition under the watchful eye of the Town of Waitsfield.

Robbins Nest Bridge

Location: 1.7 miles west of the locality of East Barre, within the Barre town line.

Directions: In East Barre, at the junction of US 302 and VT 110, go west on US 302 for 1.7 miles. The bridge is just to the left (south) at the entrance to a private residence.

GPS: 44° 10.722N 072° 28.247W

Year: 1962–64   **Truss:** Queenpost   **Waterway:** Jail Branch of Winooski River
In Use: Yes, private   **Number of Spans:** 1   **Owner:** Private
Builder: Robert R. Robbins   **Length:** 50 ft. 2¾ in.   **Width:** 12 ft. 10¾ in.
Condition: Very good   **Number:** VT-12-18   **Register:** Does not qualify

When we visited this bridge in January 2003, we found a For Sale sign posted on the portal. After inquiring further we found that the entire property on which the bridge is located was being sold by John Sell, son of the owner of the property. Mr. Sell graciously allowed us to visit and document the bridge, which is readily seen on the south side of the highway as one travels along US Route 302, just a short distance west of East Barre. Bobby Robbins built a relatively short, authentic, queenpost truss at the entrance to the private property in 1962 over the Jail Branch of the Winooski River. It is a replica of another bridge, once located about one hundred yards downstream, that was destroyed in the Flood of 1927. The truss members consist of Douglas fir from California shipped by way of the Panama Canal to New Jersey, then on to Vermont. The siding is local Vermont lumber. New owners of the property reinforced the struc-

ture, which was becoming unstable, in 1990, at which time steel beams were installed under the deck. On our visit, we found the bridge to be in very good condition. It makes an appropriate entrance to the private log home that stands on the hill beyond the bridge.

Slaughter House Bridge

Location: On Slaughterhouse Road (formerly Bailey Road), southern edge of the locality of Northfield Falls, within the Northfield town line.

Directions: In Northfield Falls, at the junction of VT 12 and Cox Brook Road (Falls General Store is on the southwest corner), go south on VT 12 for nearly 0.3 mile to an obscure road on the right (west), Slaughterhouse Road; turn right and go 0.1 mile to the bridge. When we visited in January 2003, winter parking was available up the hill beyond the bridge and railroad tracks.

GPS: 44° 10.112N 072° 39.265W

Year: ca. 1872   **Truss:** Queenpost   **Waterway:** Dog River   **In Use:** Yes
Number of Spans: 1   **Owner:** Town of Northfield   **Builder:** Unknown
Length: 59 ft. 7 in.   **Width:** 11 ft. 9 in.   **Condition:** Good   **Number:** VT-12-09
Register: June 13, 1974

Just a few tenths of a mile downstream from the Station/Northfield Falls Bridge, the Slaughter House Bridge can be found. The road to the bridge is a little obscure because it is located downhill off Vermont Route 12 on Slaughterhouse Road, which has the appearance of a private driveway. However, if you follow the directions given above, the road should be fairly easy to locate. Slaughter-

house Road dead-ends shortly after it crosses the bridge. Its name, obviously, indicates that at one time it reached a slaughterhouse. This bridge, like the other three in Northfield Falls, is painted barn red. Its sides are covered with random-width, vertical boards with a single window on each side and a narrow opening under the eaves, and its portals are covered with vertical board and batten siding. This is the only bridge in the Town of Northfield that has a rounded portal opening. There are no records of reinforcement under the deck, but a sign posted on the road displays a 16,000-pound limit, an indication that the bridge may have had steel beams placed under the deck sometime during the twentieth century. It, too, like many other bridges in the state, may have benefited from the reroofing program of the Agency of Transportation in 2001. It is covered with a standing seam, sheet metal roof. Slaughter House Bridge is another example of fine maintenance by the Town of Northfield.

Station/Northfield Falls Bridge

Location: On Cox Brook Road, just northwest of the locality of Northfield Falls, within the Northfield town line.

Directions: In Northfield Falls, at the junction of VT 12 and Cox Brook Road, go northwest on Cox Brook Road for 0.1 mile to the bridge.

GPS: 44° 10.342N 072° 39.069W

Year: 1872   **Truss:** Town   **Waterway:** Dog River   **In Use:** Yes
Number of Spans: 1+   **Owner:** Town of Northfield   **Builder:** Unknown
Length: 136 ft. 8½ in.   **Width:** 16 ft. 2 in.   **Condition:** Good   **Number:** VT-12-08
Register: Aug. 13, 1974

This is the first of the "three red jewels" refered to by Ed Barna in *Covered Bridges of Vermont*. The name Station is derived from the railroad depot that was located near the bridge. This bridge, like the other two "jewels," was built in 1872, but the builder is unknown. In 1963 the entire structure was strengthened to accommodate heavier live loads. The original deck system was reinforced with four steel beams, a central concrete pier was added, and the original, unmortared stone abutments were capped with concrete. In recent years the entire roof system has been replaced. This may have occurred in 2001, when $461,600 was awarded to Vermont for the purpose of reroofing thirty-eight of its covered spans. This award was made possible by the National Historic Covered Bridge Preservation Program, established as a result of the Transportation Equity Act for the Twenty-first Century. The good condition of this bridge, like that of the others in Northfield Falls, reflects the concern of the local authorities for the preservation of these historic remembrances of a time long past, but not forgotten.

Upper Cox Brook/Upper/Third Bridge

Location: On Cox Brook Road, just northwest of the locality of Northfield Falls, within the Northfield town line.

Directions: In Northfield Falls, at the junction of VT 12 and Cox Brook Road, go northwest on Cox Brook Road for 0.3 mile to the bridge.

GPS: 44° 10.417N 072° 39.332W

Year: ca. 1872 **Truss:** Queenpost **Waterway:** Cox Brook **In Use:** Yes
Number of Spans: 1 **Owner:** Town of Northfield **Builder:** Unknown
Length: 51 ft. 3 in. **Width:** 14 ft. $1\frac{1}{2}$ in. **Condition:** Good
Number: VT-12-11 **Register:** Oct. 1, 1974

This is the third of the "three red jewels" that are strung within a three-tenth-mile stretch of Cox Brook Road in Northfield Falls. It is also the uppermost of the two bridges that span Cox Brook. On our visit in January 2003, we could not appreciate the setting of the bridge to its fullest extent. The waterfall above the bridge and abandoned dam, referred to in *Spanning Time—Vermont's Covered Bridges* by Joseph Nelson, were not noticeable, because deep winter snow and ice covered the brook. The origin of this bridge as well as its two lower neighbors has been placed at 1872 by the Vermont Agency of Transportation. Because the road crosses the brook at a slight angle, this bridge, like several others in the state, is built on a skew. Records indicate that it, like the other two Cox Brook Road bridges, had the deck system reinforced in 1966, when four steel beams were placed beneath the floor members. It, too, may have received a new roof as a part of the reroofing program conducted by the Agency of Transportation in 2001. It is interesting to note that the upper two bridges on

Cox Brook Road are built with the queenpost truss design, while the lower bridge, also the longest of the three (across Dog River) is constructed with the Town lattice truss.

Village/Great Eddy/Big Eddy Bridge

Location: In the locality of Waitsfield on Bridge Street, within the Waitsfield town line.

Directions: In Waitsfield, at the junction of VT 100 and Bridge St. (on the east side), go east on Bridge St. for 0.1 mile to the bridge.

GPS: 44° 11.373N 072° 49.414W

Year: 1833   **Truss:** Burr   **Waterway:** Mad River   **In Use:** Yes
Number of Spans: 1   **Owner:** Town of Waitsfield   **Builder:** Unknown
Length: 107 ft. 2½ in.   **Width:** 16 ft. 2 in.   **Condition:** Good
Number: VT-12-14   **Register:** Sept. 6, 1974

The three names of this bridge, listed above, seem to be used interchangeably. We have chosen to list Village first because it seems to be the most common name given in news articles, and it is truly a "village" bridge, being located on one of the busiest streets in downtown Waitsfield. (A bronze plaque on the bridge says "WAITSFIELD VILLAGE BRIDGE . . . CONSTRUCTED 1833.") It was built to replace another span that was lost in the spring freshet of 1830, and it is considered to be the second-oldest Burr truss bridge still standing in Vermont. (The Pulp Mill Bridge in Weybridge-Middlebury is the oldest.) The names

Great Eddy or Big Eddy are derived from the eddy created in the Mad River caused by the large bedrock outcrop on which the north end of the bridge rests. In 1940, a pedestrian walkway was added to the bridge. In 1973, after 140 years of heavy use, the bridge was "returned to good health" by Milton Graton and Sons of New Hampshire. They replaced the deck support structure and flooring and the upper lateral bracing, installed new knee braces actually hewn from the branches of trees with the proper curvature, and replaced the roof with standing-seam sheet metal. In 1989, the floor was replaced again, and distribution beams were added under the deck. In 1992, structural repairs were made to the truss by Paul Ide and Jan Lewandoski, and once again in 2001. This most recent repair included replacement of eight floor beams, some deck planking, and some of the Burr truss timbers, especially a portion of one of the arches, all of this done by Restoration and Traditional Building, owned and operated by Jan Lewandoski. It is quite remarkable that even though this bridge has had many repairs and restorations and is used quite heavily, it still maintains a great deal of its original structural design and historic integrity.

Bartonsville/Williams River Bridge

Location: On the south edge of the locality of Bartonsville, within the Rockingham town line.

Directions: Just north of I-91 exit 6, at the junction of US 5 and VT 103, go northwest on VT 103 for 5.3 miles to Lower Bartonsville Road on the right (east), turn right onto Lower Bartonsville Road, and go 0.3 mile to the bridge.

GPS: 43° 13.428N 072° 32.218W

Year: 1870 **Truss:** Town **Waterway:** Williams River **In Use:** Yes
Number of Spans: 1 **Owner:** Town of Rockingham
Builder: Sanford Granger **Length:** 150 ft. 7$\frac{1}{2}$ in. **Width:** 15 ft. 1$\frac{3}{4}$ in.
Condition: Good **Number:** VT-13-11 **Register:** July 2, 1973

At one time there were seventeen covered bridges standing in the Town of Rockingham. Today there are only three—Bartonsville, Worrall, and Victorian Village. Most of the losses are attributed to the floods that seem to plague the river valleys in this area. The Bartonsville Bridge was built in 1870 by Sanford Granger when the previous bridge at this location was washed away in the spring freshet of 1869. The 150-foot Town truss structure stands within a short distance of the Green Mountain Railroad. Today, with the exception of extensive repairs done in 1983, the bridge remains primarily the way it was built 133 years ago. The repairs made by Bancroft Construction of South Paris, Maine,

included the installation of steel rods under the roadway to increase lateral strength and the addition of distribution beams that were tie-bolted under the deck. The unpainted, vertical, random-width siding has long window openings near each end giving travelers an adequate view of the railroad on one end and oncoming traffic at the bend in the road on the other. The portals are also sided with unpainted, random-width vertical boards on the artistically curved gable ends and with horizontal boards on the corbels. The deck is covered with wide planks set on edge and a pair of runners in the tire track area. The roof is covered with green, standing-seam sheet metal. Bartonsville Bridge made a striking appearance in the Williams River Valley as the sun rose when we visited it in October 2002.

Cheddar/McWilliam/MacMillan Bridge

Location: 0.5 mile south of the locality of Grafton, within the Grafton town line.

Directions: In Grafton, at the junction of Townshend Road and VT 121, go south on Townshend Road for 0.5 mile to Grafton Village Cheese Co. on the left (east) side of the road. The bridge is just north of the cheese company building.

GPS: 43° 09.974N 072° 36.799W

Year: 1960   **Truss:** Stringer with kingpost
Waterway: South Branch of Saxtons River   **In Use:** Foot traffic only
Number of Spans: 1   **Owner:** Private   **Builder:** Unknown   **Length:** 60 ft. 4 in.
Width: 12 ft. 6$\frac{1}{2}$ in.   **Condition:** Fairly good   **Number:** VT-13-E
Register: Does not qualify

Cheddar is the "official" name of this bridge, according to an executive of the Grafton Village Cheese Company, owner of the bridge. The other two names have appeared in printed information about the bridge and the cheese company. This is another nonauthentic, nonhistoric "covered bridge." It is included here because of its frequent mention in other printed literature about the covered bridges and tourist areas of the state and this area in particular. Although the structure is built on what appears to be a traditional deck with planks laid diagonally, the deck actually rests on two steel stringer beams. The simulated kingpost truss serves only to support the sides and roof structure of the span. However, it is an attractive bridge, one that is frequently photographed, and it does carry pedestrian and nonmotorized vehicles into the parklike setting beyond the bridge. It is covered with unpainted, random-width, vertical boards on both the sides and the portals. There are three windows on each side, and the gable ends of the portals have an arched white trim. The roof is covered with black, standing-seam sheet metal. Cheddar Bridge is certainly worth a visit, especially if one is in Grafton to see the Kidder Hill Bridge.

Creamery Bridge

Location: On Guilford Street in the city of Brattleboro, within the Brattleboro town line.

Directions: In Brattleboro, at the junction of US 5 and VT 9 West, go west on VT 9 for 1.4 miles to Guilford St. on the left (south); turn left onto Guilford Street to the bridge.

GPS: 42° 50.977N 072° 35.148W

Year: 1879   **Truss:** Town   **Waterway:** Whetstone Brook
In Use: Yes   **Number of Spans:** 1   **Owner:** City of Brattleboro
Builder: Team of 13 local builders and suppliers   **Length:** 80 ft. $1\frac{1}{2}$ in.
Width: 16 ft. $2\frac{1}{2}$ in.   **Condition:** Good   **Number:** VT-13-01
Register: Aug. 28, 1973

This has always been one of our favorite bridges, possibly because a photograph of it, taken at the peak of fall foliage in 1993, created a most striking picture. The bridge derived its name from the Brattleboro Creamery, which stood nearby. It is very heavily traveled, probably one of the busiest bridges in the area, because it provides a bypass of the downtown area for traffic going from Vermont Route 9 on the east end of Brattleboro to US 5 on the south end. A new bridge in this location was necessitated in 1878 when high waters in November of that year destroyed an older span. According to Ed Barna in *Covered Bridges of Vermont,* the cost of the bridge was $1,037.80, lower than the estimate of a well-known Massachusetts builder. Feeling that his bid was too high, the selectmen decided to have the bridge built by local builders. The lumber

used by the local carpenters was spruce, which was considered better (and some of it was one-half inch thicker) than the hemlock proposed by the bidder. The slate roof and the pedestrian walkway were added in 1917. The walkway is certainly a decided plus because of the heavy vehicular traffic. After the inspection by the Agency of Transportation in the 1990s, the agency recommended that the bridge be closed and a bypass be constructed. However, on our visit in October 2002, the bridge was still in very active use.

Green River Bridge

Location: On Stage Road, in the locality of Green River, within the Guilford town line.

Directions: In West Brattleboro, at the junction of VT 9 and Greenleaf St., go west on Greenleaf St. for 0.7 mile, bear left onto an unidentified road for 0.7 mile to Hinesburg Road, turn left onto Hinesburg Road, go 4.9 miles to Green River Road on the left (Hinesburg Road becomes a dirt road after 4.7 miles), turn left onto Green River Road, go 1.9 miles to Stage Road, and turn right to the bridge.

GPS: 42° 46.538N 072° 40.022W

Year: 1870   **Truss:** Town   **Waterway:** Green River
In Use: Yes   **Number of Spans:** 1   **Owner:** Town of Guilford
Builder: Marcus Worden, abutments by M. H. Day   **Length:** 104 ft. 7 in.
Width: 14 ft. 10 in.   **Condition:** Very good   **Number:** VT-13-04
Register: Aug. 28, 1973

This is a lovely bridge, located in a most spectacular setting in the southeastern corner of Windham County, just below the historic Green River Crib Dam. According to accounts by covered bridge authorities Ed Barna and Joseph Nelson, the bridge was built in 1870 by Marcus Worden with abutments by M. H. Day after an older span was destroyed in a spring freshet of 1869. Another unique feature of the bridge is that, around the 1950s, the local residents of this small rural settlement kept their mailboxes inside it. Rumor had it that even the post office had difficulty finding its way around the many unmarked roads in the area.

None of the references available to us indicate any recent work having been performed on the bridge, but we found it in very good condition when we visited it in October 2002. The sides are covered with random-width, vertical boards that have been left to weather naturally; the portals are covered with barn-red, vertical boards on the legs and random-width, horizontal board on the gables. The deck consists of wide, lengthwise planks set on edge, with runners in the tire track area, and the roof is covered with standard roof shingles. The entire structure rests on stone abutments that are extended to moderate-length, road-level wingwalls. It is obvious that the Town of Guilford is keeping this excellent Town truss structure in fine condition.

Hall/Osgood Bridge

Location: Just east of the locality of Saxtons River, within the Rockingham town line.

Directions: In Bellows Falls, at the junction of US 5 and VT 121, go west on VT 121 for 3.1 miles to Hall Bridge Rd TH 5 on the right (north); turn right to the bridge.

GPS: 43° 08.213N 072° 29.244W

Year: 1867, rebuilt 1982   **Truss:** Town   **Waterway:** Saxtons River
In Use: Yes   **Number of Spans:** 1   **Owner:** Town of Rockingham
Builder: Sanford Granger, rebuilt by Milton Graton   **Length:** 120 ft. 7 in.
Width: 12 ft.   **Condition:** Good   **Number:** VT-13-07 (2)
Register: Aug. 28, 1973

In 1867, Sanford Granger built a substantial Town lattice truss bridge in this location. It served the area well until 1980, when an overweight truck was driven onto the bridge. The bridge collapsed when the driver, hearing strange sounds as he crossed the span, stopped the truck and ran. If he had continued to travel across the bridge, it might have survived. Milton Graton and Sons were contracted to build the replacement. The Town truss of the Granger bridge had been built with three-inch-thick planks; Graton chose to rebuilt it with four-inch planks. The replacement was completed by 1982. Always trying to build in the most authentic way possible, the Gratons moved the rebuilt structure across the stream, over the falsework, with a team of oxen. The bridge now carries a four-ton limit, mostly to save it from overloading. A representative of the

Agency of Transportation, however, indicates that in its present, upgraded condition, it could probably support 22,000 pounds. According to Ed Barna in *Covered Bridges of Vermont,* another official declared: "That thing would probably take a Sherman tank." The span has always had a relatively narrow portal opening but a standard height, almost giving it the appearance of a railroad bridge. On our visit in October 2002, we found the bridge well maintained by the Town of Rockingham.

High Mowing Farm/K. Harris/ Twin Silos Bridge

Location: 1.6 miles north of the locality of Wilmington, within the Wilmington town line.

Directions: In Wilmington, at the junction of VT 9 West and VT 100 North, go north on VT 100 for 0.5 mile to Stowe Hill Road on the right (east), turn right onto Stowe Hill Road, and go 1.1 miles to farm fields on the right (east). The bridge can be seen in the valley below.

GPS: 42° 53.023N 072° 50.926W

Year: 1949   **Truss:** Town   **Waterway:** Unnamed tributary of Deerfield River
In Use: Yes, private   **Number of Spans:** 1   **Owner:** Private
Builder: Haynes Brothers, Wilmington, Vt.   **Length:** 20 ft. $1\frac{1}{2}$ in.
Width: 9 ft. 8 in.   **Condition:** Good   **Number:** VT-13-15
Register: Does not qualify

This picturesque, little bridge cannot really be considered historic, because it was not built until the middle of the twentieth century, but it certainly can be considered authentic. In 1949, Arthur D. Pinkham, owner of a five hundred-acre tract of land, required a span so that his sheep could cross over into a fifty-acre grazing area that had been cleared of rocks and turned into a pasture. He hired a local building company, Haynes Brothers, Inc., of Wilmington, Vermont, to build the bridge. The builders choose the Town lattice truss for the supporting framework, possibly patterned after the Creamery Bridge in Brattleboro. Both the sides and the portals were covered with random-width, vertical board siding, painted barn red. The upper half of each side was left open for most of its length. The deck was covered with lengthwise planks and the roof with wooden shakes. The entire structure rests on stone abutments that extend to moderate-length, ground-level wingwalls. At one time the farm containing the bridge included some other buildings across Stowe Hill Road, on which there were two silos, hence the third name of the bridge—Twin Silos. The name K. Harris is carved on a name board on the north portal of the bridge. It may be the name of one of the owners after Pinkham. The name High Mowing Farm may originate from a name given to the farm by the owner at the time the bridge was built. We've known it by that name ever since our first visit to the bridge in 1993. The property is now owned by Stephen and Susan Gross, who have graciously given permission to visit the bridge for photographs or just to spend a little time at this beautiful setting in the lower hills of the Green Mountain area.

Kidder Hill Bridge

Location: South edge of the locality of Grafton, within the Grafton town line.

Directions: In Cambridgeport, at the junction of VT 121 and VT 35, go northwest on VT 121 for 3.9 miles to Kidder Hill Road on the left (south), turn left, and go 0.2 mile to the bridge.

GPS: 43° 10.155N 072° 36.334W

Year: 1870   **Truss:** Kingpost   **Waterway:** South Branch of Saxtons River
In Use: Yes   **Number of Spans:** 1   **Owner:** Town of Grafton
Builder: Unknown   **Length:** 67 ft. 6 in.   **Width:** 12 ft.   **Condition:** Good
Number: VT-13-03   **Register:** July 2, 1973

This is another bridge that replaced an older span in 1870, after a flood caused by the spring thaw and heavy rains destroyed the former crossing in 1869. It is the longest of the kingpost truss bridges still standing in Vermont. In its early years, many wagon loads of soapstone were transported over the bridge from the quarry located on Bear Hill in the southern part of Grafton. It served the town extremely well for over 120 years. In the 1990s, the Agency of Transpor-

tation considered it to be unsafe. The townspeople, eager to save their historic span, banded together to save the bridge. Voters approved a $28,000 tax appropriation; individual contributors provided an additional $42,000; and the Grafton Improvement Association, the Windham Foundation, and the Vermont Agency of Transportation provided the balance needed. The total restoration cost $160,000. F. W. Whitcomb did the actual work on the bridge under the watchful eyes of Dion and Stevens, engineers. We have seen the restoration treatment used here in our home state, but this is only the second time we have seen it in Vermont. Two large glulam beams, one foot thick by five feet high by sixty-seven feet long, were placed on the top of the deck, on either side of the roadway, against the kingpost truss structure. These were tie-bolted to transverse, twelve-inch-wide by fifteen-inch-high glulam beams positioned under the deck. The deck planks and runners were also replaced, the bridge received new siding, and the roof was replaced with standing-seam sheet metal. In its present condition, the bridge should continue to serve the Grafton area well for quite a long period of time without another reconstruction.

Scott Bridge

Location: 1.5 miles west of the locality of Townshend, within the Townshend town line.

Directions: In Townshend, at the junction of VT 30N and VT 35, go north on VT 30 for 1.5 miles. The closed bridge is to the left (south).

GPS: 43° 02.926N 072° 41.760W

Year: 1870   **Truss:** Town and kingpost   **Waterway:** West River
In Use: No   **Number of Spans:** 3
Owner: State Division for Historic Preservation
Builder: Harrison Chamberlin   **Length:** 276 ft. $10\frac{1}{2}$ in.   **Width:** 15 ft. $3\frac{3}{4}$ in.
Condition: Fair   **Number:** VT-13-13
Register: Aug. 28, 1973

According to measurements taken on our visit in October 2002, Scott Bridge is the longest covered bridge in Vermont by nine feet eight and one-half inches—the second-longest being the West Dummerston Bridge. This is another bridge that replaced an older structure after the floodwaters of 1869 devastated a large portion of the surrounding river valleys. Harrison Chamberlin built this three-span bridge in 1870 using two different truss structures. The truss at the east end of the bridge is a Town lattice that reaches from the east abutment to a pier near the far side of the river; the western section consists of two kingpost spans. One span reaches from the pier on which the Town truss ends to a pier beyond the west bank, and the second kingpost truss portion extends from the second pier to the western abutment. The kingpost sections of the bridge were not covered until it was necessary to repair the roof on the Town truss portion in 1873. In 1955, the bridge was closed to vehicular traffic and turned over to the Vermont Historic Sites Commission. Some work has been done to maintain and stabilize the bridge since that time. A twelve-ply laminated arch was added to the Town truss section at one time in its history, but according to the historic marker at the bridge site, it was not successful. Even though the bridge is open only to pedestrian traffic at this time, it is certainly worth seeing this rather different use of two conventional truss systems.

Snow Bridge

Location: Approximately 26 miles north of the locality of Wilmington, within the Stratton town line.

Directions: From the south, starting in Wilmington at the junction of VT 9 and VT 100, go north on VT 100 for 13.8 miles to West Wardsboro; at the junction of VT 100 and Stratton/Arlington Road, go left (west-northwest) on Stratton/Arlington Road for 3.4 miles to West Jamaica Road on the right (northeast), turn right onto West Jamaica Road, go 2.2 miles to Mountain Road on the left (north), turn left onto Mountain Road, go 4.4 miles to T with Brazer's Way (Stratton Mountain Road), turn left (northwest) onto Brazer's Way, go 1.4 miles to North Brookwood Road on the left (south), turn left onto North Brookwood Road, and go 0.65 mile to the bridge on the left. The bridge is on Snow Bridge Road. Or from the north, starting in Rawsonsville at the junction of VT 100 North and VT 30 West, go west on VT 30 for 1.7 miles to Bondville; at the junction of Stratton Mountain Ski Resort Road on the left (south), turn left onto Stratton Mountain Ski Resort Road and go 3.3 miles to North Brookwood Road on the right (south); turn right onto North Brookwood Road, and go 0.65 miles to the bridge on the left.

GPS: 43° 06.674N 072° 55.002W

Year: 1998   **Truss:** Stringer with Town
Waterway: Ski Run on Stratton Mountain   **In Use:** Yes
Number of Spans: 1   **Owner:** Snow Bridge Town Homes Project

Builder: Intra West Stratton Development Corp.   **Length:** 61 ft. 5½ in.
Width: 11 ft. 11¼ in.   **Condition:** Very good   **Number:** VT-13-P
Register: Does not qualify

This is one of the bridges referred to in the introduction to the Vermont section as a nonhistoric and nonauthentic structure. However, it is a very attractive contemporary structure that provides a most appropriate entrance into the Snow Bridge Town House Project located in the Stratton Mountain Ski Area. It was built by the Intra West Stratton Development Corporation in 1998. Even though it must be classified as a stringer bridge because its deck rests entirely on four heavy steel I beams, its cover has been built with a true Town lattice truss design. An interesting feature of this bridge is that it does not span a waterway, a railroad, or another highway; it spans one of the downhill ski runs that descend from the peak of Stratton Mountain. Notice, in the photo, the warning to skiers located on the side of the bridge. The barn-red siding with white trim is quite attractive, especially in the winter against the snow-clad ski slope and mountain background, and in typical nineteenth-century fashion, its roof is covered with wooden shakes. If you are looking for another photogenic covered bridge subject, it is worth your while to take the time and travel the distance to see this late-twentieth-century span.

Victorian Village/Depot Bridge

Location: In the locality of Rockingham at the Vermont Country Store, within the Rockingham town line.

Directions: Just north of I-91 exit 6, at the junction of US 5 and VT 103, go northwest on VT 103 for 2.5 miles. The bridge provides one of the entrances to the Vermont Country Store to the left.

GPS: 43° 11.810N 072° 30.240W

Year: 1967   **Truss:** Kingpost (modified)   **Waterway:** Unnamed brook
In Use: Only as entrance to parking lot   **Number of Spans:** 1   **Owner:** Private
Builder: Aubrey Stratton   **Length:** 43 ft. 7¼ in.   **Width:** 14 ft. ½ in.
Condition: Good   **Number:** VT-13-23   **Register:** Does not qualify

This bridge is part of the Depot Bridge that was built in Townshend in 1872 by Harrison Chamberlin. In 1959, when the U.S. Army Corps of Engineers was preparing to build dams for the Townshend flood control project, it was necessary to remove the bridge from the area. At the time, Vrest Orton, founder of a chain of shops known as Vermont Country Store, happened to be chairman of the Vermont Historic Sites Commission. He was able to save the bridge from annihilation by having it dismantled, carefully labeled, and stored on the farm of Aubrey Stratton. In 1967, when the Rockingham outlet of Orton's Vermont

Country Store was built, Mr. Stratton, using timbers from the original Depot Bridge, rebuilt a shortened version of it spanning a small, unnamed brook on the country store property between the main store building and a restored nineteenth-century gristmill. The restructured span is now a forty-three-foot seven-and-one-quarter-inch kingpost truss bridge, one of only four such designs in Vermont.

West Dummerston / Dummerston Bridge

Location: On East-West Road, just east of the locality of West Dummerston, within the Dummerston town line.

Directions: In Williamsville Station, at the junction of Williamsville Road and VT 30, go south on VT 30 for 3 miles to East-West Road on the left. The bridge is just to the left (east). Or, in Brattleboro, at the junction of US 5 and VT 30, go north on VT 30 for 6.6 miles to East-West Road on the right (east). The bridge is just to the right (east).

GPS: 42° 56.194N 072° 36.805W

Year: 1872, rebuilt late 1990s **Truss:** Town **Waterway:** West River
In Use: Yes **Number of Spans:** 2 **Owner:** Town of Dummerston
Builder: Caleb B. Lamson **Length:** 267 ft. 2 in. **Width:** 18 ft.
Condition: Very good **Number:** VT-13-02 (2) **Register:** May 8, 1973

This is the fourth bridge to be built over this stretch of the wide West River during the 1800s. The first one was lost in the spring freshet of 1826, the second

one in the same location was lost in 1839, and the third one, built farther downstream, was lost in the "famous flood" of 1869. The townspeople debated for an extensive period of time as to where the new bridge should be located. Finally, in 1872, a two-span, Town lattice truss bridge was built by Caleb Lamson, then only twenty-two years old. The bridge was in constant use until November 1993. There are records of Jan Lewandoski making emergency repairs to maintain the stability of the structure until major restoration could take place. In December 1994, at a special town meeting, an appropriation of $621,000 was approved for the project. Fay, Spofford, and Thorndike of Bedford, New Hampshire, were hired as the engineers. Final approval of the plans for rehabilitation was granted in 1996. The plans called for contractors to replace the top chords and two sets of bottom chords with slightly larger glue-laminated materials, replace the floor beams with glue-laminated beams, replace the deck with a new laminated timber deck, add knee braces to the roof structure, and repair or replace roof framing and hardware as needed. It was estimated that 85 percent of the existing Town lattice truss was replaced with new timbers, and new trunnels were also installed. A new seamed metal roof was also part of the project. All of this seems to indicate that the bridge now standing in this location is really a replica of the original bridge.

Williamsville Bridge

Location: Just west of the locality of Williamsville, within the Newfane town line.

Directions: At the junction of VT 30 and Williamsville Road, approximately 3 miles south of Newfane, go west on Williamsville Road (which becomes Depot Road within 0.1 mile) for 1.9 miles to a T, turn left (southwest) toward South Newfane, and go 0.4 mile to a fork. Take the left fork for 0.2 mile to the bridge.

GPS: 42° 56.571N 072° 41.215W

Year: 1870   **Truss:** Town   **Waterway:** Rock River   **In Use:** Yes
Number of Spans: 1   **Owner:** Town of Newfane   **Builder:** Eugene P. Wheeler
Length: 117 ft.   **Width:** 13 ft. $10\frac{1}{2}$ in.   **Condition:** Fair   **Number:** VT-13-05
Register: Aug. 14, 1973

There are several confusing facts that should be mentioned about this bridge. According to the DeLorme *Vermont Atlas & Gazeteer,* 2000 edition (the most recent available) and current town records, this bridge crosses the Rock River. Several other historians list the waterway as Stoney Brook, Marlboro, or South Branch. The exact date of construction and the builder are also in question. In one account, Caleb B. Lamson, builder of the original Dummerston Bridge, is credited with having built this one as well around 1870, but some reports indicate that the bridge preceding this one survived the flood of 1869. Another account indicates that this bridge was built around 1860 by Eugene P. Wheeler.

Because of its location on a very busy connecting road between two relatively major Vermont highways, the bridge has required frequent repairs. Ac-

cording to Doris Knechtel, adminstrative assistant, Newfane Board of Select-men, there has been considerable discussion about its future. In relatively recent years, the Vermont Agency of Transportation has installed two large glulam beams inside the bridge, tie-bolted to the deck, that extend the entire length of the bridge to provide adequate live load capacity. The Town lattice truss has been repaired many times and should really be completely rebuilt. Plans at the time of this writing are to remove the large glulam beams, replace them with appropriate-sized glulam beams under the deck, raise the South Newfane end of the bridge, and replace the truss timbers as needed to provide a totally restored bridge. This restoration will probably also include new siding and a new deck. It will be the kind of restoration preferred by the town selectmen, who since the beginning of discussions wanted to preserve the historic authenticity of this century-plus-old span.

Worrall Bridge

Location: Approximately 0.5 mile south of the locality of Bartonsville, within the Rockingham town line.

Directions: Just north of I-91 exit 6, at the junction of US 5 and VT 103, go northwest on VT 103 for 4.9 miles to Williams Rd TH 14 on the right (east), turn right onto Williams Rd TH 14, and go 0.2 mile to the bridge.

GPS: 43° 12.713N 072° 32.147W

Year: 1868   **Truss:** Town   **Waterway:** Williams River   **In Use:** Yes
Number of Spans: 1   **Owner:** Town of Rockingham
Builder: Sanford Granger   **Length:** 82 ft. $4\frac{1}{2}$ in.   **Width:** 14 ft. $1\frac{3}{4}$ in.
Condition: Good   **Number:** VT-13-10   **Register:** July 16, 1973

This bridge is another of the three spans in the northern part of Windham County that are credited to Sanford Granger as the builder. He completed the bridge in 1868, just before the floodwaters of 1869 destroyed many other structures in the Williams River Valley. The Worrall Bridge, although threatened by the rising waters of the river, remained standing after the floodwaters receded. Through its history, like most covered bridges, it has seen a variety of changes. Another flood in 1936 washed away much of the riverbank behind the northeast abutment. According to the nomination information provided when the bridge was submitted for inclusion in the National Register of Historic Places, that damage was repaired with a nineteen-foot span of steel beams that carries the approach road across the washed-out area to the end of the bridge. That end of the bridge rests on the original abutment of stonework, which has been reinforced with concrete. The bank behind the reinforced abutment has been partly excavated, leaving the abutment nearly freestanding, much like a pier. According to Ed Barna in *Covered Bridges of Vermont,* this modification is referred to

as a "wooden ramp." The southwestern end of the bridge still rests on the original abutment of stone. The lattice truss system has also been reinforced—with six pairs of vertical posts, six inches by seven inches that are further steadied by iron rods and steel cables. On our visit in October 2002, there was no evidence of any recent work having been done on the bridge, but it is still serving the residents in this rural part of the county.

Baltimore Bridge

Location: In the locality of Goulds Mill, within the Springfield town line.

Directions: Just southeast of Goulds Mill, at the junction of US 5 and VT 11 West, go west on VT 11 for 0.6 mile to Eureka Schoolhouse and the Baltimore Covered Bridge site on the right (north) side of the highway.

GPS: 43° 16.202N 072° 26.876W (coordinates recorded in parking lot of Eureka Schoolhouse)

Year: 1870   **Truss:** Town   **Waterway:** Small Brook
In Use: Foot traffic only   **Number of Spans:** 1   **Owner:** State
Builder: Granville LeLand and Dennis Allen   **Length:** 44 ft. $11\frac{1}{2}$ in.
Width: 15 ft. 2 in.   **Condition:** Very good   **Number:** VT-14-03
Register: Does not qualify

In its original location, the Baltimore Bridge spanned the Great Brook in the Town of North Springfield, approximately ten miles northwest of its present location. There it carried the main road to the small mountain town of Baltimore, hence its name. The Town lattice truss structure was built in 1870 by Granville LeLand and Dennis Allen. By 1967, the ninety-seven-year-old span was badly twisted, and the town declared it unsafe for travel and closed it. In an account of this situation, Milton Graton in *The Last of the Covered Bridge Builders* states: "We were asked for a price for making it safe again but at a town meeting it was decided that our price *was not high enough.* The matter stood still for two years. The water from the roof dripped into the bottom chord on alternate corners."

In 1969, after the historic Eureka Schoolhouse was preserved in a state historic site, a committee, headed by former U.S. Senator Ralph E. Flanders, was formed to rescue the Baltimore Bridge, restore it, and move it to a new location next to the school. Mr. Graton was again contacted to do the job. He offered to do what was necessary for a sum of $10,000, but before an agreement was signed, the committee increased the amount to $10,500. Abutments were built at the new location from stones salvaged from the original bridge site; the bridge was completely, authentically restored; and it was dedicated at its new home. Unfortunately, Senator Flanders did not live to see the project completed, but the bridge was dedicated to his memory in 1970. It is now readily available for all to see and enjoy along busy Vermont Route 11 at Goulds Mill.

Best/Bests/Swallows Bridge

Location: Approximately 2.2 miles west of the locality of Brownsville, south of VT 44, within the West Windsor town line.

Directions: Approximately 3.7 miles west of Brownsville, at the junction of VT 106 and VT 44, go east on VT 44 for 1.5 miles to Churchill Road on the right (south), turn right onto Churchill Road, and go 0.05 mile to the bridge.

GPS: 43° 27.315N 072° 30.973W

Year: 1889   **Truss:** Tied arch   **Waterway:** Mill Brook   **In Use:** Yes
Number of Spans: 1   **Owner:** Town of West Windsor   **Builder:** A. W. Swallows
Length: 37 ft. 4½ in.   **Width:** 13 ft. 11½ in.   **Condition:** Very good
Number: VT-14-10   **Register:** July 2, 1973

This is one of three surviving tied arch truss bridges still standing in the state of Vermont. Town records indicate that the thirty-seven-foot, four-and-one-half-inch structure was built in 1889 by A. W. Swallows—note that the third name listed for the bridge is that of the builder. Some accounts of this bridge list the date as 1890. However, according to Ed Barna in *Covered Bridges of Vermont,* "a memoir by longtime resident Mary Beardsley Fenn mentions seeing the date 1889 neatly chiseled into the bridge." When originally built, the arch truss members consisted of five laminates of approximately two-inch-thick planks, bolted together and tied to the bottom chord. In 1991, when the bridge was refurbished, an additional two planks were added to each arch. The actual bridge covering consists of a simple post and beam shed.

Ed Barna also tells the story of the six Best girls "who lived in the little house

The tied arch system of the Best Bridge.

nearby, decorating the knotholes and cracks in the bridge with daisies, black-eyed Susans, devil's paintbrushes, and Queen Anne's lace, especially if a wedding or funeral was to be held in town; the girls holding their own funerals in the bridge for dead birds or other animals they found; the older girls quieting fussy babies in the heat of summer by taking them in carriages to the bridge, the coolest place, and pushing them back and forth; town children coming across to sing Christmas carols for old Mr. Best, who was then 101; and paddling in the brook beneath, even though it was too small and shallow to learn to swim."

Bowers/Brownsville Bridge

Location: Approximately 1 mile west of the locality of Brownsville, within the West Windsor town line.

Directions: Approximately 3.7 miles west of Brownsville, at the junction of VT 106 and VT 44, go east on VT 44 for 2.8 miles to Bible Hill Road on the left (north). (A town maintenance building and gravel pit are on the south side of the road.) Turn left onto Bible Hill Road and go 0.3 mile to the bridge.

GPS: 43° 27.676N 072° 29.442W

Year: ca. 1919   **Truss:** Tied arch   **Waterway:** Mill Brook   **In Use:** Yes
Number of Spans: 1   **Owner:** Town of West Windsor   **Builder:** Unknown
Length: 45 ft. 4 in.   **Width:** 13 ft. 9 in.   **Condition:** Very good
Number: VT-14-11   **Register:** Aug. 28, 1973

This is another one of the three tied arch truss spans that are still standing in Vermont; the other two are the Best Bridge, just two miles away, and the Lake Shore Bridge located in Charlotte, Chittendon County. It was built around 1919, but there is no record of the builder. The tied arch trusses of this relatively short span consists of five laminates of two-by-ten-inch planks tied to the bottom chords with three-quarter-inch rods. The bridge covering is a simple post and beam shed with no openings other than the two portals. It is covered with well weathered, vertical boards on both the sides and the portals. The deck consists of lengthwise planks, and the roof is covered with green, standing-seam sheet metal. The bridge may be one of the thirty-eight in the state that received new roofs through a $461,600 grant from the National Historic Covered Bridge Preservation Program in 2001. We considered the bridge to be in fine condition on our visits to it in September 2002 and February 2003.

Frank Lewis Bridge

Location: On the farm property of Mr. and Mrs. Frank Lewis, 3.7 miles northwest of the locality of Woodstock, within the Pomfret town line.

Directions: In Woodstock, at the junction of US 4 East or West and VT 12 North, go north on VT 12 for 3.7 miles. At this point VT 12 is a straight highway with a house on the right side of the road and farm buildings on the left side of the road. The covered bridge is the most southern structure in the field on the left side of the highway.

GPS: 43° 39.232N 072° 33.883W (coordinates recorded in the Lewises' driveway)

Year: 1981   **Truss:** Town/kingpost variation   **Waterway:** Gulf Stream
In Use: Yes, private   **Number of Spans:** 1   **Owner:** Private
Builder: Frank Lewis   **Length:** 40 ft. 4 in.   **Width:** 10 ft. 1½ in.
Condition: Fair   **Number:** VT-14-116   **Register:** Does not qualify

This is a covered bridge that most people would not recognize as such, because of its location among other farm structures on the Frank Lewis property just a short distance from Woodstock. It has received little mention in covered bridge literature, but because of its unique truss structure it certainly deserves documentation. It was built by Mr. Lewis himself when he was sixty-one years old. According to Ed Barna in *Covered Bridges of Vermont,* Frank's family has commented: "Grandpa, he can make anything out of wood." In 1981, Lewis needed a way to get his farm animals and machinery across the small Gulf Stream, which runs through his farm property, so he devised his own bridge with a rather unusual truss. It will not be found on any other bridge in the New England area. It is a combination of an expanded, modified Town lattice truss that is sandwiched between two sets of elongated kingpost diagonals (see the interior photo). The only covering on the structure is the roof, along with the vines that have grown up and twined around the truss structure. Most of the lumber for the forty-foot span Frank acquired through the company for which he worked. Barna tells that the "company bought a lot of plywood, which came in bundles with scrap lumber (known as dunnage) protecting the sheets from being damaged by the binding. Lewis scrounged as much dunnage as he could, and now it constitutes the bulk of the bridge." On our visit to the bridge in September 2002, Mr. Lewis, now eighty-two years old, accompanied us to his bridge so that we could measure it, photograph it, and record the usual statistics that we acquire on every bridge visit.

The unusual Town and kingpost truss of the Frank Lewis Bridge.

Lincoln Bridge

Location: Approximately 1.5 miles west of the locality of West Woodstock, within the Woodstock town line.

Directions: In West Woodstock, at the entrance to Woodstock Union High School and Middle School on the south side of US 4, go west on US 4 for 1.5 miles to the road on the left (south); turn left to cross the bridge.

GPS: 43° 36.047N 072° 34.126W

Year: 1877   **Truss:** Pratt with tied arch   **Waterway:** Ottauquechee River
In Use: Yes   **Number of Spans:** 1   **Owner:** Town of Woodstock
Builder: R. W. and B. H. Pinney   **Length:** 137 ft. 1 in.   **Width:** 14 ft. 5$\frac{1}{4}$ in.
Condition: Very good   **Number:** VT-14-13   **Register:** Aug. 28, 1973

This bridge was named for a family who owned land nearby at the time the bridge was built. A notice posted by the Woodstock Historical Society on the vertical board covering inside the portal states:

> Town Reports indicate that this bridge was built in 1877 by the brothers R. W. and B. H. Pinney of Bridgewater and Woodstock respectively, at a cost of $1,732.23. It is the only known remaining wooden bridge in America of its kind and design. In 1844, T. Willis Pratt invented and patented the bridge plan which bears his name. The design utilized vertical wooden posts and crossed iron rods through the arch to the lower chords.

This style found increased favor with the advent of iron construction and literally hundreds of steel bridges in use across the nation can trace their origin back to this surviving example of Pratt's truss [see the interior photo].

The single span is 134 feet long and in it the truss is in the form of an arch. The bridge was completely renovated in 1947.

In 1998, the bridge was completely renovated again by the Wright Construction Company. In this restoration high-strength steel rods were added below the bottom chords, and distribution beams were installed under the floor. The town selectmen also specified that green fiberglass panels—"the

The modified Pratt truss system of the Lincoln Bridge.

kind used to make chicken coops"—be installed in the roof, which greatly disturbed lovers of authentic, historic bridges. One of these called the installation "honky-tonk." Otherwise the structure remains true to the original intent of the builders. In all of our bridging experiences, this is the only bridge we have seen with such a roof treatment.

Martin's Mill/Martinsville Bridge

Location: On Martinsville Road, just east of the locality of Hartland, within the Hartland town line.

Directions: In Hartland, at the junction of US 5 and VT 12, go south on US 5 for 0.5 mile to Martinsville Road on the left (east), turn left onto Martinsville Road, and go 0.5 mile to the bridge.

GPS: 43° 31.930N 072° 23.776W

Year: 1881   **Truss:** Town   **Waterway:** Lulls Brook   **In Use:** Yes
Number of Spans: 1   **Owner:** Town of Hartland   **Builder:** James Tasker
Length: 139 ft. 1 in.   **Width:** 16 ft. 3¾ in.   **Condition:** Good
Number: VT-14-01   **Register:** Aug. 28, 1973

A complex of mills that date back to 1823 stood near the site of this bridge when it was built in 1881 by James Tasker. One of those mills was owned by Frank Martin, who made sashes, blinds, and turbine pipe. Frank's brother, Ernest, had a competing mill nearby. In its early years, this was a very busy bridge because the former Connecticut River Turnpike used it to cross Lulls

Brook. Today, nothing but the ruins of the mills exist, but the bridge, not nearly as busy, still carries traffic over the Martinsville Road. In 1979, repair work was done to strengthen the span. According to Nelson in *Spanning Time—Vermont's Covered Bridges*, "distribution beams were tie-bolted under the deck, diagonal steel sway braces were installed, and steel cables were added to lend lateral support. Except for additions like these, James Tasker's bridge remains much as he left it more than one hundred years ago." On our visits in September 2002 and February 2003, we found that, with the exception of a few missing side boards, the bridge was being well maintained by the Town of Hartland.

Middle/Union Street Bridge

Location: In the locality of Woodstock on Union Street/Mountain Ave., within the Woodstock town line.

Directions: In the village of Woodstock where the town green divides US 4, East and West, Union St./Mountain Ave. goes north from the US 4 West portion of the divide. Turn north onto Mountain Ave. to the bridge.

GPS: 43° 37.477N 072° 31.203W

Year: 1969 **Truss:** Town **Waterway:** Ottauquechee River **In Use:** Yes
Number of Spans: 1 **Owner:** Town of Woodstock **Builder:** Milton Graton
Length: 143 ft. **Width:** 14 ft. 9 in. **Condition:** Excellent **Number:** VT-14-15
Register: Does not qualify

The best information for this bridge is that which appears on a notice by the Woodstock Historical Society displayed along the walkway of this lovely, twentieth-century structure in downtown Woodstock:

> Several covered bridges spanned the Ottauquechee River at this point. The 1877 iron bridge which succeeded them was condemned in 1966. Estimates for a modern concrete and steel span started at $75,000, whereas this comparable wooden bridge was constructed for approximately $65,000. The State of Vermont paid 80% of the cost and the balance was raised by private subscription. Full State specifications of 15-ton capacity have been more than fulfilled. The roadway is 14' 5" with a 5' sidewalk.
>
> Graton Associates of Ashland, N.H., the designer and builders, have had extensive experience in repairing and moving covered spans. This was their first complete building project and it employs the Town Truss construction. . . . The span is the first truly authentic highway covered bridge to be built in either New Hampshire or Vermont since 1895.
>
> There is no functional metal in the trusses, the lattice members being held in place with some 1,400 trunnels, turned from 23 white oak trees from

New Hampshire. The necessary 80,000 board feet of lumber is mostly Douglas fir from Oregon.

The estimated weight of one side member is 19 tons. Total weight of the bridge is approximately 100 tons and the length of the bridge is 150 feet. It was assembled on Union St. and ox-drawn across the river on cribwork in June of 1969.

In May of 1974, on the night of the Firemans' Ball, the bridge was set afire by a group of local youths. The roof and siding was destroyed and extensive damage was done to the lattice trusses on the north end. Fortunately, Mr. Graton's genius was available for the intricate reconstruction, but the cost of the repairs exceeded $87,000. Some few thousand of this was retrieved by court order as a percentage of wages during a two year period of those old enough to work.

Even after the fire, the State has rated the span at 16-ton capacity, and there is still no structural steel in the bridge.

Quechee Bridge

Location: In the locality of Quechee, within the Hartford town line.

Directions: Just west of Quechee Gorge, at the junction of US 4 and Waterman Hill Road, go north on Waterman Hill Road for 0.1 mile to the bridge.

GPS: 43° 38.727N 072° 25.146W

Year: 1970　**Truss:** Stringer with Town　**Waterway:** Ottauquechee River
In Use: Yes　**Number of Spans:** 1　**Owner:** Town of Hartford
Builder: Quechee Lakes Development Corp.　**Length:** 68 ft. 11in.
Width: 24 ft. 7 in.　**Condition:** Good　**Number:** VT-14-A
Register: Does not qualify

This is another of the twentieth-century, nonauthentic covered bridges that we have chosen to include in our guide. It has been included because it is mentioned in tourist literature and spans the Ottauquechee River where it carries Waterman Hill Road into the town of Quechee. It was built by the Quechee Lakes Development Corporation in 1970. It is definitely of the stringer variety, built on steel girders with a macadam deck, but is attractively covered with a simulated Town lattice truss. The deck, obviously, supports the live load, and the truss structure supports only the sides, portals, and roof. The lower portion of each side is covered with natural, vertical boards, and the portals are covered with similar material, painted gray. The roof is covered with wooden shakes. A walkway has been provided to accommodate pedestrian traffic along this busy span. The entire structure is supported on concrete abutments and lies across a very rocky portion of the river where a waterfall flows past the famous Simon Pearce glass showroom and restaurant. Anyone visiting the town of Quechee, especially the Pearce showroom, is certain to see this modern example of an older era.

Salmond Bridge

Location: Just east of the locality of Amsden, within the Weathersfield town line.

Directions: In Downers, at the junction of VT 106 and VT 131, go east on VT 131 for 2.4 miles to Henry Gould Road on the left (north). (Henry Gould Road is easy to miss; watch for a field on the left/north side of the road at 2.2 miles with many large boulders. Henry Gould Road is just ahead on the left/north.) Turn left and immediately bear to the right. The road is closed ahead. The bridge is just beyond on the closed road.

GPS: 43° 25.575N 072° 29.331W (coordinates recorded at parking area near the bridge)

Year: ca. 1880   **Truss:** Multiple kingpost   **Waterway:** Sherman Brook
In Use: Closed to vehicular traffic   **Number of Spans:** 1
Owner: Town of Weathersfield   **Builder:** James F. Tasker   **Length:** 53 ft. 2 in.
Width: 16 ft. 4 in.   **Condition:** Good   **Number:** VT-14-05
Register: Does not qualify

A bronze plaque located near the present site of this bridge states:

> Salmond Bridge was built by James F. Tasker c1880. This 54' multiple king post structure spanned the Black River near Stoughton Pond and was named after the Salmond family living near the bridge. It remained in this area until 1959, when it was relocated beside route 131 in Amsden in order to remove it from the flood control area. There it was used as a town storage shed.
> It was restored and moved to this site over Sherman Brook in 1986, through the efforts of the townspeople of Weathersfield.

The first move of the bridge was necessitated because the U.S. Army Corps of Engineers was building the North Springfield Lake Flood Control Reservoir and the bridge would have been lost. According to Milton Graton, who assisted with the move, the bridge did not receive much care in the Amsden location. In his book *The Last of the Covered Bridge Builders*, Mr. Graton says: "The floor had been removed and imitation brick siding had been nailed all over the outside. A good servant had been exposed to a shameful end." Fortunately, in the mid-1980s the Committee for the Restoration of the Salmond Covered Bridge was formed and headed off the idea of having the ill-fated bridge serve as the glass-recycling center at the town dump. The restored bridge was dedicated in its present location in 1986, at which time Karl Stevens, the town's first manager, led his pair of oxen across the span as part of the ceremony.

Seven Cedars Farm Bridge

Location: Approximately 7 miles southeast of the locality of Gaysville, within the Barnard town line.

Directions: Approximately 3.5 miles northeast of Gaysville, at the junction of VT 107 and VT 12 South, go south on VT 12 for 4.2 miles to the bridge on the left (east) side of the highway.

GPS: 43° 45.229N 072° 37.966W

Year: 1985   **Truss:** Stringer with kingpost   **Waterway:** Pond Brook
In Use: Yes, private   **Number of Spans:** 1   **Owner:** Private
Builder: Neal Campbell   **Length:** 24 ft. 5½ in.   **Width:** 13 ft. 2 in.
Condition: Good   **Number:** VT-14-D   **Register:** Does not qualify

This is another twentieth-century stringer bridge that deserves documentation in this guide. It is frequently visited by tourists traveling in the Barnard area, and is located within easy driving distance of the cluster of nine covered bridges in the southern part of neighboring Orange County. It was built by Neal Campbell, owner of the Seven Cedars Farm, in 1985 using timbers from an old barn on the property. At first glance, one would consider this short, twenty-four-and-one-half-foot span to be an authentic kingpost truss structure. But careful examination of the deck, even during the winter (February 2003, with a heavy snow cover), indicated that the bridge is actually supported on two steel girders. The kingpost, while probably sufficiently substantial to support both the live load and the dead load of the bridge, actually supports only the sides and the roof. The sides and the portals are covered with unpainted, random-width, vertical boards, the deck consists of crosswise planks laid over the steel girders, and the roof is covered with regular roof shingles. The bridge is in a lovely, rural setting crossing Pond Brook and is certainly worth taking the time to visit if one is traveling the central Vermont area.

Taftsville Bridge

Location: In the locality of Taftsville, within the Woodstock town line.

Directions: In Taftsville, Woodstock Road forks off and parallels US 4 on the north side of the highway; Quechee Main St. goes north from Woodstock Road. The bridge is on Quechee Main St.

GPS: 43° 37.840N 072° 28.103W

Year: 1836
Truss: Multiple kingpost, queenpost, and arch (a unique combination)
Waterway: Ottauquechee River   **In Use:** Yes   **Number of Spans:** 2
Owner: Town of Woodstock   **Builder:** Solomon Emmons III
Length: 193 ft. 6 in.   **Width:** 17 ft. 9 in.   **Condition:** Fairly good
Number: VT-14-12   **Register:** Aug. 28, 1973

An account of this bridge posted on the inside covering relates the following:

> This is the oldest covered bridge in Windsor County and the fourth oldest in
> the state of Vermont.
>
> The bridge was built in 1836 by Solomon Emmons. It stretches 194 feet
> across the Ottauquechee River (an Indian name meaning "winding water").
>
> It was built completely from local forests at a cost of $1800.00. Eight huge trees
> were cut to 90 feet each & made into four spliced "stringers". . . . timbers that
> span the distance and hold the bridge together. There is a stone pier in the
> middle for support and the style of construction is called "QueenPost" design.
>
> The original bridge was built with solid side walls and was very dark. The
> walls were papered with ads for various "miracle drug" ads and notices for
> upcoming events. It was a favorite spot for young lovers to meet. The win-
> dow holes were cut out after 1914.

According to Jan Lewandoski, a twenty-first-century restorer of covered
bridges, the truss structure of this two-span bridge is quite different, "an almost uncategorizable truss." He claims that it has features of both a queenpost

The unique combination of kingpost, queenpost, and arch truss system of the Taftsville
Bridge.

and multiple kingpost truss. In other accounts it is described as a multiple kingpost truss with arches (see the interior photo).

Through the middle of the 1800s, the bridge was maintained by the original builder and later his son. In the early 1900s, the four laminated arches were added to the multiple kingpost trusses—the south arches consist of ten laminates, and the north arches consist of twelve laminates. In a 1953 renovation, the entire structure was raised on its abutments to prevent water from running onto the bridge deck, and steel gussets replaced the overhead knee braces. One other change took place in 1980, when distribution beams were installed under the deck system.

Teago / South Pomfret / Smith Bridge

Location: On the south edge of the locality of South Pomfret, within the Pomfret town line.

Directions: In Woodstock, at the junction of US 4 East or West and VT 12 North, go 1.1 miles north on VT 12 to a fork in the road (VT 12 bends left); go straight on the road to South Pomfret for 1.9 miles to a private dirt road on the left (west). The bridge can be seen from the South Pomfret road. The owners welcome visitors to the bridge but request that visitors do not drive across the bridge. We suggest parking along South Pomfret road.

GPS: 43° 39.680N 072° 32.254W

Year: 1973   **Truss:** Town   **Waterway:** Barnard Brook
In Use: Yes, private   **Number of Spans:** 1   **Owner:** Private
Builder: H. P. Cummings Construction Co.   **Length:** 38 ft. 1 in.
Width: 14 ft. 4½ in.   **Condition:** Good   **Number:** VT-14-18
Register: Does not qualify

The first name listed above may not be familiar to "bridgers" who have heard this bridge referred to as the Smith or South Pomfret Bridge. The new owners of the property on which the bridge is located have indicated that they are now calling the bridge the Teago/South Pomfret Bridge. According to one of the owners, Missy Middleton, the Teago name makes the most sense to her because "the hill across the street from us is called Teago Hill and they began to refer to this area of South Pomfret as Teago. The general store just one-quarter mile from here is the Teago General Store." The information provided here is for the span formerly known as the Smith/South Pomfret Bridge.

In 1973, a one-hundred-foot, covered bridge that was no longer in use, located over the Green River in Garfield in the Town of Hyde Park, Vermont, was purchased by a housing developer, Thurston Twigg-Smith. He had the bridge divided into two spans, one of which was placed in the present location of the Teago Bridge, at the entrance to a proposed housing development. The second

portion of the Town truss system was moved to another housing project in West Windsor, Windsor County, and became known as the Twigg-Smith Bridge or Smith Bridge at Brownsville. The second bridge served well as an entrance to the West Windsor housing development until a severe windstorm in the summer of 2002 blew it over. Since replacing it was the responsibility of the property owners in the development, they chose the most expedient and economical way to proceed, which was to replace it with a concrete stringer bridge. Meanwhile the other span remained in South Pomfret. In recent years the property beyond the Teago Bridge was purchased by Missy Middleton and Richard Balser. They have built a lovely home on the property and have maintained the bridge in fine condition. Bridgers are welcome to visit the bridge, but please do not block the driveway or drive onto the bridge.

Titcomb/Stoughton Bridge

Location: Just south of the locality of Perkinsville, within the Weathersfield town line.

Directions: In Downers, at the junction of VT 106 and VT 131, go south on VT 106 for 2.5 miles to an open field on the left (east) side of the road (just south of Weathersfield Elementary School on the right/west). The bridge can be seen 0.15 mile to the left (east). The Titcombs welcome visitors to the bridge. It is possible to drive over an obscure lane to get closer to the bridge if the field is not planted; however, do not drive over the bridge.

GPS: 43° 22.009N 072° 31.073W (coordinates recorded in the Titcombs' driveway)

Year: 1880 **Truss:** Multiple kingpost **Waterway:** Schoolhouse Brook
In Use: Yes, private and snowmobile **Number of Spans:** 1 **Owner:** Private
Builder: James and Henry Tasker, moved by Milton Graton
Length: 46 ft. 1½ in. **Width:** 11 ft. 5 in. **Condition:** Good
Number: VT-14-04 **Register:** Does not qualify

This is another bridge that found a new home in 1959, when the U.S. Army Corps of Engineers started to work on the Black River Flood Control Project, which resulted in the North Springfield Lake Flood Control Reservoir. The bridge originally was built in 1880 by James and Henry Tasker over the North Branch of the Black River in Weathersfield, where it provided access to the Stoughton property. Milton Graton was contracted to move this bridge as well as the nearby Salmond Bridge, but when it was time to move this bridge, no one was sure where it was to be placed. According to Graton's book *The Last of the Covered Bridge Builders,* Andrew Titcomb, an architect and owner of a piece of farm property and woodlot, and also an active member of the Weathersfield Historical Society, said: "Take it to my pasture. There is a very small brook there on which we can place it." The move proceeded, and classes at the elementary school halted as the students eagerly watched the covered bridge go by. The bridge was unloaded in the Titcomb meadow, where it awaited the building of abutments, which the Gratons built out of stones taken from the original Stoughton site. Today, the bridge is known as the Titcomb Bridge and is still owned and well maintained by them. It is a favorite location along one of the Weathersfield area snowmobile trails. On our visit to the bridge, Mrs. Titcomb welcomed us and encouraged us to drive in the farm lane toward it. If the field is not planted, visitors are allowed to do the same, but please do not drive onto the bridge.

Upper Falls/Downers Bridge

Location: Just west of the locality of Downers, within the Weathersfield town line.

Directions: In Downers, at the junction of VT 106 and VT 131, go west on VT 131 for 0.3 mile to Upper Falls Road on the left (south), turn left onto Upper Falls Road, and go 0.1 mile to the bridge.

GPS: 43° 23.923N 072° 31.316W

Year: 1840   **Truss:** Town   **Waterway:** Black River   **In Use:** Yes
Number of Spans: 1   **Owner:** Town of Weathersfield
Builder: James F. Tasker   **Length:** 121 ft. 1½ in.   **Width:** 15 ft. 10 in.
Condition: Fairly good   **Number:** VT-14-08   **Register:** Aug. 28, 1973

This is another covered bridge attributed to James F. Tasker. Its exact date is in question. Joseph Nelson in *Spanning Time—Vermont's Covered Bridges* and Ed Barna in *Covered Bridges of Vermont* place it circa 1840, the *World Guide to Covered Bridges* places it at 1851, and Milton Graton in *The Last of the Covered Bridge Builders* places it "about 1870." When the date is unknown, Mr. Graton has been able to approximate it by examining the kind of lumber and construction methods used.

When contracted to do a restoration of the bridge in 1975, the "Last of the Covered Bridge Builders" wrote:

> This bridge was once one of the most tidily built bridges in Vermont. From the splendid, well laid, stone approach walls and abutments to the portal finish with splined boarding, it was outstanding.
>
> Filling the approaches over the years had left the bridge floor as the lowest place and water running into the bridge had caused much rot.

We rebuilt the trusses and raised the bridge $2\frac{1}{2}'$ for drainage and also built new backwalls. We re-framed the floor system with heavier joists. Time would not permit of our doing more so others covered the floor and south side.

On our visits in September 2002 and February 2003, we noticed that although the bridge is in fair condition, it might be in store for some restoration in the near future. Upon returning home and researching the bridge further, we discovered that there are plans for a complete restoration. The project is expected to cost $450,000. We anticipate that much of this sum will be requested from the National Historic Covered Bridge Preservation Project. Tentative plans are to refurbish the abutments, restore necessary truss members, adopt an adequate live load limit, and do cosmetic work on the exterior, which could include sides, portals, and roof. Avid "bridgers" are encourage to "stay tuned" to their bridge society newsletters for updates.

Willard/Willard's/North Hartland (East Twin) Bridge

Location: On Mill Street in the locality of North Hartland, within the Hartland town line.

Directions: In White River Junction, at the junction of US 4 and US 5, go south on US 5 for 4.7 miles to the I-91 underpass in North Hartland. Just beyond the underpass turn left (east) onto Evarts Road, go 0.1 mile to Mill Street, turn left onto Mill Street, and go 0.2 mile to the Willard Bridges.

GPS: 43° 35.621N 072° 20.974W

Year: 1870 **Truss:** Town **Waterway:** Ottauquechee River **In Use:** Yes
Number of Spans: 1 **Owner:** Town of Hartland **Builder:** Unknown
Length: 125 ft. **Width:** 16 ft. 6 in. **Condition:** Very good
Number: VT-14-02 **Register:** Aug. 28, 1973

There is some question regarding the date of origin of this bridge. The *World Guide to Covered Bridges* lists the date as unknown, Ed Barna in *Covered Bridges of Vermont* lists it as "1870, according to town records," and Joseph Nelson in *Spanning Time—Vermont's Covered Bridges* lists it as circa 1919, "Unconfirmed VAOT date." There is no available record of the builder. At one time this Town lattice truss bridge had a "twin" just down the road, in the form of a queenpost covered bridge. That twin was lost in a flood of 1938 and replaced with a steel and concrete bridge. On our visit to the Willard Bridge in September 2002, we were delighted to see that it once again had a twin—this time a nearly identical twin (more about that on the following pages; see the photo of both bridges). The East Twin, which we will call the original Willard Bridge, is in very good shape. A renovation project in 1953 replaced the siding with vertical board and batten left to weather naturally. The two windows on each side were also added at this time. According to Barna, the sides were originally completely covered to prevent horses from "shying at the sight of the river and falls below." At some time in recent years, the roof was replaced with a standing-seam, sheet metal roof. The present deck consists of lengthwise planks with wide plank runners. The dark, weathered siding of the East Twin creates an interesting contrast to the new wood of the West Twin.

The Willard Twins. The one on the left is the "old," East Twin; the one on the right is the "new," West Twin.

Willard/Willard's/North Hartland (West Twin) Bridge

Location: On Mill Street in the locality of North Hartland, within the Hartland town line.

Directions: In White River Junction, at the junction of US 4 and US 5, go south on US 5 for 4.7 miles to the I-91 underpass in North Hartland. Just beyond the underpass turn left (east) onto Evarts Road, go 0.1 mile to Mill Street, turn left onto Mill Street, and go 0.2 mile to the Willard Bridges.

GPS: 43° 35.615N 072° 21.027W

Year: 2001   **Truss:** Town   **Waterway:** Ottauquechee River
In Use: Yes   **Number of Spans:** 1   **Owner:** Town of Hartland
Builder: Jan Lewandoski, Restoration and Traditional Building
Length: 81 ft. $5\frac{1}{2}$ in.   **Width:** 16 ft. $5\frac{1}{2}$ in.   **Condition:** Excellent, new
Number: VT-14-64 (2)   **Register:** Does not qualify

"Man bites dog! A steel and concrete bridge is being replaced by a wooden covered bridge instead of the other way around!" This was the lead sentence in the fall 2001 issue of *The Bridger*, the newsletter of the Vermont Covered Bridge Society. We were absolutely delighted to find this newly constructed covered span in place next to the older Willard or North Hartland Bridge when we visited the site in September 2002. We have chosen to refer to this newer twin as the Willard/Willard's/North Hartland West Twin because up to the present time we have not seen another name for it. Even at the time of its dedication on October 13, 2001, it remained unnamed. The West Twin was built by Jan

Lewandoski, Restoration and Traditional Building, Inc. It is a Town lattice truss structure like its East Twin, and it, too, is covered with unpainted, vertical board and batten siding—quite a contrast to its older twin with dark, naturally weathered siding. In his remarks about the bridge, Lewandoski indicated that sixteen of the eighteen ship's knees used to brace the trusses were cut from the stumps of tamarack trees and two were cut from spruce. Be sure to look for these on a visit to the bridge. The truss members themselves are three-by-eleven-inch spruce timbers secured with seven hundred trunnels. The deck is constructed of oak and hickory. This is truly a twenty-first-century covered bridge built in the tradition of the nineteenth century. Don't miss it on your next trip to Vermont.

Bibliography

Books

Allen, Richard Sanders. *Covered Bridges of the Northeast.* Lexington, Mass.: The Stephen Green Press, 1985.

Barna, Ed. *Covered Bridges of Vermont.* Woodstock, Vt.: The Countryman Press, 2000.

Congdon, Herbert Wheaton. *The Covered Bridge.* Middlebury, Vt.: Vermont Books, 1979.

Evans, Benjamin D., and June R. Evans. *Pennsylvania's Covered Bridges: A Complete Guide.* Pittsburgh, Pa.: University of Pittsburgh Press, 2001.

Graton, Milton S. *The Last of the Covered Bridge Builders.* Plymouth, N.H.: Clifford-Nichol, 1990.

Hammer, Arthur F. *Romantic Shelters.* Marlboro, Mass.: The National Society for the Preservation of Covered Bridges, 1989.

Helsel, Bill. *World Guide to Covered Bridges.* Marlboro, Mass.: The National Society for the Preservation of Covered Bridges, 1989.

Howard, Andrew R. *Covered Bridges of Maine, a Guide.* Unionville, Conn.: The Village Press, 1982.

Howard, Andrew R. *Covered Bridges of Massachusetts, a Guide.* Unionville, Conn.: The Village Press, 1996.

Knoblock, Glenn A. *Images of America: New Hampshire Covered Bridges.* Charleston, S.C.: Arcadia Publishing, 2002.

Krekeler, Brenda. *Covered Bridges Today.* Canton, Ohio: Daring Publishing Group, 1988.

Nelson, Joseph C. *Spanning Time—Vermont's Covered Bridges.* Shelburne, Vt.: The New England Press, 1997.

New Hampshire Department of Transportation. *New Hampshire Covered Bridges: "A Link with Our Past."* Manchester, N.H.: Lighthouse Press, 2000.

Robertson, Doris K., and Edwin "Bill" Robertson. *Covered Bridges in the Saco River Valley.* Westbrook, Maine: Robertson Books, 1983.

Robertson, Doris K., and Edwin "Bill" Robertson. *Maine Covered Bridge Finder.* Westbrook, Maine: Robertson Books, 1983.

Walker, C. Ernest. *Covered Bridge Ramblings in New England.* Contoocook, N.H.: The Capital Offset Co. of Concord, N.H., 1959.

Walker, Janice R., and Todd Taylor. *The Columbia Guide to Online Style.* Chichester, West Sussex, N.Y.: Columbia University Press, 1998.

Wilson, Raymond E. "Twenty Different Ways to Build a Covered Bridge." In *American Wooden Bridges.* New York: American Society of Civil Engineers, 1976.

Data

Reinhold, Rebecca M. *New England States Map File.* Indiana, Pa.: Spatial Science Research Center, Indiana University of Pennsylvania, 2002.

Electronic Mail (email)

Bonta, Susie. "Dummerston/Vermont Covered Bridge." Personal email (14 Feb. 2003).

Boudreau, Christine. "Swiftwater Covered Bridge." Personal email (1 July 2003).

Brock, Dan J. "Massachusetts Covered Bridge Info." Personal email (14 Feb. 2003).

Crowe, Anne. "Dover Pedestrian Bridge." Personal email (24 Feb. 2003).

Crowe, Anne. "Dover Pedestrian Bridge." Personal email (4 Mar. 2003).

Foster, James. "Watson Covered Bridge # 1006." Personal email (27 June 2003).

Garvin, James. "Cornish-Windsor Covered Bridge." Personal email (9 July 2003).

Garvin, James. "Covered Bridge Rehabilitation." Personal email (22 Nov. 2002).

Garvin, James. "Info Request." Personal email (2 May 2003).

Garvin, James. "Jackson Covered Bridge." Personal email (22 Nov. 2002).

Garvin, James. "Jackson Covered Bridge." Personal email (2 May 2003).

Garvin, James. "Jackson Honeymoon Covered Bridge." Personal email (2 May 2003).

Garvin, James. "New England's Covered Bridges." Personal email (26 Mar. 2003).

Garvin, James. "Rehabilitation of New Hampshire Covered Bridges." Personal email (2 May 2003).

Gilbertson, Eric. "Covered Bridge Rehabilitation Standards." Personal email (25 Nov. 2002).

Hamel, Heidi. "Henniker Covered Bridge." Personal email (12 Feb. 2003).

Jamele, Suzanne. "Vermont Covered Bridges on the National Register." Personal email (12 Nov. 2002).

Loether, Paul. "CT's Historic Covered Bridges." Personal email (26 Nov. 2002).

Maurais, Marcia. "Vermont Covered Bridges." Personal email (19 Nov. 2002).

Mohney, Kirk. "Covered Bridge information for the state of Maine." Personal email (14 Feb. 2003).

Mohney, Kirk. "Covered Bridge Rehabilitation." Personal email (22 Nov. 2002).

Philbrick, Stephanie. "Covered Bridges." Personal email (25 Feb. 2003).

Preservation. "Owners of New Hampshire's Covered Bridges." Email (12 Nov. 2002).

Roper, Stephen J. "Massachusetts Covered Bridges listed on the National Register." Personal email (13 Dec. 2002).

Russo, Kristin B. "Information regarding the Battleground Covered Bridge." Personal email (17 Feb. 2003).

Sayers, Debra. "Orne Covered Bridge, Irasburg, VT." Personal email (11 Apr. 2003).

Zurier, Sarah. "Covered Bridges in RI." Personal email (25 Nov. 2002).

Maps

AAA North America Road Atlas. Canada: Quebecor Aurora, 2001.

AAA Special Area Series: New England. Heathrow, Fla.: AAA, 2003.

Barna, Ed, and Peter Mason. *Vermont Covered Bridges: Illustrated Map & Guide to 107 Authentic Vermont Covered Bridges.* Freeport, Maine: Hartnett House Map Publishers, 1998.

The Main Atlas and Gazetteer. Eighteenth edition. Freeport, Maine: DeLorme Mapping, 1995.

New Hampshire Atlas & Gazetteer. Fourteenth edition. Yarmouth, Maine: DeLorme, 2002.

Russo, Doreen; Peter Mason; and Robert Hartnett. *New Hampshire Covered Bridges: Map & Guide.* Freeport, Maine: Hartnett House Map Publishers, 1999.

The Vermont Atlas & Gazetteer. Eighth edition. Freeport, Maine: DeLorme Mapping, 1988.

Vermont Atlas & Gazetteer. Tenth edition. Yarmouth, Maine: DeLorme, 2000.

Pamphlet

Swiftwater Covered Bridge, Bath, New Hampshire, $573,383, May 1999. Mt. Holly, Vt.: Wright Construction Company, 2003.

Periodicals

The Bridger. The Vermont Covered Bridge Society. August 2000, winter 2000, spring 2001, summer 2001, fall 2001, winter 2001, spring 2002, summer 2002, fall 2002, winter 2002, spring 2003, and summer 2003.

Fischetti, David C. "Conservation Case Study of the Cornish-Windsor Covered Bridge." *APT Bulletin, The Journal of Preservation Technology.* Fredericksburg, Va.: Association for Preservation Technology, November 1, 1991.

Garvin, James L. "Discoveries at the Haverhill-Bath Covered Bridge." *New Hampshire Preservation Alliance News.* Concord, N.H.: New Hampshire Preservation Alliance, fall 2002.

"Grant to Help Protect Covered Bridges." *Manchester Union Leader.* Manchester, N.H., September 29, 2001.

Lewandoski, Jan Leo. "The Restoration of the Cornish-Windsor Bridge." *Society for Industrial Archeology: New England Chapters.* Greensboro Bend, Vt., November 1, 1990.

"Massachusetts Bridges in Disrepair." *Pennsylvania Crossings.* Lancaster, Pa., winter 2003 (vol. 26, no. 2).

"Preservation Resources." *New Hampshire Preservation Alliance News.* Concord, N.H.: New Hampshire Preservation Alliance, fall 2002.

Walsh, Kate. "Charlemont and the Battle over the Bissel Covered Bridge." *Shirley Oracle.com.* Shirley, Maine, December 19, 2002.

The World Wide Web (WWW)

50states.com. "State Nicknames." http://www.50states.com/bio/nickname5.htm (5 Mar. through 1 Apr. 2003).

Andover, New Hampshire, Genealogy. "Andover Covered Bridges." http://www.rootsweb.com/~nhcandov/Bridges.html (17 June 2003).

Boston Phoenix. "Pittsford—Hammond Covered Bridge." http://www.bostonphoenix.com/supplements/summer/01/listings/sight_vt_hammond_covered_bridge.html (7 Apr. 2003).

Carter Notch Inn—Jackson, New Hampshire. "Why Jackson, N.H.?" http://www.carternotchinn.com/jackson.html (5 Mar. through 1 Apr. 2003).

Citizens for New Hampshire Land and Community Heritage. "Funded Projects 2001." http://www.specialplaces.org/fundedprojects2001.htm (22 June 2003).

Clark's Trading Post. "The Clark Museum." http://www.clarkstradingpost.com/museums.html$more (17 June 2003).

Clark's Trading Post. "White Mountain Central Railroad." http://www.clarkstradingpost.com/images/ticket.gif (17 June 2003).

Conn River Historic Sites Database & Heritage Trails. "Connecticut River Historic Sites Database & Connecticut River Heritage Trails." http://members.valley.net/~connriver/index.html (13 Apr. through 17 Apr. 2003).

Connecticut Department of Transportation. "Connecticut's Historic Highway Bridges." http://www.past-inc.org/historic-bridges/titlephoto3web.JPG (5 Mar. through 1 Apr. 2003).

Corinth Historical Society. "Robyville Covered Bridge." http://www.angelfire.com/me2/corinthhistorical/juliecorinth/robyville.html (21 June 2003).

Covered Bridges of the Northeast USA. "Index Page." http://www.coveredbridgesite.com/index.html (1 Mar. through 17 July 2003).

Haverhill-Bath Bridge Committee. "Haverhill-Bath Covered Bridge Committee (Copied from the Annual Town Report)." http://www.town.haverhill.nh.us/haverhill-bathbr.html (15 Feb. 2003).

The Herald of Randolph, VT. "Eight Covered Bridges in Valley Area to Get New Roofs." http://www.rherald.com/News/2002/0704/Front_Page/f07.html (8 Apr. 2003).

The Independence Hall Association. "Philadelphia Timeline: 1875." http://www.ushistory.org/philadelphia/timeline/1875.htm (5 Mar. through 1 Apr. 2003).

INHALE. "How to Reference Web Sites." http://inhale.hud.ac.uk/perl/printunit.pl?folio=1&unit=6 (15 July 2003).

Land & Community Heritage Investment Program. "All LCHIP Grant Awards to Date, by Town." http://www.lchip.org/GrantRndInfo/AllAwards.htm (17 June 2003).

Maine Department of Transportation. "The Covered Bridges of Maine." http://

www.state.me.us/mdot/maint_op/covered/splash.html (1 Mar. through 17 July 2003).

Maine Department of Transportation. "Hemlock Bridge—Fryeburg, ME." http://www.state.me.us/mdot/maint_op/covered/hemlock.htm (21 June 2003).

Maine Legislature. "Title 23: Highways, Part 1: State Highway Law, Chapter 9: Bridges, Subchapter 5: Bridges of Historic Significance." http://janus.state.me.us/legis/statutes/23/title23sec603.html] (21 June 2003).

National Historic Covered Bridge Preservation Program—Allocation Plan Project Descriptions. "Bennett Covered Bridge—Oxford County, Maine." http://www.fhwa.dot.gov/bridge/cbfy00pd.htm#bennett (21 June 2003).

National Park Service. "National Register Information System." http://www.nr.nps.gov/nrname1.htm (12 Nov. through 17 July 2003).

National Register of Historic Places. "Home Page." http://www.nationalregisterofhistoricplaces.com (1 Mar. through 17 July 2003).

New Hampshire Department of Transportation. "New Hampshire Bridges." http://www.state.nh.us/nhdhr/bridges/intro.html (1 Mar. through 17 July 2003).

New Hampshire dot com. "The Gateway to New Hampshire: The Granite State." http://www.newhampshire.com/pages/coveredbridgeswhitemtns.cfm#albany albany (1 Mar. through 17 July 2003).

New Hampshire Preservation Alliance. "N.H. Preservation Achievement Awards Honor Thirteen." http://www.nhpreservation.org/html/news_23.htm (17 June 2003).

Newfane, Vermont. "2. Scheduled Members of the Public, A. Roger Whitcomb, Vaot—Review Proposed Covered Bridge (Cb#17) Plans." http://www.newfanevt.com/selectmen/041901.html (13 Apr. 2003).

Newfane, Vermont . "Minutes—Regular Meeting—Board of Selectmen, March 1st, 2001." http://www.newfanevt.com/selectmen/030101.html (13 Apr. 2003).

Newfane, Vermont. "Minutes—Special Meeting of the Board of Selectmen, June 28th, 2001." http://www.newfanevt.com/selectmen/062801.html (15 Apr. 2003).

NH Dept. of Transportation. "Planned Rail-Trail & Bikeway Projects." http://members.tripod.com/Kenyon_Karl/NH-DOT.htm (17 June 2003).

The Rutland Herald Online. "Pittsford's Closing of Bridge Annoys Those on Other Side." http://rutlandherald.nybor.com/News/AtAGlance/Story/10864.html (7 Apr. 2003).

The Times Argus Online. "Kent's Corners Museum Proposed." http://timesargus.nybor.com/Local/Story/16922.html (16 June 2003).

U.S. Congress. "Compilation of Selected Surface Transportation Laws Volume 1—Laws Relating to Infrastructure." http://www.house.gov/transportation/highway/compilations/surfacecomp.html (5 Mar. through 1 Apr. 2003).

U.S. Department of Transportation, Federal Highway Administration. "National Historic Covered Bridge Preservation (NHCBP) Program." http://www.fhwa.dot.gov/bridge/covered.htm (1 Mar. through 17 July 2003).

U.S. Department of Transportation, Federal Highway Administration. "President Ronald Reagan and the Surface Transportation and Uniform Relocation Assistance." http://www.fhwa.dot.gov/infrastructure/rw01e.htm (5 Mar. through 1 Apr. 2003).

University of Vermont. "Vermont, the Green Mountain State." http://www.uvm .edu/state/GreenMount/verdmont.html (7 Apr. 2003).

Vermont Agency of Transportation. "Historic Bridge Rehabilitation or Restoration Projects for Continued Highway Use." http://www.aot.state.vt.us/progdev/ Sections/LTF/VermontHistoricBridges (13 Apr. 2003).

Vermont Agency of Transportation. "Mill Covered Bridge Replaced. Original Destroyed by Flood in March of 1999." http://www.aot.state.vt.us/archaeology/ design/tunbridge.htm (7 Apr. 2003).

———. http://www.aot.state.vt.us/archaeology/design/tunbridge.htm (15 Apr. 2003).

Vermont Agency of Transportation. "Williamsville Covered Bridge (No. 17), Newfane BHF 0106(4)S." http://www.vermontbridges.com/williams.ville.notes.htm (15 Apr. 2003).

Vermont Historical Society Library. "Biographical Sketch, Louise Andrews Kent (1886–1969)." http://www.vermonthistory.org/arccat/findaid/kent.htm (16 June 2003).

Vermont League of Cities and Towns. "Brief Overview of Town Offices." http:// www.vlct.org/local/townoff1.htm (16 Apr. 2003).

Vermont Only. "Vermont Covered Bridges." http://www.vtonly.com/bridges.htm (1 Mar. through 17 July 2003).

Vermont's Covered Bridges, Vermont, Tours, History, Trusses. "The Changing Scene." http://www.vermontbridges.com/changes.htm (7 Apr. 2003).

———. http://www.vermontbridges.com/changes.htm (11 June 2003).

Vermont's Covered Bridges, Vermont, Tours, History, Trusses. "Irasburg's New Covered Bridge Opens to Traffic." http://www.vermontbridges.com/irasnew.htm (10 Apr. 2003).

Vermont's Covered Bridges, Vermont, Tours, History, Trusses. "New Covered Bridge Slated for North Hartland." http://www.vermontbridges.com/bridger .aug00.htm (17 Apr. 2003).

Vermont's Covered Bridges, Vermont, Tours, History, Trusses. "New North Hartland Covered Bridge Replaces Concrete Span." http://www.vermontbridges .com/nhartlnd.htm (17 Apr. 2003).

Vermont's Covered Bridges, Vermont, Tours, History, Trusses. "North Hartland Celebrates Bridge Opening!" http://www.vermontbridges.com/bridger.winter01 .htm (17 Apr. 2003).

Vermont's Covered Bridges, Vermont, Tours, History, Trusses. "North Hartland Celebrates Bridge Opening!" http://www.vermontbridges.com/nhartlnd.opening .htm (17 Apr. 2003).

Vermont's Covered Bridges, Vermont, Tours, History, Trusses. "Plans Made for Weathersfield's Upper Falls Covered Bridge (Wgn 45–14–08)." http://www .vermontbridges.com/bridger.winter01.htm#downers (15 Apr. 2003).

———. http://www.vermontbridges.com/bridger.winter01.htm#downers (17 Apr. 2003).

Vermont's Covered Bridges, Vermont, Tours, History, Trusses. "Randolph Refurbishes Gifford Covered Bridge." http://www.vermontbridges.com/bridger.fall01.htm (17 Apr. 2003).

Vermont's Covered Bridges, Vermont, Tours, History, Trusses. "Thetford's Covered Bridges." http://www.vermontbridges.com/thetford.htm (18 Apr. 2003).

Vermont's Covered Bridges, Vermont, Tours, History, Trusses. "Town of Johnson Covered Bridge News." http://www.vermontbridges.com/johnson.meeting.htm (7 Apr. 2003).

Vermont's Covered Bridges, Vermont, Tours, History, Trusses. "The Town of Newfane May Save the Williamsville Covered Bridge." http://www.vermontbridges.com/bridger.winter00.htm (15 Apr. 2003).

Vermont's Covered Bridges, Vermont, Tours, History, Trusses. "V.A.O.T. Historic Bridge Committee Proceedings." http://www.vermontbridges.com/newfane.selbd.meeting.htm (15 Apr. 2003).

Vermont's Covered Bridges, Vermont, Tours, History, Trusses. "Weathersfield Plans Upper Falls Covered Bridge Restoration." http://www.vermontbridges.com/bridger.fall01.htm#upper (17 Apr. 2003).

Vermont's Covered Bridges, Vermont, Tours, History, Trusses. "Williamsville Covered Bridge Plans." http://www.vermontbridges.com/bridger.fall01.htm#william (15 Apr. 2003).

Virtual Vermont. "Vermont Covered Bridges." http://www.virtualvermont.com/coveredbridge/(1 Mar. through 17 July 2003).

What You Need to Know about Portland, ME. "Covered Bridges of Maine." http://portlandme.about.com/library/weekly/aa053001a.htm (1 Mar. through 17 July 2003).

Index of Bridges

Chase Bridge. *See* School House Bridge, Lyndon, Caledonia Co., Vt.

Cheddar Bridge, 292

Chester H. Waterous Bridge, 75

Chiselville Bridge, 189

Chub Bridge. *See* Fisher Railroad Bridge

Chubb Bridge. *See* Fisher Railroad Bridge

Church Street Bridge, 225

Cilley Bridge, 244

Cilleyville Bridge, 137

Clark's Bridge, 117

Clark's Trading Post Railroad Bridge. *See* Clark's Bridge

Coburn Bridge, 276

Cocheco River Foot Bridge. *See* Cocheco River Pedestrian Bridge

Cocheco River Pedestrian Bridge, 148

Codding Hollow Bridge. *See* Jaynes Bridge

Cold River Bridge. *See* McDermott Bridge

Cole Land Transportation Museum Bridge, 50

Columbia Bridge, 167

Comstock Bridge, East Hampton, Middlesex Co., Conn., 25

Comstock Bridge, Montgomery, Franklin Co., Vt., 212

Contoocook Bridge. *See* Railroad Bridge

Cooley Bridge, 263

Coombs Bridge, 98

Corbin Bridge, 152

Cornish-Windsor Bridge, 169

Cornwall-Salisbury Bridge. *See* Salisbury Station Bridge

County Bridge, 133

County Farm Bridge. *See* County Bridge

Coventry Bridge. *See* Irasburg Bridge

Creamery Bridge, Ashfield, Franklin Co., Mass., 68

Creamery Bridge, Brattleboro, Windham Co., Vt., 293

Creamery Bridge, Montgomery, Franklin Co., Vt., 214

Creek Road Bridge. *See* Salisbury Station Bridge

Cresson Bridge, 99

Crystal Springs Bridge. *See* Creamery Bridge, Montgomery, Franklin Co., Vt.

Dallas Bridge. *See* Montgomery Bridge

Dalton Bridge, 139

DeGoosh Bridge. *See* Scribner Bridge

Depot Bridge, Pittsford, Rutland Co., Vt., 264

Depot Bridge, Rockingham, Windham Co., Vt. *See* Victorian Village Bridge

Dingleton Hill Bridge, 154

Dover Pedestrian Bridge. *See* Cocheco River Pedestrian Bridge

Downers Bridge. *See* Upper Falls Bridge

Drewsville Bridge. *See* Prentiss Bridge

Dummerston Bridge, Dummerston, Windham Co., Vt. *See* West Dummerston Bridge

Dummerston Bridge, Sturbridge, Worcester Co., Mass., 77

Durgin Bridge, 87

East Fairfield Bridge, 215

East Johnson Bridge. *See* Scribner Bridge

East Shoreham Railroad Bridge. *See* Shoreham Railroad Bridge

Edgell Bridge, 118

Emily's Bridge. *See* Gold Brook Bridge

Eunice Williams Bridge. *See* Green River Pumping Station Bridge

Fairfax Bridge. *See* Maple Street Bridge

Field of Dreams Bridge, 55

Fisher Railroad Bridge, 227

Flint Bridge, 245

Florence Station Bridge. *See* Depot Bridge, Pittsford, Rutland Co., Vt.

Flume Bridge, 120

Foster Bridge. *See* A. M. Foster Bridge

Frank Lewis Bridge, 311

Fuller Bridge, 216

Gates Farm Bridge, 228

Gibou Bridge. *See* Hectorville Bridge

Gibou Road Bridge. *See* Hectorville Bridge

Gifford Bridge, 246

Gilbertville Bridge, 73

Gold Brook Bridge, 230

Goodnough Bridge. *See* Gorham Bridge

Goodrich Bridge, 72

Gorham Bridge, 265

Grand Canyon Bridge. *See* Grist Mill Bridge

Library of Congress Cataloging-in-Publication Data

Evans, Benjamin D., 1929–

New England's covered bridges : a complete guide / Benjamin D. Evans and June R. Evans.

   p.   cm.

ISBN 1–58465–320–5

1. Covered bridges—New England.   I. Evans, June R., 1931–   II. Title.

TG23.E93 2004

624.2'18'0974—dc22   2004002193